THE
REBEL
PUBLISHING
HOUSE

TALKS GIVEN TO THE
OSHO INTERNATIONAL UNIVERSITY OF MYSTICISM
IN GAUTAMA THE BUDDHA AUDITORIUM
POONA, INDIA

THE ZEN MANIFESTO
FREEDOM FROM ONESELF

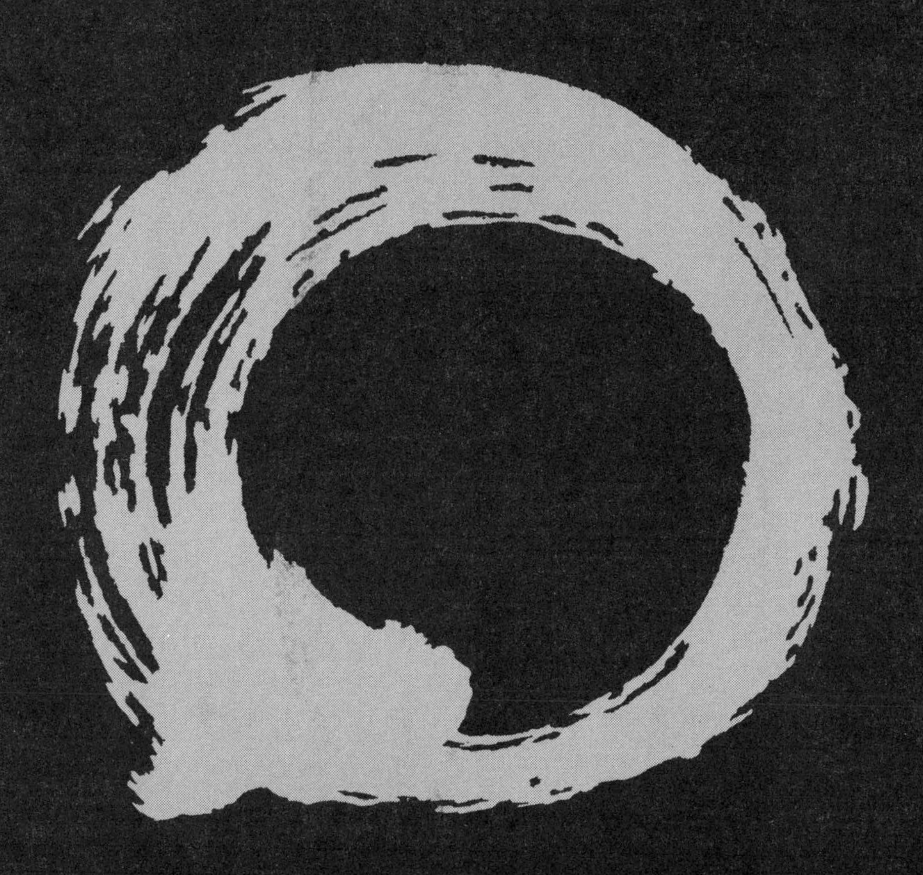

OSHO

Editing by Ma Dhyan Sagar, B.A.

Typesetting by Ma Prem Arya

Design by Swami Dhyan Jayadip, B.A.

Photography by Swami Premgit

Cover Painting by Ma Yoga Shakti

Endpaper Paintings by Swami Atit Kaivalya (Zupo)

Calligraphy by Qui Zheng Ping

Production by Swami Prem Prabhu
Ma Deva Mahabub

Printing by Mohndruck, Gütersloh, Germany

Published by The Rebel Publishing House GmbH
Venloer Str. 5-7, 5000 Cologne 1, Germany

Second Edition

ISBN 3-89338-121-X

TABLE OF CONTENTS

1. THIS DISAPPEARANCE IS ANATTA

2. LET THE CHRISTIAN SHIP DROWN

3. TO WAIT, TO WAIT FOR NOTHING

4. FREEDOM NOT LICENTIOUSNESS

5. THE SKY OF COMPLETION

6. CHAOS – THE VERY NATURE OF EXISTENCE

7. MIND ONLY THINKS, MEDITATION LIVES

8. INSCAPE – THE ULTIMATE ANNIHILATION

9. SMALL INTERVALS OF LIGHT

10. THE LESS YOU ARE, THE MORE YOU ARE

11. SAMMASATI – THE LAST WORD

INTRODUCTION

INTRODUCTION TO THE INTRODUCTION

Robert Rimmer has written this introduction to the book, and in his covering letter he has said:

"Here's the introduction to *The Zen Manifesto*. If the powers don't like it, don't want to use, or want to change it anyway, modify, or correct it anyway…it's okay with me."

We have not changed a single word and we have not added anything to it; but that does not mean that Osho agrees with all that he says. Of course, He loved it all, and we think that Robert Rimmer would also like it that we have not changed it. Whether we agree or not, that is not the point. The introduction is beautiful.

Ma Dhyan Sagar, Editor

ON THE ROAD TO BUDDHAHOOD
or, Thoughts on The Zen Manifesto
by Robert H. Rimmer

I have never personally met Shree Rajneesh, the Bhagwan, Zorba the Buddha, Osho, or whatever name Osho may decide reflects his current "anatta" or freedom from oneself. Even though I think the idea of changing names to give yourself, and others, new perspectives is a delightful idea, I am a long way from becoming Swami Robert, or Bob, a more laughing side of my personality. But I love Osho, and admire his courage in permitting an "intellectual" to write an introduction to *The Zen Manifesto*. I am more likely "to take arms against a sea of troubles" than "not to be" in the Zen sense.

And that's probably one reason why this book exists. It is produced for people like me, and hopefully thousands of readers who are searching for the roots of their own and all existence. Osho is well aware that, while I am not a sannyasin, I am very much "deprogrammed," and like you, perhaps, have thought that Zen was too ascetic and esoteric to offer a way of life. But not after Osho takes you by the hand. He knows the problem: "If Zen remains hard, it will disappear from the world." But, he tells you, "If you can just be – only a few minutes in twenty-four hours – that is enough to keep you alert to your buddhahood."

Although I admire Osho, I have no need to sit in his physical presence. In a very real sense he doesn't need my physical presence either. He once told a sannyasin who believed that meditation was the best when sitting in his presence that "Once you have learned the art of opening, the art of being silent, it doesn't matter whether I am present or not."

Nearly twenty years ago, before the arrival and sad debacle of his departure from United States, I had discovered his *Book of the Secrets*, and in its many volumes was relearning Eastern philosophy. I was also discovering that my own fascination with the experience of non-being in extended sexual intercourse (tantra) had been thoroughly explored by Osho in his books *The Tantra Vision* and *From Sex to Superconsciousness*.

While Osho has gradually come to the conclusion, emphasized in this book, and tells us in his discourses published in *Zen: All the Colors of the Rainbow,* that "Zen has taken the ultimate standpoint about man," Osho has never been to Japan where the Zen masters first began and, as he is now doing completely, tried to separate Zen from the Buddhist religion, or any religion. Osho's library of writings about Zen (listed in the Osho Times, March 1989) and his discourses about Zen in this book will prove to you that he is the greatest living Zen master. But unlike Father Merton, who never realized his wish, Osho has no need to go to Japan and live in a Zen monastery.

As radio and television have proved, seeing or hearing a person, whether it be Osho or another Zen master, is not so effective a way of learning as the printed word. Joseph Campbell inadvertently proved this in his six-hour television talks with Bill Moyers on *The Power of Mythology*. If you want to learn, and retain, what Campbell really thought don't buy the tapes, read his books.

Sadly, we live in a world where millions of people aren't literate enough to read a book like this or even the daily newspaper. I want to emphasize the point because many readers may be unaware that, like most of his writings, *The Zen Manifesto* was originally spoken by Osho as he continues to explore every aspect of human beliefs and thinking in his lectures, discourses, and darshans (more private conversations). That any human being can pursue erudite philosophies so thoroughly in verbal form is an amazement in itself. You have to go back to Plato to discover similar abilities and these were dialogues. Osho does it without an interlocutor.

I have no need to listen to Osho speak. Listening to him and seeing him as I have done via video tape (many of his lectures are available in this form) too often the medium (Osho himself) becomes the message. Then, like his devoted sannyasins, even though I am aware that it is carefully staged, and Osho should be eligible for a Motion Picture Academy Award, I become hypnotized by his sage-like manner and appearance. Or if he suddenly plunges into the "real" world as he often does and ad libs a joke, I'm so happily laughing that I often lose the real meat of what he is saying. There isn't time (provided by a printed book) to assimilate or correlate his insights. Listening to him on tape, I often feel as if I were back in a college philosophy class and should be scribbling notes, lest I forget.

The Zen Manifesto, like all of Osho's books, eliminates these problems. As you read these eleven chapters (my advice is to take them one at a time) read each one twice before you continue. If you do, you'll not only experience the great joy of slowly sipping a Zen master's words but you can re-read them, when you haven't grasped them thoroughly. If you're like me, you'll soon be writing your own comments, enthusiasms and dissents in the margins. (I don't agree with Osho all the time and I'm sure he doesn't expect me to.)

If this is your first experience with Osho's writings, you'll gradually discover that each of these lectures, from which these chapters have been carefully structured, not only try to show you the way of Zen but give Osho a chance to answer questions raised by those who have listened to a previous discourse. And then after a heavy session of philosophic ideas and before you begin to gaze at the two inches surrounding your navel (Don't miss Osho's delightful discussion of where the "hara" of your being may be found) Osho suddenly tells you that it's time for Sardar Gurudayal Singh, and he's telling you really funny and often quite sexy jokes. There are more than thirty of them in this book and I guarantee that you'll be repeating them to your friends. Why the jokes? Because Osho is leading you out of the trap. Don't take enlightenment too seriously. It must be approached with laughter and dancing, too! And your laughter makes it possible for you to relax, let your brain cells unwind and listen to the poetry of his dreamy words – leading you to witnessing and non-being. Relax. Nivedano....

Through his writings – and I hope this book will eventually appear in a low-priced American edition, and will be read by many of the sixty million Americans who may still claim they are Christians but never attend church – Osho has catalyzed my own thinking. He starts the axons and dendrites in my brain cells dancing. As you savor the chapters, you'll discover that Osho is like a Zen archer. Almost poetically he circles his target, surveying it over and over again from many positions, before he draws back his bow and lets the arrow fly. But the bow, the arrow, and the target are all relative, and if Osho occasionally hits a target he didn't aim at, he's still showing you the way.

Osho is well aware that I am not a Zen scholar. Like many of you reading his book I am a contemporary man, and as Osho points out I am too busy (probably not accomplishing much) for "zazen," or sitting. But Osho straddles both the "real" world and the world of non-being. Five years ago in my novel *The Immoral Reverend*, my character, Mat Chilling, who is both a graduate of Harvard Divinity and Harvard Business School suggests that Harvard should give Osho a Master's Degree in Business Administration based on his belief that philosophy is not for the poor. Unlike the popular Western conception that Zen is an escape from reality, Osho has stated, and he was probably chuckling: "When you are hungry you cannot think of the divine. But when your stomach is full you don't know what else to do, so you think about art and God." His solution, which should win the approval of both George Bush and Donald Trump is: "Get off your ass and start working. Life offers everything that is available. It's up to you to take advantage of it."

That approach, plus his caution in this manifesto that Zen is not escapism but "inscapism" and a recognition that the search for nothingness does not give you freedom from responsibility is a point of view that the directors of Harvard Business School should appreciate. With business takeovers that do little more than churn money for the wealthy, and insider trading becoming an American way life, HBS is belatedly trying to indoctrinate future graduates with some kind of moral ethical feelings and convince them that the world isn't really their private oyster. On the other hand, while Osho can't tolerate Pope John and calls him Pope the Polack, they do have something in common, an enjoyment of luxury. In a full-page, four-color montage photo in the July 1989 Osho Times, Osho – sitting in front of the grillwork of one of his Rolls Royces, with a superior expression on his face, makes the statement, "I am a man of simple tastes – I like the best." I'm sure that Pope John would concur, but silently, of course.

Does enjoyment of the finer things in life contradict the message in this book? That is a problem that confronts many people trying to understand what Osho is saying which often contrasts with his life-style. "Life has no purpose," Osho tells you in one of these chapters. "You have become the world's richest man, and suddenly you find that you are surrounded with all kinds of junk. You cannot live if you are trying to be richer. You will be richer if you live."

I don't know whether Osho has ever contrasted his own "need" for personal luxury with the asceticism of the early Zen masters who proclaimed that Westerners cannot accept impermanence or non-being because of the Three Fires burning within us. Wanting, hating and delusion. Osho, in these pages, extols Tanka Tennen, a Zen master who he talks about at some length. He doesn't seem to emulate him. But watch out! Perhaps he does. When Lord Teiko found Tanka lying naked on a bridge, and Tanka told him "I am a monk of nothing," Teiko provided Tanka's food and clothing for the rest of his long life.

Chuckling, Osho might agree that Lord Teiko made Tanka's fame possible in the same way that Osho's followers make "the unbearable lightness of being" tolerable for him. You can't achieve non-being when the hungry I inside you is gnawing for sustenance.

One thing is certain. Most of Osho's life is an open book which has been explored in great detail by believers and non-believers. If you have read the middle of the roaders like Frances Fitzgerald's *Cities on a Hill*, or the nay sayer's like Hugh Milne who in his book, *Bhagwan, The God that Failed*, reveals among other things that loving women have played a continuing role in Osho's life, you'll have fun trying to reconcile the worldly realities of Osho's life with his search for no-thing. Laughing, I dissent when, in this book, Osho tells me that by the time I'm fifty I can escape the bondage of my sex drives. No way, Osho. At seventy-two, although I no longer have the physical appearance to attract young females, as the guru of X-rated films, I still enjoy watching young people using their bodies and genitals in search of a moment of non-being. But at the same time I'm well aware that Osho is showing me, and you who read this book, a new kind of Zen, and Tao (the Way) for men and women of the 21st century.

While I'm not quite sure whether Osho would accept an honorary MBA from Harvard, he does make it abundantly clear in this book that he doesn't want to become a member of any organization, including the American Academy of Humanists. In my essay, *Rajneesh, The Enlightened Humanist* which appeared both in the Summer issue of Free Inquiry (a Humanist based American magazine that sponsors the Academy) and the Osho Times (March 1989) (largely because of his book *The Greatest Challenge: The Golden Future)* I proposed that he should be elected to the Academy. Humanism, rejecting an omnipotent power, is in one sense a Zen way of thinking, but without meditation or the recognition of non-being. Most Humanists are totally disinterested in the search, or recognition of non-being, nor would they accept Osho's playing with astrology and numerology (means to nothingness that I'm sure he'd reject as quickly as he does God). Since Osho enjoys jokes I presume that he knows the one about the Indian guru who after many years of sitting in silence tells his acolytes to bring him a gold-plated screwdriver. When it finally arrives the Indian saint very slowly unscrews his navel and his asshole falls out.

Humanists can't appreciate that Osho might not only chuckle at a joke like this, but use it to help you find the Way. It doesn't matter. I haven't convinced Paul Kurtz, who founded the Academy of Humanism, and I'm sure that Osho would be uncomfortable to have his name listed with Steve Allen, Issac Asimov, Sir Alfred J. Ayer, Kurt Baier, Sir Isaiah Berlin and Sir Hermann Bondi, to mention a few of the members. But many Humanists were shocked that I agreed with Osho that we must work toward a governing world based on meritocracy along with a deprogramming of those who will become our future leaders. Humanists can't comprehend the kind of deprogramming that can occur through the Zen experience, or even my more practical approach – the compulsory teaching of the entire range of Human Values at the undergraduate level (detailed in my novels *The Harrad Experiment* and *The Premar Experiments)*.

Our goals are similar. As Osho tells you in the chapter To Wait, to Wait for Nothing, "Wherever you end up, that is the place you were destined to end. Wherever the boat leads you, and wherever the river moves, that is the direction." Life has no purpose. But Osho, you mention destiny. Doesn't destiny reflect someone's purpose? I'm chuckling. I'm trying to be, at least, what Osho calls a man of Zen. But my previous teachers D.T. Suzuki, Krishnamurti, Thomas Merton, Alan Watts, Fritjof Capra, Philip Kapleau, and many others who Osho has evaluated in these pages have led me astray.

Never mind, as an intellectual I'm still trying. When Osho describes the joy of witnessing as he does in many pages of this book, I realize that what Abraham Maslow described as peak experiences, even extended sexual intercouse and the fleeting moment of orgasm, is a temporary form of the Zen experience. But with them, I have momentarily achieved buddhahood.

I've enjoyed my trip aboard *The Zen Manifesto*, and hope you will, too. If a few million of us try to make the leap from intellect to non-being, at least some of the time, we can achieve Osho's mission "to change the world."

Not the meek, but those who achieve buddhahood should inherit the earth.

Okay Osho?

NOTE TO THE READER

THE END OF EACH DISCOURSE in this series follows a certain format which might be puzzling to the reader who has not been present at the event itself.

First is the time of Sardar Gurudayal Singh. "Sardarji" is a longtime disciple whose hearty and infectious laughter has resulted in the joke-telling time being named in his honor.

The jokes are followed by a meditation consisting of four parts. Each stage of the meditation is preceded by a signal from Osho to the drummer, Nivedano. This drumbeat is represented in the text as follows:

The first stage of the meditation is gibberish, which Osho has described as "cleansing your mind of all kinds of dust...speaking any language that you don't know...throwing all your craziness out." For several moments the hall goes completely mad, as thousands of people shout, scream, babble nonsense and wave their arms about.

The gibberish is represented in the text as follows:

The second stage is a period of silent sitting, of focusing the consciousness on the center, the point of witnessing.

The third stage is "let-go" – each person falls effortlessly to the ground, allowing the boundaries that keep them separate to dissolve.

A final drumbeat signals the assembly to return to a sitting position, as they are guided in making their experience of meditation more and more a part of everyday life. The participants are guided through each stage of the meditation by the words of the Master, and the entire text of each evening meditation is reproduced here.

THIS DISAPPEARANCE IS ANATTA

BELOVED OSHO,

When Tenjiku was asked about the incident of Tanka burning the statue, he replied, "When it is cold we gather around the hearth by the fire."
"Was he wrong or not?" persisted the monk.
"When it is hot we sit in a bamboo forest in the valley," said Tenjiku.

The day after the burning of the statue, Tanka Tennen went to see Nan-yō, who had once been a disciple of Enō and was the emperor's Zen master. When Tanka unrolled his Zazen rug, Nan-yō said, "There's no need."
Tanka took a few steps backward.
Nan-yō said, "That's right."
At this, Tanka took a few steps forward.
Nan-yō said, "That's not right."
Tanka walked around Nan-yō one time and left.
Nan-yō commented, "The old, golden days are far away, and people are now so lazy. Thirty years from now, it will be difficult to get hold of this fellow."

FRIENDS,

It is time, ripe time for a Zen manifesto.

The Western intelligentsia have become acquainted with Zen, have also fallen in love with Zen, but they are still trying to approach Zen from the mind. They have not yet come to the understanding that Zen has nothing to do with mind.

Its tremendous job is to get you out of the prison of mind. It is not an intellectual philosophy; it is not a philosophy at all. Nor is it a religion, because it has no fictions and no lies, no consolations. It is a lion's roar. And the greatest thing that Zen has brought into the world is freedom from oneself.

All the religions have been talking about dropping your ego – but it is a very weird phenomenon: they want you to drop your ego, and the ego is just a shadow of God. God is the ego of the universe, and the ego is your personality. Just as God is the very center of existence according to religions, your ego is the center of your mind, of your personality. They have all been talking about dropping the ego, but it cannot be dropped unless God is dropped. You cannot drop a shadow or a reflection unless the source of its manifestation is destroyed.

So religions have been saying continuously, for centuries, that you should get rid of the ego – but for wrong reasons. They have been asking you to drop your ego so you can surrender to God, so you can surrender to the priests, so you can surrender to any kind of nonsense, any kind of theology, superstition, belief system.

But you cannot drop the ego if it is a reflection of God. God is a lie, out there in the universe, and ego is a lie within your mind. Your mind is simply reflecting a bigger lie according to its size.

Religions put humanity in a great dilemma: they went on praising God, and they went on condemning the ego. So people were in a very split state, in a schizophrenic space. They tried hard to drop the ego, but the harder they tried, the harder it became to drop it – because who was going to drop it? The ego was trying to drop itself. That's an impossibility. So even in the humblest so-called religious people, the ego becomes very subtle, but it is not dropped. You can see it in the eyes of your saints.

One of my sannyasins went to see U.G. Krishnamurti, and because he argued with him, U.G. Krishnamurti immediately became angry. And these people like U.G. Krishnamurti are telling people to drop anger, to drop greed, to drop the ego. But if you provoke them… Their whole religion is just skindeep. Inside is hiding a very pious ego, and when ego becomes pious it becomes poisonous. It is more dangerous because you become absolutely unaware of it, it goes so deep down in the unconscious.

U.G. Krishnamurti lived with J. Krishnamurti for twelve years, and he never mentions his name. If somebody brings up J. Krishnamurti's name, he immediately condemns J. Krishnamurti – and whatever he is saying is just an imitation of J. Krishnamurti, paraphrasing. The reason he cannot accept the fact that he has been with J. Krishnamurti for twelve years is very simple. The moment he accepts it, then you can compare his statements with J. Krishnamurti's, and you will find they are simply paraphrasing. He is repeating, imitating, he knows nothing.

These people have been around in the world all the time. They have tried whatever the religions have been telling them, but their effort cannot remove the shadow. If there is a shadow of the bamboos, you cannot remove the bamboo shadows unless you remove the bamboos. You cannot directly remove the shadows; they are a by-product. If the bamboos remain there, the shadows are going to remain there. They can become very subtle.

I have heard a story about a fox coming out of the cave where she used to live….

Early in the morning, as the sun was rising behind her, her shadow was very long. She said, "My God! I am this big? I will need almost a camel for my breakfast!" And she started searching for a camel for her breakfast.

But the fox could not manage to find a camel. It was just the middle of the day and the sun was over the head of the fox. The fox was feeling very hungry. She had another look at the shadow, and the shadow had disappeared.

It had not disappeared, it had just gone underneath the fox. As long as the fox was there, the shadow was going to be there – but now it was absolutely invisible to the fox. Everybody else could see it, but the fox could not see it; it had just gone underneath the fox.

That's what happens to so-called religious people. They force their shadows, their egos, their anger, their greed, their ambitions, into the unconscious. But in the unconscious these things are still there, and far more dangerous because you are not aware of them. You think they have disappeared.

Before my sannyasin started arguing with U.G. Krishnamurti, he was just a great saint, so silent, so peaceful. As the argument began, he was afraid to be caught, he could not answer the questions, and anger suddenly arose. He may not have been aware of that anger, but my sannyasin helped him! He wanted to get rid of the sannyasin.

It is U.G. Krishnamurti who is not an authentic or sincere man – but you can fall into the trap because he is repeating beautiful phrases. His memory is good, and his intellect is good, but this is the shadow.

Even the original man, J. Krishnamurti, used to become very angry just seeing my sannyasins. I had told my sannyasins everywhere that wherever J. Krishnamurti speaks, you just sit in the front row. At that time sannyasins were wearing red clothes, they had the mala with my photo in the locket, so they were absolutely recognizable.

The moment J. Krishnamurti would see my sannyasins all around, he would forget on what subject he was going to speak. He would start condemning me, and condemning sannyas. This man was talking for his whole life about awareness, and he had forgotten the subject completely. And it was not only once...because my sannyasins were everywhere. Wherever he was going to speak – in London, in San Francisco, in Bombay, in New Delhi, in Madras – wherever he was going to speak, my sannyasins were there just in the front rows.

He was so allergic to me that the moment he would see the sannyasins he would lose all control. At some times he even started beating his head saying, "Why do you come here? I am against sannyas." And I had told my people, "Laugh joyously! Make him as angry as possible! That will bring out the original man which is hiding behind." He could not even understand why this was happening everywhere, that he was being distracted. He would start condemning me, condemning sannyas, and become almost neurotic.

Seeing my sannyasins laughing was almost like putting more fuel on the fire, and he would become more and more angry. He could not understand why these people didn't feel offended, but on the contrary, they were laughing. His whole time would be taken up by the sannyasins.

It is very easy to talk about beautiful things, to have an intellectual grasp. Krishnamurti had been forced by the theologians of a particular brand, the Theosophical Society. It was a worldwide organization in the beginning of this century, and it was preparing J. Krishnamurti to be a world teacher.

Nobody can prepare anybody to be a world teacher; anything that has been prepared is going to be false. They almost tortured him in the name of discipline. They got hold of him at the age of nine, and from that moment he was not allowed to move in the world, he was not allowed to go into society. He was continuously hammered with scriptures. Early in the morning at three o'clock, he had to get up, take a cold bath, and be ready for the theosophists, the leaders of the movement, who would recite Sanskrit scriptures, Tibetan scriptures, Zen scriptures. And he was almost asleep – a nine-year-old child... And this went on up to his twenty-fifth year.

They managed to create a certain personality – you can only create a personality – and they had the hope that they had succeeded in creating a world teacher. Now he was writing beautiful poems, beautiful articles which were published by a section of the Theosophical Society which had been created especially for J. Krishnamurti. The organization was called the Star of the East, and they used to publish magazines, periodicals, literature, all about Krishnamurti, creating the atmosphere around the world to receive him as a world teacher.

But it was all forced from the outside. J. Krishnamurti had no realization, but he was intelligent enough to grasp slowly all the scriptures. He was honest also; U.G. Krishnamurti is not even honest.

Finally, when they thought that he was ready, they called a world conference in Holland – which used to be their great world center. Six thousand leaders of the theosophical movement from all the countries gathered to receive J. Krishnamurti and declare that he was the world teacher.

He came onto the stage.... And it was in a very historical moment of honesty that he said, "I am not a world teacher." It was a shock to the whole theosophical movement. It shattered the whole movement. But he had become completely familiar with all the great literature of mysticism. He dissolved the organization, the Star of the East, which had been specially created for him, and he left the Theosophical Society, and lived his whole life in reaction.

He was a giant in intelligence. The reaction was against all those people who had forced him to do things which were not coming naturally to him. He was not allowed to be natural at all. He was not allowed to meet any girls, he was not allowed to mix with ordinary people. He was not allowed to enter into any ordinary school or college, but had only private tutors, so that he could be proved to the world a superior being, as if he were coming directly as a messiah from God.

And obviously, if he had been dishonest, he could have told the world, "I am a world teacher." He was ready for it; intellectually his memory was completely programmed. But because everything was imposed, it also created deep down in him a rebellion. He knew nothing of what he was talking about, of what he was writing. He knew nothing.

One of his best books is *At the Feet of the Master*. That was published when he was just thirteen or fourteen years old, just to prove that even at the age of fourteen he could produce such a great book. It was not written by him; it was written by a man called Leadbeater. Leadbeater was one of his tutors, and a very profound scholar of Eastern religions.

I have looked into all the Theosophical Society's literature of that time to find out the style, to whose style that book fits. Leadbeater had already written many books, showing great intelligence and scholarship. The book that was published in J. Krishnamurti's name was written by him, and perhaps polished by others. J. Krishnamurti did not even remember when he had written that book.

When he left the theosophical movement, he was asked, "What about the book, *At the Feet of the Master*, which has become a worldwide bestseller?" It is a beautiful book. But he said, "I don't know. I don't remember having written it."

He was honest, but because all these things were imposed on him, there was a constant reaction, rebellion, and he lived in that reaction his whole life. The theosophical movement destroyed the man. He might have become a Gautam Buddha – he had every possibility – but because of this reaction, he fought those dead tutors, those dead Theosophical

Society leaders, Annie Besant, Leadbeater, and others, his whole life. He was fighting with those shadows his whole life – against masters, against mystics, against scriptures – but it was not coming as a revelation, it was coming as a reaction.

His whole life was wasted by the theosophical movement. If they had allowed him to grow naturally, there would have been a possibility; the man had the potential of being a Gautam Buddha. But they destroyed him, and he could not get rid of them. Those shadows he lived with in his early childhood became so ingrained that he was fighting against them. He lived in a negativity, and one cannot live in a negativity and be nourished and blossom into a lotus flower.

So even J. Krishnamurti was not enlightened, and U.G. Krishnamurti is a shadow of an unenlightened intellectual giant. U.G. Krishnamurti is not even an intellectual giant, but he goes on preaching the same words, the same language, and tries to hide the fact.

Just the other day I saw an article about him in a newspaper. He was asked by the interviewer, "When and where did you become enlightened?" And his answer was, "I don't know when and where."

Enlightenment does not happen in time or in space. "When" and "where" are time and space. It happens when you are nowhere, no one. It happens when there is eternity, no time. But his answer may impress many people – people are very gullible.

I am taking his case for a particular reason – because the whole of the Western intelligentsia has become immensely interested in Zen, but their interest remains intellectual. They have written great books, and we will be discussing in this manifesto almost everyone who has written books on Zen.

My effort is to make you really clear that all these intellectuals may have written very beautiful books...I appreciate their scholarship, I appreciate their articulateness of expression, but they are not men of Zen, to say nothing of masters of Zen. Hence this manifesto is absolutely needed to make the whole world clear that Zen is not a mind affair. It is a no-mind space.

I told you that all the religions are saying, "Drop the ego." Zen goes beyond the ego and beyond the self. Except Zen, no religion has come to the point of going beyond the self, beyond the *atman*, beyond your spirit, beyond your individuality. It is absolutely a single man's contribution to human consciousness – Gautam the Buddha's.

Zen is the ultimate flowering. Slowly, slowly improving the image of Gautam the Buddha, each master has contributed something, a new dimension to it. Gautam Buddha is the only person in the whole history of mankind who said, "Just dropping the ego will not help. It can be easily dropped if you drop God." He dropped God, the ego disappeared. The moon disappeared. The reflection disappeared. He went away from the mirror, the mirror was empty. His reflection in the mirror disappeared. He had been fighting with the reflection.

I have heard about an ugly woman....

She was so neurotic about mirrors – because only mirrors made her aware that she was ugly. Otherwise, without mirrors, as far as she was concerned, she was beautiful. Wherever she would see a mirror – even in somebody else's house – she would immediately break it. The reason was that mirrors made her look ugly.

Those poor mirrors had nothing to do with her ugliness. She was ugly, but she was forcing the responsibility on the mirrors, fighting with the mirrors.

That is the essence of all your religions: fighting with the mirrors, with the shadows, trying to drop the ego without dropping God. The ego is just a reflection of a lie in the small pond of your mind.

Gautam Buddha dropped the idea of God, and was amazed that as God disappeared, the ego disappeared. It was just a reflection of God. Hence my effort to remove God. Without removing God you cannot remove the ego. It is the shadow, in the small pond of your mind, of the ultimate lie. Then, as the ego disappeared with God, Buddha came to understand that even *self* has to disappear.

There are religions who have God, ego, and the self: Judaism, Christianity, Mohammedanism, Hinduism. And there are religions which don't have God – Taoism, Buddhism, Jainism – but they have the self. Because they don't have God, the ego disappears on its own. Now their whole effort is how to make their self pure, pious. Now a different kind of effort starts.

Buddha is the only man who said, "If there is no God and there is no ego, the self is also arbitrary, artificial. As you go deeper in your interiority, you suddenly find yourself disappearing into the oceanic consciousness. There is no self as such. You are no more, only existence is.

Hence, I call Zen essentially freedom from oneself. You have heard about other freedoms, but freedom from oneself is the ultimate freedom – not to be, and allow the existence to express itself in all its spontaneity and grandeur. But it is existence, not you, not me. It is life itself dancing, not you, not me.

That is the Zen Manifesto: freedom from oneself.

And only Zen has refined, in these twenty-five centuries, methods, devices to make you aware that you are not, that you are only arbitrary, just an idea.

As you go beyond the mind, even the idea of "I am" disappears. When the "I" also disappears and you start feeling a deep involvement in existence, with no boundaries, then only has Zen blossomed in you. In fact, that is the state, the space of the awakened consciousness. But it has no "I" at the center, no *atman*, no self.

To make it clear to you… Socrates says, "Know thyself." Gautam Buddha says, "Know – just know, and you will not find thyself." Enter deeper into your awareness, and the deeper you go, your self starts melting. Perhaps that is the reason why none of the religions except Zen have tried meditation – because meditation will destroy God, will destroy the ego, will destroy the self. It will leave you in absolute nothingness. It is just the mind which makes you afraid about nothingness.

I receive questions almost every day, "Why are we afraid of nothingness?"

You are afraid because you don't *know* nothingness. And you are afraid only because you figure out intellectually, "What is the point? If in meditation you have to disappear, then it is better to remain in the mind." At least you are – maybe illusory, maybe just an idea, but at least you are. What is the point of making all this effortless effort just to disappear into nothingness?

The mind simply makes you beware of going beyond the boundaries of the mind, because beyond the boundaries of the mind you will be no more. That will be the ultimate death.

A Gautam Buddha dies ultimately, you die only temporarily. Just maybe a few minutes, a few seconds, and you enter into another womb.

Some idiots are always making love around the world, twenty-four hours, and you don't have to travel far away, just in the neighborhood. Around the clock millions of couples are making love, so whichever is the closest couple, here you die and there you are born. The gap is very small.

But an enlightened man, a man who has come to know his nothingness, his no-selfness, his *anatta*, simply disappears into the cosmos.

Mind is afraid, and it seems logical, obvious: What is the point? Why should one do such a thing in which he disappears?

Gautam Buddha was asked again and again, "You are a strange fellow. We came here to realize our self, and your meditation is to *un*realize our self."

Socrates was just a great genius, but confined to the mind: "Know thyself." There is no self to be known. That is the Zen Manifesto to the world. There is nothing to know. You have just to be one with the whole. And there is no need to be afraid....

Just think for a moment: When you were not born, was there any anxiety, any worry, any angst? You were not there, there was no problem. *You* are the problem, the beginning of the problem, and then as you grow, more and more problems.... But before your birth, was there any problem?

Zen masters continuously ask the newcomers, "Where have you been before your father was born?" An absurd question, but of immense significance. They are asking you, "If you were not, there was no problem. So what is the worry?" If your death becomes the ultimate death and all boundaries disappear, you will not be there, but the existence will be there. The dance will be there, the dancer will not be there. The song will be there, but the singer will not be there.

This is only possible to experience by falling deeper, beyond the mind, to the very depth of your being, to the very source of life from where your life is flowing. Suddenly you realize the image of yourself was arbitrary. You are imageless, you are infinite. You were living in a cage. The moment you realize your sources are infinite, suddenly the cage disappears and you can open your wings into the blue sky and disappear. This disappearance is *anatta*, this disappearance is freedom from oneself. But this is possible not through intellect, it is possible only through meditation. Zen is another name for meditation.

Hundreds of beautiful books have appeared in the West since a very strange man, D.T. Suzuki, introduced Zen to the West. He did a pioneer job, but he was not a Zen master, or even a man of Zen. He was a great scholar, and his impact spread through all the countries to the intelligentsia. He immediately had a great appeal.

As the old religions are crumbling, particularly in the West... Christianity is just a name, the empire is crumbling. They are trying to hold onto it, but it is not possible. It is falling apart and a vacuum is growing every day, bigger and bigger, like an abysmal depth which creates nausea.

Jean-Paul Sartre's book, *Nausea*, is very significant. Once you see the bottomless pit, this meaningless life – that you are utterly arbitrary, unnecessary, accidental – you lose all dignity. And for what are you waiting? – there is nothing to wait for, only death. This creates a great anxiety: "We are worthless...nobody needs us...existence is care-less."

At that very moment D.T. Suzuki appeared on the horizon in the West. He was the first man to talk about Zen in the Western universities, colleges, and he attracted immensely the intelligent people, because they had lost faith in God, they had lost faith in the Holy Bible, they had lost faith in the pope.

Just today, almost a dozen German bishops have come together to make a declaration that the pope is going beyond his limits, that his continuous preaching against birth control is bringing humanity to a point where half of the world is going to die from starvation; the pope should not be listened to anymore.

Now, this is pure rebellion. These one dozen bishops in Germany have formed a committee, and they are collecting more and more bishops to rebel against the pope, and they are declaring that he is not infallible. The whole of history shows that the popes and archbishops are fallible. So this whole idea of the pope being infallible was making him an absolute dictator. Now it is intolerable.

The beginning of this century was the start of a boiling up of energy against all old religions, particularly in the rich countries of the West. Poor countries don't have time; they don't have even food enough, no nourishment. Their whole time is involved in getting food, clothing, in getting a shelter. They can't discuss the great problems of life, they can't even conceive of them. The question is food, not God!

That's why it is so easy to convert poor people to Christianity – just by providing food, just by providing shelter, service. But they are not converted to Christianity. They are simply not concerned about God. They are not concerned about any system of belief, their basic thing is that they are hungry and starving!

When you are hungry and starving you don't think of God, you don't think of hell and heaven. The first thing you think about is where to get some bread and butter. And if anybody gives you bread and butter with the condition that you have to be a Catholic, you will agree, rather than die of starvation.

So poor countries are becoming more and more Catholic, more and more Christian. But in the West itself, Christianity is losing its hold. Not more than twenty-five percent of people attend the churches. Seventy-five percent of people are completely disappointed. Those twenty-five percent are mostly women, and they go for a particular reason: that is the only place where you can gossip and meet all the other women, and see who has got better clothes, better fur coats, better jewelry, a better car. The church is the only club where the women are accepted. All other clubs are boys' clubs, where old boys talk about women but don't allow women in.

Even at parties, as the dinner is complete, the women retire to a separate room and leave the boys alone. The boys will be drinking and shouting and fighting, and talking all kinds of nonsense which they cannot say in front of women because they feel a little embarrassed. So the women retire. And this is good, because the women have their own gossiping: who is falling in love with whom. Let the boys do their work, the old girls are doing their work.

The church is the only place in which all the religions have allowed women to gather; otherwise they are boycotted from every other social congregation. They cannot be members of many organizations, many clubs; they are all male-oriented. The woman's area, her territory, is the home. She has to be confined in that territory. So the church has been the only outlet; they wait for Sunday.

So these twenty-five percent are women. A few men may be there who cannot leave their wives alone out of fear, and a few men may be there to find a new girlfriend. But this has nothing to do with religion.

D.T. Suzuki appeared in the West with a new approach to existence. He appealed to people because he was a man of great scholarship, profound scholarship, and he brought to the Western mind a totally new concept of religion. But it remained a concept, it remained an argument in the mind; it never went deeper than that.

A parallel exists in China. Before Bodhidharma appeared in China, China was already converted to Buddhism. Bodhidharma went there fourteen hundred years ago, but Gautam Buddha's philosophy and religion had reached China two thousand years ago, six hundred years before Bodhidharma went there. In those six hundred years scholars had converted the whole of China to Buddhism.

In those days it was very easy to convert the whole country. You simply converted the emperor, and then his whole court got converted, then his whole army got converted, then his whole bureaucracy got converted. And when the emperor and the whole bureaucracy and the army, and all the so-called wise people of the emperor's court were converted, the masses simply followed.

The masses have never decided anything for themselves. They simply look at the people who proclaim themselves great, in power, in intelligence, in riches. If these people are converted, the masses simply follow.

So in those six hundred years, thousands of Buddhist scholars reached to China, and they converted China – the emperors, the governors. But it was not the true message of Gautam Buddha yet. Although China had become Buddhist, Buddha had not yet appeared.

Bodhidharma was sent by his master, who was a woman. She said, "Scholars have prepared the way, now you go. You are immensely needed there." Bodhidharma was the first buddha to enter China, and he brought a totally different vision, not of the mind but of no-mind.

The West is absolutely ready for a Zen manifesto. Intellectually, D.T. Suzuki, Alan Watts, and many others – we will be discussing each one – have prepared the road. Now only a Bodhidharma is needed, a Gautam Buddha is needed, or a Mahakashyapa – someone whose Zen is not just a philosophy but an actual experience of no-self, an actual experience of entering into nothingness.

And once you enter into nothingness, you will be surprised that it is nothing to be afraid of. This is your real home. Now you can celebrate, because there is nothing more than this mystery. That nothingness opens all the doors. As long as you are confined by the self, the very idea of separation from existence keeps you miserable.

You have to find ways – and these ways can be found easily only when you have somebody who has already traveled the path, who knows that nothingness is not something empty. By disappearing, you are not really disappearing, you are becoming the whole. From this side, it looks like you are disappearing; from that side, it looks like you are becoming the whole. Just ask a dewdrop.

I have told you about Kabir....

When he first entered into this nothingness, he immediately wrote a beautiful poem, in which comes the sentence, "The dewdrop has fallen into the ocean." His own sentences are very beautiful:

Herat herat hey sakhi, rahya Kabir herayi – "O, my friend, my beloved, I had gone to search, to seek myself, but something strange has happened. Rather than finding myself, I have disappeared just like a dewdrop disappearing in the ocean."

Bunda samani samunda men so kat heri jayi – "The dewdrop has disappeared in the ocean. Now how can you find the dewdrop again?"

That was his first experience. Then he became more and more aware of the ocean, and forgot all about the dewdrop. Before dying he called his son, Kamal. He was certainly rightly named by Kabir. *Kamal* means a miracle – and the son of Kabir was certainly a miracle. He called Kamal and said to him, "I am going to leave my body soon. Before I leave, you have to correct one of my poems. Just a little change...

"I have written, *Bunda samani samunda men* – the dewdrop has entered into the ocean. You have to change it. Just reverse it. *Samunda samana bunda men* – the ocean has disappeared into the dewdrop – because now I know from the other side.

"My first experience was from *this* shore; now I am talking from the further shore, the beyond. Now I know the dewdrop has not fallen into the ocean, it is the ocean that has fallen into the dewdrop."

Kamal said to him, "I have always suspected that line. I can show you my copy." And he showed Kabir. He had crossed out that line.

Kabir said, "You are really a *kamal*. You are a miracle. You came to know it before me." The line was crossed out.

Kamal said, "I was suspicious from the very beginning, that this is the statement of a beginner, the first statement when he comes to see the nothingness. But when he *becomes* nothingness, this statement will be absolutely wrong. So now that you have come to your senses, just before dying, I can rejoice that you are no longer just a beginner, you have become part of the whole." Then he wrote the new line: the ocean has fallen into the dewdrop.

I said to you that Kabir had named his only son "Kamal," a miracle, because the young man was certainly not an ordinary man. At one point, even Kabir was angry with him, because he used to raise questions which even Kabir could not answer. And this was always happening when thousands of Kabir's followers would be there. His own son would stand up and make him feel very embarrassed because he was not able to answer the question.

One day he was very angry – it must have happened before his enlightenment – and he said to Kamal, "*Buda vansh Kabir ka* – my family ends with me, Kamal!"

He means the same by "my family" as what Zen people call their heritage, their family, their masters. They are not talking about their parents.

Kabir said, "My family ends with me. I cannot trust you."

Kamal said, "If you cannot trust me, you cannot trust yourself. But because you have disowned me by making this statement, I will not be staying in your cottage. I am going to make a small hut just next to you, so when gullible people come to you and they are going back home, I can deprogram them." And he remained just in front of Kabir's house, and because everybody knew he was Kabir's son, before leaving Kabir they would go to pay tribute to his son also.

Even the emperor of Varanasi was a devotee of Kabir. Kabir was a poor man, a weaver. The emperor of Varanasi asked one day, when he had not seen Kamal for a few days – he was coming almost every day to listen to Kabir, and he saw that Kamal was missing – he asked Kabir, "Where is Kamal?"

Kabir said, "It is a sad story. I was just angry, and I told him that my family ends with me, and he immediately left, saying, 'If your family ends with you, I no longer belong to your family.' He remains outside, just in front, disturbing my disciples. He is a pain in the neck! Now he has gone outside, so I cannot even say anything. He just sits there."

The emperor of Kashi said – Kashi is the older name of Varanasi – "I would go and see him, but what is your problem with him?"

Kabir said, "Thousands of problems. People come with money, diamonds, emeralds, and all kinds of valuable things, and I don't need them, so I refuse them. And he is just sitting by my side, and he tells those people, 'Okay, if he is refusing, bring them to me. Anyway it doesn't look good that you have come to offer and you are going rejected. Offer them to me.'

"So I reject, and he goes on collecting. And I told him that this is not right, but he said, 'You think about yourself. I know on my own accord what is right and what is wrong. Don't tell me! I am not your disciple, I am your son.'"

So the emperor said, "Don't be worried, I will go and see and check." So he brought with him a very big diamond, and he told Kamal, "I have brought this most valuable diamond in the country as an offering to you."

He said, "You can put it into the bamboos of the roof of my hut. If somebody does not take it away, it will remain there. Once in a while I can see that I have got the most valuable stone in my hut. I don't have much decoration here."

The emperor thought, "Kabir seems to be right, he is very clever and cunning. He is not taking it, but he is telling me, 'Just put it there. If somebody does not take it away, I will enjoy seeing it.' And as I go out he will take it, that is certain." So the emperor stayed away for one week, did not come.

After one week he came, and he asked Kamal, "Where is that diamond?"

Kamal said, "If somebody has taken it, then it will not be in the roof; otherwise it is bound to be in the roof. You have put it there yourself, so you can find it easily. I had no opportunity to look at it. I am looking inwards and your diamond is outside."

The emperor said, "Great!" And he looked and found the diamond exactly where he had put it in the roof.

He told Kabir, "You are in a misunderstanding. Your son is really a miracle. I was thinking that he was cheating me, deceiving me, but he has not even looked at the diamond, to say nothing of touching it. He said to me, 'If anybody has taken it, then I don't know, because I am looking inwards. Anybody can take it. There is no guard on the hut, there is no door. And sometimes I have to go to the Ganges to take a bath, and anybody can take it. So if it is still there, you will find it.' And I have found it; it was there. He has not even looked at it. So your whole idea is wrong. Your idea that he is interested in wealth is absolutely wrong."

Finally, Kabir had to go to the hut and ask Kamal, "Forgive me, come back. I was wrong. You were just trying to test me, whether I get angry or not – and I certainly got angry. I thought it was your greed."

Kamal said, "I am your blood, your bones, your very marrow. How could you ever think that I should be greedy? You became angry, and you exposed yourself, that all your teaching not to be angry, not to be greedy, is just superficial.

"It is not your concern. If I am taking things, why are you interested? There must be some greed in you. Just as anger came up, your greed may come up any moment. If there was no greed in you, you would have simply witnessed that Kamal is taking things, that's all. It is Kamal's business to take care of his own being, it is not your business. I'm not your disciple. I am a master on my own authority."

And Kabir looked into himself and agreed with Kamal: "Perhaps you are right. My being interested and being angry that you are gathering money shows *my* greed, not your greed, shows *my* anger, not your anger. And you left so joyously, touching my feet, saying, 'If you say your family ends with yourself, then a new family starts with me, just after you.'"

So Kamal was persuaded back into the family. He was the successor of Kabir, a far greater man, far more aware, alert, far more conscious. But strangely, it is Kabir who is remembered. He has an organized religion following him – *Kabir Panth*, "Path of Kabir." Kamal has nothing. He never created any following. Although hundreds of people listened to him, he remained only a friend. He helped them, shared his light with them, but never gave any discipline, any commandments, any principles to be followed.

Once you know meditation, you don't have to follow anybody. You have your own eyes open, and you have your light just ahead of you showing the path, and all that is right and all that is good happens choicelessly. It is not that you are doing it, you cannot do otherwise.

For six hundred years in China, Buddhism was only an intellectual exercise, good gymnastics. But as Bodhidharma entered China, he changed the whole idea about Zen. People were talking about Zen as if it was another philosophy, which it is not; as if it is another religion, which it is not. It is a rebellion against mind, and all your religions and philosophies are part of the mind.

This is the only rebellion against mind, against self, the only rebellion of withdrawing all the limits that imprison you and taking a quantum leap into nothingness. But this nothingness is very alive. It is life, it is existence. It is not a hypothesis. And when you take the jump, the first experience is that you are disappearing. The last experience is, you have become the whole.

A few questions.

The first question:

Why have so many Western intellectuals been drawn to an examination of Zen?

They are feeling a great vacuum, and they want to fill the vacuum. You cannot live with a vacuum. The vacuum is empty, and out of that emptiness, life becomes sad, serious.

All the religions have been filling your vacuum with lies. Now those lies are exposed. Science has done much in exposing those lies, and great meditators, mystics, have done tremendous work around the world in exposing all the lies of religions.

The contemporary man stands in a strange position: the old has fallen, it was a deception, and the new has not yet arrived. So there is a gap, an interval, and the Western intelligentsia is trying to find something which will not be again a lie, which will not just give you consolation, but which will transform you, which will be a deep revolution in your very being.

Zen certainly is the right approach towards existence, the ultimate truth. Without believing in anything, without being a follower or a believer, you simply enter into your own interiority, and you are entering into the immense nothingness of the whole. But it is the same nothingness from where you had come and to where you are going again.

When the source and the goal become one, you will have a great celebration. In that celebration you will not be, but the whole existence will be participating. The trees will be showering flowers, and the birds will be singing songs, and the oceans and the rivers will all be rejoicing.

The whole existence becomes your home the moment your heart melts into the universal heart. That is where Zen is happening. In that melting into the universe you are back to the original source, fresh, eternal, timeless, spacious. The only thing needed is freedom from the self. That is the very essence of Zen.

You have heard about many freedoms: political freedom, psychological freedom, economic freedom – there are many kinds of freedom. But the ultimate freedom is Zen, freedom from yourself. That is not to be accepted as a belief, that has to be experienced. Only then you know. It is a taste. Anybody can describe that sugar is sweet, but if you have not tasted sugar, you hear the word 'sweet' but you don't understand what it is. The only way is for somebody to force some sweetness into your mouth.

The master's function in Zen is to force nothingness into your experience, or in other words, to bring you to your own nothingness. The master devises methods, and when they become old and routine he drops them, finds new methods, new ways.

But it has been twenty-five centuries since Gautam Buddha gave a lotus flower to Mahakashyapa, without a single word, and told his congregation, "What I could say I have told you. What I cannot say – although I want to, but it is simply not possible – I am transferring to Mahakashyapa." That lotus flower was just a symbol: unless you open up like a lotus flower in the early morning sun when the dewdrops are shining like pearls on the lotus leaves… It is a silent transmission of the lamp. Nothing is said.

Mahakashyapa came for the first time close to Buddha, took the lotus flower, touched his feet, went back and sat silently under his tree. Mahakashyapa is the first patriarch of Zen. So the lineage of Zen, the family of Zen, is a branch, a very silent branch of Buddhism. They love

Gautam Buddha, because Zen really originated in his disappearance. He transferred it to Mahakashyapa, and then it was the responsibility of Mahakashyapa to go on finding people to whom he could transfer it.

So since that moment, twenty-five centuries ago, it has been transferred without any arbitrary means, without any language, from master to disciple; from one who has come home to one who is just wandering around but cannot find the way.

The master functions as a friend. He holds your hand and takes you on the right path, helps you to open your eyes, helps you to be capable of transcending the mind. That's when your third eye opens, when you start looking inwards. Once you are looking inwards, the master's work is finished. Now it is up to you.

You can travel that small gap between your mind and no-mind in a single moment of tremendous intensity and urgency. Or you can travel slowly, hesitantly, stopping, being afraid that you are losing grip of your mind, you are losing grip of your individuality, that all boundaries are disappearing. What are you doing? You may think for a moment, "This may bring a breakdown, you may not be able to come back to the mind again. And who knows what is going to happen ahead? Things are disappearing..."

If you pay too much attention to the things that are disappearing you may stop out of fear. The master goes on focusing your mind on things that are happening, not on things that are disappearing. He goes on forcing you to look at the blissfulness, look at the silence that is descending on you. Look at the peace, look at the joy, look at the ecstasy. He is continuously emphasizing that which is happening, not that which is going away – the anxiety, the despair, the angst, the anguish, he is not allowing you even to take note of them. What is disappearing is not worth keeping. Just go on looking at what is appearing out of nothingness.

So you gather courage, you become more daring. You know that nothing is going to be wrong. With every single inch of movement, something greater is happening. And finally, as you enter the very source of your being, the center of your being, the whole universe falls upon you, just as Kabir said before he died: "The whole ocean has fallen into the dewdrop."

Once you have experienced this beautitude, this ecstasy, this divine drunkenness, who cares about individuality? Who cares about the self? What has the self given to you except anxiety, except hell? And this nothingness is so pure, without boundaries. For the first time you find the infinity, the eternity, and all the mysteries of existence are suddenly opening their doors to you. And they go on opening...door after door....

There is no end to this journey, it is an endless pilgrimage. You are always arriving and arriving and arriving, but you never arrive. But each moment you are going deeper into bliss, deeper into ecstasy, deeper into truth, and there is no full stop.

The Zen Manifesto is absolutely needed, because all old religions are falling apart, and before they fall apart and humanity goes completely bananas, Zen has to be spread wide around the whole earth. Before the old house falls down, you have to create a new house.

And this time don't commit the same mistake. You have been living in a house which was not there; hence you were suffering rain, winter, sun, because the house was only an imagination. This time really enter into your original home, not into any man-made temple, any man-made religion. Enter into your own existence. Why be continuously a carbon copy?

This time is very valuable. You are born in a very fortunate moment, when the old has lost its validity, its proof, when the old is simply hanging around you because you are not courageous enough to get out of the prison. Otherwise the doors are open – in fact, there have never been any doors, because the house you are living in is completely imaginary. Your gods are imaginary, your priests are imaginary, your holy scriptures are imaginary.

This time don't commit the same mistake. This time humanity has to take a quantum leap from the old rotten lies to the fresh, eternally fresh truth.

This is the Manifesto of Zen.

The second question:

D.T. Suzuki, the man who introduced Zen to the Western intelligentsia, said: "Zen must be seized with bare hands, with no gloves on."
Would You like to comment?

His statement is rationally beautiful. You should seize Zen with your bare, naked hands, with no gloves on. He means by that that you should enter into the world of Zen without any beliefs, without any security, without any safety, without any gloves. You should enter into Zen with naked hands, with nudity.

But his statement is still intellectual. He was neither a master of Zen nor even a man of Zen. If he had been a master of Zen, he could not have said it. A master of Zen cannot say that Zen must be *seized*. It is not a question of seizing Zen. This is the old language of the mind, of "conquering nature." Now it becomes conquering Zen.

Zen is your reality. Whom are you going to seize? Whom are you going to conquer? You *are* Zen.

And what does he mean by "with bare hands"? Hands will not reach there, bare or with gloves on. Hands symbolize the movement outwards, they always point towards the outside. All your senses open to the outside, they are all extrovert. Your ears hear the sound that is coming from the outside, your eyes see colors, light that is coming from the outside, your hand goes on grabbing – that is outside you. None of your senses can reach to the inside. For the inside there is a different sensitivity, the third eye. There are no hands.

Just between your two eyebrows, exactly in the middle, is the place which can look inwards. When you are with closed eyes, trying to look inwards, rushing towards your center, you are hitting on the third eye continuously. Because it has not been opened for centuries, it has forgotten how to open. Hence, every day meditation...and one day suddenly you will find the eye has opened, and the whole path is clean and clear. You have simply to walk to the center.

Now there are no hands, and there is no question of conquering. It is your nature. The very idea that Zen must be seized creates a duality: you are the person who is going to seize Zen, and Zen is something other than you. It creates a duality. That's what gives me a clear-cut idea whether the man is just intellectual or has the experience. I have my clear-cut criteria how to know that a man is talking only from the mind. Howsoever clever D.T. Suzuki may be, I say unto you that he is not a master, he is still living in duality.

Mind is dual, it always divides things into polar opposites: the conqueror and the conquered, the observer and the observed, the object and the subject, the day and the night. It goes on dividing things which are not divided. Neither is the day divided from the night, nor is birth divided from death. They are one energy. But mind goes on dividing everything into polarities, opposites. Nothing is opposite in existence; every contradiction is only apparent. Deep down all contradictions are meeting together.

So when somebody says, "Seize, conquer," he is still talking in the language of the mind and is still being violent. His words show it.

Zen has to be neither the object nor the subject. It is a transcendental experience. Duality of all kinds is transcended: the observer and the observed become one, the knower and the known become one. So it is not a question of conquering or seizing, it is a question of relaxing into yourself.

It is not a fight or a war, it is pure resting, sinking into your rest deeply. And as you sink deeper and deeper you find you are melting. The moment you come to oneness with existence, you have arrived to your nature. It can be possible only through relaxation, through rest.

Suzuki's statement is rational, but not existential, and Zen is the only existential approach in the whole world.

A little biographical note:

Once, when he was traveling, Tanka Tennen stopped overnight in a temple.

You know the meaning of Tennen; it means "absolutely natural."

Zen is your nature; whether you know it or not does not make any difference. If you know you will not stumble unnecessarily, you will not go on falling into the same ditches again and again. If you know, you will walk like a man with eyes. If you don't know, you will walk with eyes, but closed. Your whole life you will suffer unnecessary misery, tension, anxiety. But there is no difference as far as your inner nature is concerned. You are a buddha all the time – sleeping, waking, whether you know it or not. If you know, life becomes a bliss. If you don't know, life becomes a misery.

So it is simply you. If you are ready to sink deep within yourself, being in deep rest… It is not a victory, it is just remembering that buddhahood is your nature, it is your *dhamma*.

Tanka Tennen stopped overnight in a temple. It was so cold that he made a fire of one of the wooden Buddha statues. When he was chastised the following morning by the temple monks, Tanka explained that he had burned the statue so he could take Buddha's bones.
"How could a wooden statue have bones?" a monk asked Tanka Tennen.
"Then why have you chastised me?" replied Tanka.

Only a man of immense insight, only a man who knows his buddhahood, can burn a statue of Buddha in the night. The night was so cold, the real buddha was suffering from cold, and the unreal buddha was enthroned, so he took one of the statues – it was a wooden statue – and he burned it and was quite happy.

In the morning, when the monks of the temple found that he had burned a statue of Buddha, obviously they were very angry. "What kind of man are you? We thought you were a Zen master, and you have destroyed one of our most valuable Buddhas. What was the purpose?"

He said, "The night was very cold." He was simply showing those monks, "You have forgotten your buddha nature and you are worshipping statues made by man. Buddhas are worshipping statues of wood or stone or marble – this is absurd! What kind of spiritual sleep are you suffering from? Have you completely forgotten who you are?"

So he said, "It was a cold night, and the buddha was feeling the cold very much. A false buddha was just sitting there. I burned the statue; it was just wood." To make it completely clear, he said, "I was trying to find Buddha's bones."

In the world of the Buddha, the bones of a buddha are called flowers. When a buddha has awakened, even his bones are no longer bones, so they are not referred to as bones, they are referred to as flowers. Slowly, slowly it has become widespread in India that now everybody's bones, when somebody dies…

In India the body has to be burned on a funeral pyre, and on the third day, when the fire has completely cooled down and the body is completely burned, the relatives and the friends go to the burning place to collect the "flowers." That is the expression. They are going to collect the bones. Those bones have to be dissolved either into a river or into the ocean for eternal rest – but they are not referred to as bones.

The first time it was Gautam Buddha's bones which were referred to as flowers. How can you say Gautam Buddha's bones are just bones? In that body lived the foremost awakened man; in that body radiated the splendor, the bliss arising from nowhere. It is because of this that Buddha has said, "This very body the buddha, and this very earth the lotus paradise."

When you know your nothingness, it radiates. Even from your bones, your eyes, your skin, everything takes a new grace, a new grandeur, a new majesty. Your words become golden, your silence becomes so precious – a song without sounds. Even when the buddha walks, his body is expressing his buddhahood. If the buddha looks into your eyes, his eyes are expressing the ultimate truth. Whether he says anything or not, he is continuously diffusing a certain energy all around him. He is a radiator, a radiation of the ultimate bliss.

So naturally, if a man like Gautam Buddha became enlightened when he was forty-two years old, and lived for forty years afterwards – for forty years continuously the Buddha was inside these bones and the flesh and the skin – how is it possible that all these bones and skin will not be affected by this tremendous metamorphosis? Hence came the expression, "flowers."

The man who translated it has forgotten. He simply says that Tanka Tennen said, "I had to burn the statue so I could take Gautam Buddha's *bones*" – not flowers. But everything changes with your change of consciousness. Everything becomes tremendously beautiful.

This was just to provoke those monks so they were cornered. Immediately, the high priest of the temple must have said, "*How could a wooden statue have bones?*" How could a wooden statue have flowers?

Tanka had made his point. He is saying that a wooden statue is not a buddha; it has not even the bones, it has not even the flowers of Buddha. It is simply wood, cut in a certain shape. You have given the shape to the wood, but you cannot make it a buddha.

Once the monks were cornered, Tanka said, "*Then why have you chastised me?*" Then why are you angry at me?

There are many versions of this story. The version that I love – and I don't know whether it is in the scriptures or not – I don't know from where I got it, but I am absolutely certain that is the right version.

It was not in the morning that Tanka Tennen was found, it was in the middle of the night when the priests saw a fire burning in the temple, because they were sleeping in the temple. The high priest came running: "Are you mad or something? What are you doing? You have burned one of my most valuable Buddhas!"

Then Tanka took his staff – and the Buddha was almost burned – and he started looking for flowers with his staff in the ashes of the Buddha. The high priest said, "What are you doing?"

He said, "I am looking for Buddha's flowers. I have heard that Buddha has bones, and those bones turn into flowers. I am looking for those flowers."

The high priest laughed. He said, "You are certainly insane. It was just a wooden statue, it was not a buddha!"

And Tanka Tennen said, "Aha! So it was not the Buddha! And the night is still long and very cold, and you have so many wooden statues; just bring one or two more."

The high priest said, "You are a very dangerous fellow! I cannot allow you to stay in the temple." And he forced Tanka Tennen outside the temple in the middle of the night.

It was cold winter, icy cold, and Tanka Tennen said, "What are you doing? You are *my* high priest, and you are throwing *me* out. Just to keep your wooden statues safe, you are throwing the buddha out!"

But the high priest did not listen, he just pushed him out and closed the doors.

And in the morning when he opened the doors, Tanka Tennen was sitting by the side of the road by a milestone. He had collected a few wildflowers, and he had put those wildflowers on the milestone, and he was sitting there reciting a beautiful mantra that the disciples of Buddha used to recite before him: *Buddham sharanam gachchhami* – I go to the feet of the buddha; *Sangham sharanam gachchhami* – I go to the feet of those who are the commune of the awakened one; *Dhammam sharanam gachchhami* – I go to the feet of the ultimate truth.

The priest said, "Listen, you burned my Buddha – that was an insane act. Now you are doing even more mad behavior. This is a milestone, not a Buddha, and you have put flowers on it, and you are going to the feet of this milestone!"

Tanka Tennen said, "It is the same, just an excuse. You have wooden statues as an excuse, I have this stone. Hidden in it there is a stone Buddha. If some sculptor takes out all the unnecessary pieces, a Buddha will appear. Any excuse will do. I burned one of your excuses and you were so angry. This is just the same as your wooden statue; and neither does this stone have Buddha's bones.

"I was simply wanting, in the early morning sun, with this beautiful breeze, and flowers fragrant all around, and the birds chirping and making their joyful sounds... I have to show my gratitude to the man who is the source of my family. Without him, perhaps, there would not have been so many enlightened people.

"Gautam Buddha started a new chapter in the consciousness of humanity. Obviously, I go to his feet, and I go to the truth that he revealed, and I go to the feet of those who became enlightened because of his sharing the enlightenment. I would not have been the light that I am right now if Buddha had not transferred to Mahakashyapa that which cannot be said in a lotus flower. I am showing my gratitude to the greatest man in the history of mankind who has risen above mind."

This, I know, is the right story. If you don't find it in the scriptures, correct them. Wherever you find those scriptures, correct them, because they do not show exactly Tanka Tennen's approach; they are very poor. I love riches – and the real richness comes from your awareness, your consciousness.

In this way, Tanka Tennen was trying to make all those priests and monks aware: "What are you doing? You have forgotten the real thing, and you are worshipping statues. Any stone will do, because in every stone the Buddha is hidden."

I remember one story about Michelangelo....

He was passing by the market where marble was sold, and he saw a big piece of marble in front of a shop. He asked the owner, "How much will it cost?"

The owner said, "Nothing, because it has been there for ten years and nobody has even asked about it. I don't have space in my shop, so I have thrown it out on the other side of the road. You can take it, it will give me space to put a few other rocks. This rock seems to be absolutely absurd, of no use."

So Michelangelo took that rock, and after a year he invited the owner of the shop, "Now you can come and see. Your rock has blossomed." And it was Michelangelo's greatest work of art – which has been destroyed just a few years ago by a madman. It was a statue of Jesus Christ. His mother, Mary, has taken the body of Jesus Christ from the cross. Jesus is lying almost naked in her lap, and she is looking at his face. It was one of the most beautiful statues in the world.

The shop owner could not believe his eyes. He said, "How did you manage it?"

He said, "It was not me. When I passed by the side of the rock, Jesus called to me, 'I am lying down in this rock. Just remove the unnecessary parts and I will be revealed.'

"And as I looked at the rock, I could see Jesus in the lap of his mother by the side of the cross. It looked strange, because this statue was hidden inside it – the cross, Jesus lying in the lap of his mother, and Mariam. So it looked a very strange type of rock. But I have just done a little work of chipping away unnecessary parts, and you can see the miracle that has happened."

That statue was in the Vatican, and just a few years ago – perhaps ten years ago – a madman with a hammer just went in and broke the heads of Jesus and Mariam, and destroyed that beautiful statue, the like of which may not be made again, because Michelangelos don't happen that often.

That man was caught, but it was too late. And in the court he said, "I am not a Michelangelo so I cannot create, but I can destroy. And I wanted my name to become history, I wanted to see my picture in all the newspapers on the front page. I have succeeded in it, and I am ready for any punishment."

The judge was at a loss what to say to this man. He had destroyed one of the most precious things, one of the most beautiful works of art, just to have his photograph in the newspapers on the front page, and his name in history: "Michelangelo created it, and this man destroyed it." He was ready...he said, "I am ready even to go to the gallows. It doesn't matter."

If you have eyes like Michelangelo, then every stone becomes something that ordinary people cannot see. Only a Michelangelo can penetrate just like an X-ray deep into the stone, and it can become a Jesus, it can become a Buddha.

Tanka Tennen was saying, "What is the need of all those statues when the real buddha was feeling the immense cold of the night? You pushed me out. And this has been the story of all the religions. They push the buddha out and they worship Buddha's statues."

The sutra:

BELOVED OSHO,
When Tenjiku was asked about the incident of Tanka burning the statue, he replied, "When it is cold we gather around the hearth by the fire."

Tenjiku is another master. When he was asked about the burning of the statue of Buddha by Tanka Tennen, he replied, "There is nothing wrong." He didn't say it directly, he simply said, *"When it is cold we gather around the hearth by the fire."*

"Was he wrong or not?" persisted the monk.
"When it is hot we sit in a bamboo forest in the valley," said Tenjiku.

He is not saying it is right or wrong – that is the way of Zen, not to decide right or wrong – he is simply saying, "Every Zen master behaves spontaneously. When it is hot he goes into the shade of a bamboo forest; when it is cold he burns wood." He is not mentioning at all whether Tanka Tennen has done anything wrong. He is simply saying, "Everybody who is aware functions spontaneously. Finding no other wood, Tanka Tennen found the wooden statue of Buddha. There is nothing wrong in it. When it is cold one needs fire, and when it is hot one needs shade."

Zen is absolutely natural. You should function according to your nature, and out of your spontaneity should come your response.

The day after the burning of the statue, Tanka Tennen went to see Nan-yō, who had once been a disciple of Enō and was the emperor's Zen master. When Tanka unrolled his Zazen rug, Nan-yō said, "There's no need."

That reminds me.... Perhaps little Siddhartha is still here, or maybe he has gone. When he first came, many many years ago, he was a small child, very small, maybe three years old or four years old. I can see exactly the moment he came to me.

He had brought a small rug, and he came as if he was a grown-up. Perhaps Maneesha will remember, she was present. He unrolled the rug like the Zen disciples do, and he touched my feet. All those who were present started laughing. This little boy was doing a real thing, which is not expected from such a little boy. He touched my feet with great gratefulness, with grace, and then sat down on his rug.

That's why I gave him the name Siddhartha. Siddhartha was Gautam Buddha's name given by his father. It is as beautiful as Buddha. It means one who has arrived: Siddhartha, one who has found the meaning, one who has found the significance of existence.

Just now he has been here for almost one month. I don't know whether he is still here or not. Now he has come with a girlfriend, has become very grown-up. It was reported to me by Anando that when he entered the gate after so many years, he had tears in his eyes. He must have remembered the first day he had come to me, almost twenty years ago.

He was such a lovely child.... His mother reported to me, "It is very difficult to find where he is, because he goes with everybody. He has such a great friendship with all the sannyasins" – and he was a little child.

He used to ask anybody, "Just give me ten rupees. I am going to see the movie." And it was not only one-sided; if somebody was in need of money, he would bring the money from others and give it to the person, saying, "Keep it, but remember, whenever I need it... Pay whenever you can."

So people used to ask Siddhartha, "Can you manage twenty rupees?" He would immediately go. He had the whole commune as his friends, and nobody could refuse him, he was so lovely, so innocent. With those tears he must have remembered the first day he had come.

Still he is innocent, and he is growing well on his own. His father has died. He is in a very good art school, learning acting. I was happy when he informed me that he is learning acting. Actors can be meditators very easily, because they are always acting somebody else's role, so they can witness also that it is not their identity. They may become Jesus Christ in a film, but they know they are not Jesus Christ. So to recognize that their performance is not their being, is very easy.

To me, acting is one of the best professions for meditators, because it will teach you that your identity can change every day. An actor is moving from one film to another. In one film he is one thing, in another film he is something else, in a third film he is somebody else. So slowly, slowly he can become aware – if he knows the art of becoming aware – that all these identities come and go. And finally, he can recognize that his own personality is nothing but an act taught by his parents, and the priests, and the politicians, and the professors.

All these people are creating a certain personality around you which is not your real being; it is just for convenience's sake. They are creating a social being out of a spiritual being. A social being is an ordinary thing. Your spiritual being is vast and immense.

The day after the burning of the statue, Tanka Tennen went to see Nan-yō, who had once been a disciple of Enō and was the emperor's Zen master.

Certainly he was a very important man, the emperor's Zen master.

When Tanka unrolled his Zazen rug, Nan-yō said, "There's no need, because that rug is spread only by disciples, and you are already a master. You don't have to do it."

Tanka Tennen was doing it just out of respect, because this man Nan-yō was very old, the emperor's master, and Tanka Tennen was a young man, although he had become enlightened. This is the Eastern way of always being respectful to the elders...because it used to be a part of natural growth. If a man lives naturally, then just as he becomes sexually mature at the age of fourteen, he will become capable of going out of sexual, biological bondage by the age forty-two – if he lives very naturally. And by the time he gets out of the control of biology, it is very easy for him to get out of the mind.

The ancient calculation is that by the age of forty-nine, a man can meditate easily, without any effort. The only condition is that he has lived without repressive religions, gods and priests. If he has lived just like a simple, natural human being, without any inhibition, without any guilt, then at the age of forty-two he gets out of the biological control.

Your sex is your bondage; it is a biological bondage. Don't fight against it. If you fight against it, you will not be out even at the age of eighty, or ninety. You will not be out of it at any point. Even when you are dying, your last thought will be about sex.

It has been calculated that every man thinks at least once about sex in three minutes, and every woman thinks about sex once every seven minutes. That is a disparity. That is why men look more sex-oriented than women. The difference is not much – three minutes or seven minutes is not much of a thing. The man has to wait only for four minutes. In that four minutes the woman can have the headache and take two aspirins, and she will be ready!

Your religions are responsible for keeping you in the bondage of sex by teaching you celibacy. Celibacy is a perversion of your nature. I want you to be absolutely natural: when it is time for sex, it is time for sex. Then you will be out of it by the age of forty-two, just simply out, with no question of making any effort to be celibate. Whenever you make any effort it is against nature. Nature does not allow any effort; it wants you to be utterly relaxed with it, and then it goes on doing things to you. By the time you are forty-nine you are really mature, and you have passed seven years without the bondage of sex.

One of the best novelists of this century, Kazantzakis, who wrote *Zorba the Greek*, also wrote a book about Jesus, *The Last Temptation*. Jesus was only thirty-three...and I agree with Kazantzakis that on the cross came the last temptation.

On that hot summer day, he was hanging on the cross. Do you think he was thinking about God? He started having a dream about Mary Magdalena, a fantasy that, "Perhaps if I had lived differently, and I had loved Mary Magdalena, and I had not got into this trip, I would not be hanging on this cross..."

In *The Last Temptation*, Kazantzakis depicts this whole dream. Because of this dream he was expelled from the Greek Orthodox church. His book was banned all around the world, because everywhere Christians were protesting against it: "This is too much!" When the film was made into a movie, everywhere there were great demonstrations against the movie. And Kazantzakis, one of the best novelists of this century, lived in utter misery and trouble, because the church had condemned him, expelled him.

He is dead, but just now my sannyasin, Amrito, who knows his wife in Greece, has been to see her. She asked her, "Would you like to become part of this sannyas movement?"

She said, "I would love to, but I am afraid. I have suffered so much because of my husband's suffering, the utter condemnation everywhere – and he had not done anything wrong."

I absolutely support him; his insight is clear. It's absolutely natural that a man of thirty-three hanged on the cross is bound to think, "My God! What have I done? If I had lived a different life with a beautiful woman who always wanted to live with me... I was trying to tell her, 'Get away! You are a temptation, get away!'" At the last moment the temptation must have come to him.

I can say with absolute authority that Kazantzakis is right. It is absolutely natural to remember Mary Magdalena, one of the most beautiful women, whom he had been denying. That was unnatural. And when God failed to do any miracle, he certainly would have thought, "It would have been right for me to have a wife, children, and live naturally. I unnecessarily went onto this number of being the only begotten son of God, and there seems to be no God at all!" Six hours on the cross are enough to bring anybody to his senses.

Now there is a movement amongst the intelligentsia of Europe that Kazantzakis should be accepted by the church again, posthumously. But the church is absolutely adamant: that man cannot be accepted back as a Christian, he has done immense harm to the image of Jesus Christ.

To me, he has done immense good to the image of Jesus Christ. He is saying that Jesus Christ was not a pervert, he was a natural human being. He has given more respect to Jesus Christ than anyone else, because of this dream.

His wife said, "I am simply afraid. Your master is continuously in trouble, is going to be in trouble, and I have suffered too much and I am old, too old. I would have loved to, but my whole life I suffered because my husband wrote *Zorba the Greek* and the church was angry. Then he wrote *The Last Temptation*, and the whole world was protesting, burning his books – and now they are banning the film."

Religions have done such harm that it is almost unbelievable – and they are still doing it.

In the East, particularly when religions were not organized, when religion was a freedom, an individual affair, people were very natural, and they came to celibacy naturally. When celibacy comes naturally it has a totally different flavor. There is no suppression, there are no sexual dreams, there is no question. And by the time you come to the age of fifty...

In India, the age of fifty is called "getting ready for the forest" – *vanprastha*. By the time you are fifty your children will be coming back from their schools, colleges, universities; now they will take care of your business. You can look now towards the forest.

Perhaps you will have to wait for a few days to teach your children the practical aspects of life. They have been in the universities, and they don't know anything about practical life. They have been meditating, they have been learning, they have been with great seers, and they are coming utterly innocent about the practical aspects of the world. So perhaps for twenty-five years... That was the Indian calculation: twenty-five years for education, twenty-five years for living as a householder, twenty-five years preparing to go to the Himalayas or to go to the forests, twenty-five years – the last twenty-five years – absolutely devoted to meditation. If life is one hundred years, then it was divided absolutely naturally into four parts.

By the time one is seventy-five he should retire into the forest. Now it is time to prepare for death, for another journey, for another experience. Life has passed away. Because of this, more respect was shown to the older man – and he was worthy of it. If he had lived naturally, he was worthy of it.

So *when Tanka Tennen unrolled his Zazen rug, Nan-yō said, "There's no need."* He was an old man. He could recognize Tanka Tennen immediately.

Only the enlightened person can recognize another enlightened being. There is no other way. The unenlightened cannot recognize the enlightened. The enlightened can recognize both the unenlightened and the enlightened. The higher can recognize the lower, but the lower cannot recognize the higher, because the higher has both the experience of the lower and of the higher. The lower has only the experience of the lower; he does not know anything beyond it.

But the difficulty is that the lower, the masses who have never known anything of the higher – they decide things. They decide who is enlightened, who is not enlightened. It is so hilarious....

One newspaper from Indore has written an editorial, and asked its readers to vote whether I am enlightened or not. So I have informed Chaitanya Keerti to write to them, "How many of your readers are enlightened? And first you should think about yourself: Are *you* enlightened? Can you recognize an enlightened person without being enlightened?" But this kind of stupidity goes on and on.

The people who had the experience were naturally respected by the younger generation, because they knew all the parts of life; they had been through all the stages, and they had passed beyond. Now they have become again innocent like a child; they are getting ready to enter again into existence.

But Nan-yō immediately said, "*There is no need.* You are as enlightened as I am. You are as much a master as I am. Here, age does not matter. Here, time is of no account."

Tanka took a few steps backward.

These are the ways of Zen. Unless you understand their symbology, their whole metaphoric language, you will miss the point.

Tanka took a few steps backward. What does it show? He is saying, "I have gone deep into myself. You are right." Taking a few steps backward means going inwards.

Nan-yō said, "That's right. You have gone really deep."

At this, Tanka took a few steps forward – just to check on the master, what he says.

Nan-yō said, "That's not right." Taking a few steps forward is going outward; taking a few steps backward is going inward. Backward and inward are equivalent, forward and outward are equivalent.

Nan-yō said, "That's not right."
At this, *Tanka walked around Nan-yō one time and left.*

He has paid the tribute: "I had come to see whether you are really as great as everyone says, and I have found you are simply the right man to be the master of the emperor himself."

On each point, Nan-yō proved right. When he was trying to unroll his rug, he stopped him, "There is no need." Then he took a few steps backward, and Nan-yō immediately said, "That is right."

At this, Tanka took a few steps forward.
Nan-yō said, "That's not right."

Tanka walked around Nan-yō.... Walking around Nan-yō is a symbol of great respect – making the circle complete: going from the source, and coming back again to the source as a goal. By making this circle complete, he expressed, "You are entirely enlightened, completely enlightened. I have nothing to ask, nothing to say." He simply left, with no word, no question. Those symbols were enough.

Nan-yō commented, when Tanka left, *"The old, golden days are far away."*

It used to be very common – enlightenment. It used to be very common to find such a man as Tanka Tennen, but those golden days are far away, and people are now so lazy that they will not even take a few steps backward, inward.

"Thirty years from now" – he made a prophecy – *"it will be difficult to get hold of this fellow."*

He was so young, and he had already expressed his immense clarity and his enlightenment. After thirty years, when he becomes a ripened being and his circle is complete – it has already begun to move towards completion – he said, "Thirty years from now, this man will be one of the greatest masters ever known. It will be very difficult to get hold of this fellow."

It is in deep respect and love that old Nan-yō recognized, not only his enlightenment, but also recognized that it is not far away...only thirty years and he will be a perfect buddha. Then it will be very difficult to get hold of this fellow.

Hyakusai wrote:

First frost.
My way lies northeast
facing the stars.

That is the way for everyone who is going deeper into meditation. It seems you are going deeper into meditation, but simultaneously something in you is going higher towards the stars. It is happening simultaneously. The roots go deeper and the tree goes higher.

In your meditation you are creating roots deep into your sources. When the nourishment is available your consciousness will start moving towards the stars – a pillar of light going towards the beyond. "First frost. My way lies northeast facing the stars."

A man of meditation, wherever he goes, is always moving towards the stars, because he is always moving towards the very source of nourishment. Once he gets his roots fixed into the earth, then there is no problem. Wherever he is, he is moving higher and higher like a Cedar of Lebanon. Those ancient trees – hundreds, thousands of years old, are standing, still growing towards the stars. The beauty of those trees is simply a reminder that the same is the way for human consciousness: deeper into the earth, higher into the sky.

Maneesha's question:

BELOVED OSHO,

D.T. Suzuki describes two different kinds of "seeing" as denoted by two different Chinese characters.

I have just told you, D.T. Suzuki is still in the mind; hence the division. Even seeing becomes of two kinds.

D.T. Suzuki describes two different kinds of "seeing" as denoted by two different Chinese characters. "K'an" consists of a hand and an eye and means "to watch an object as independent of the spectator" – objective knowledge.

You are watching a tree. The tree is different from you, this is one kind of seeing.

"The seen and the seeing are two separate entities." On the other hand, the character "chien" is composed of an eye alone on two outstretched legs, and signifies the pure act of seeing.

Suzuki considers the difference between these two kinds of seeing as "revolutionary in the history of Zen thought."

In the first place, Zen is not a thought. In the second place, the act of pure seeing cannot be called at all an "act of pure seeing." What are you seeing? For seeing to be seeing, you need an object.

The meditator goes beyond the object and beyond the subject, beyond the first Chinese character, "k'an," which signifies duality – the seer and the seen, the knower and the known – and the second character, "chien," which signifies the pure act of seeing. But the very word 'seeing' means something is there, otherwise how can you see? What can you see? If there is nothing, seeing disappears, being appears.

Hence I will not agree with D.T. Suzuki at all. These two kinds of seeing are just mind, logic, rationality, but not meditation, not Zen. Zen is going beyond the seeing and beyond the seen. It is going into being – just being, utterly silent, at ease with existence.

There is no duality, and there is no oneness either – you have to understand it – because if there is no duality, you cannot call it oneness. "One" suggests immediately the two; hence Gautam Buddha does not use the word 'oneness'. He uses the word *advaita,* not twoness. It makes a great difference.

When you say one, immediately you are reminded of two. How can one exist without two and three and four and five and six and seven...? One is a digit; it is just below two. If one exists, then thousands of numbers will follow, or millions, or trillions. There is no end to it. If you have started on one, you are on a long journey without end.

To avoid this, a roundabout way has been found: not to say "oneness with existence" but to say "not twoness." It exactly means oneness, but to say that in language creates the difficulty. Without two, how can there be one? So don't say "one," just say, "not two." The one is understood, it has not to be said. It is the inexpressible. But by saying "not two," you have indicated towards it. A simple gesture – without making any noise about it, you have hinted at it. It is a pure hint.

Suzuki misses the point. The revolutionary step is not Zen thought, but Zen experience. That experience is of "not twoness." There is no seer and no seen, but just being.

It is time for Sardar Gurudayal Singh.

Put the lights on! I love to see my people laughing. I am absolutely against seriousness, but unfortunately I have to discuss serious things. But it is good to make you first serious, then laughter comes more easily. Then it gives a great relaxation.

Little Albert comes running into the village store and races up to the counter. "Hey, mister," he cries to old Jock, the owner. "My dad was fixing the roof when the ladder slipped from under him! Now he is hanging by his fingers from an upstairs window ledge!"

"Well, son," says old Jock, "you have come to the wrong place! You want the police station across the road – and hurry!"

"No," says Albert, "you don't understand. I want some more film for my camera!"

One Sunday morning at the Loony Tunes Funny Farm, old Father Fungus is the guest preacher in the lunatic asylum's small chapel. He is ranting and raving in the pulpit, screaming all about damnation and hellfire, God's sweet love and the nocturnal emissions of the Holy Ghost, when suddenly, Mad Melvin jumps up out of his seat, raises both arms high in the air and shouts, "Bullshit! Do we have to listen to this idiot?" Then Mad Melvin smiles and sits back down.

There is pindrop silence. Father Fungus is extremely embarrassed, and turns to the hospital director Doctor Dumshit.

"Oh dear!" stammers the priest. "Shall I stop speaking?"

"No need for that, Father," sighs Dumshit, yawning. "It won't happen again. Mad Melvin only makes a true statement once every seven years."

Two famous music lovers, Cardinal Catsass and Pope the Polack, are sipping wine and having an intimate chat in the pope's private Vatican chambers. "Did you know," says Catsass, confiding in the old papal fruitcake, "that I have a very special musical friend?"

"Really?" says the pope.

"Yes," continues Catsass. "I treat her just like a guitar – I finger the top and play the bottom and get beautiful music!"

"Well," says Pope the Polack, "I must confess that I have a very special musical friend, too."

"Really?" exclaims Catsass.

"Yes," continues the Polack pope. "I treat mine more like a pop record. I place her on the deck and we make beautiful music. And then three minutes later, I turn her over!"

Nivedano...

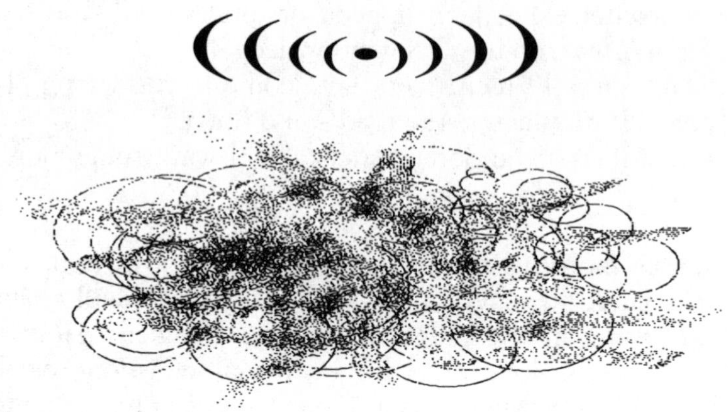

Nivedano...

Be silent...

Close your eyes...and feel your body to be completely frozen.

This is the right moment to look inwards.

Gather your energies and your total consciousness, and rush towards your very center of being. It is just below the navel, exactly two inches below, inside you.

But only those will succeed who rush with an urgency and intensity, as if this is the last moment of life. You have to make it now or never.

Faster and faster... Deeper and deeper...

You are coming closer to the center of your being.

A great silence is descending over you like soft rain. You can feel the coolness. With you, the whole night has become silent.

A little closer to your center, and a great peace surrounds you, engulfs you. You are drowned in it. It is the peace that mystics have called "the peace that passeth understanding."

A little closer...and blossoms, flowers start showering over you, of bliss, of ecstasy. You are starting to feel like a drunk – but this is not an ordinary drunkenness, it is divine drunkenness. And only in this divine drunkenness can you take the last step. Enter into your center.

This is the opening into the beyond, this is the place where you are joined with the cosmos. You will meet here your original face. The face of Gautam the Buddha has been accepted in the East as a symbol of everybody's original face.

Meeting the buddha is a very strange experience, because you start disappearing, fading away. And as you fade away, the buddha becomes more and more solid and strong. It is your very essential being.

The only quality the buddha has is witnessing. You have to get more and more attuned with this quality, because only this quality can bring your buddha from the center to the circumference. He can become your whole life. He is the ultimate dance.

Gautam the Buddha is the Zen Manifesto.

Witnessing, you start disappearing.

That's what I have called freedom from the self.

Witness that you are not the body.

Witness that you are not the mind.

Witness that you are only a witness, and everything starts settling.

To make this witnessing more clear and deeper,
Nivedano...

Relax...

It is only a question of relaxing, it is not an effort. It is just falling deep into your own depth, resting at the very center of your life source.

This life source, this juice that is flowing all around you, will start a tremendous metamorphosis within you. You will feel you are melting, melting, melting...

Gautama the Buddha Auditorium is becoming an ocean of consciousness. Ten thousand buddhas have disappeared into one oceanic experience.

This is the Zen Manifesto: freedom from oneself.

Gather all these experiences, the grace, the beauty, the truth, the blissfulness. You have to bring them with you. They have to become your day-to-day life. I don't teach any other morality. I teach spontaneity, and the morality follows like a shadow. And because it comes from your very sources you never feel you are being commanded, you never feel you are being dominated, you never feel you are being a slave, you never feel you are being a sheep. You start being a lion.

Your morality, your response to existence becomes a lion's roar.

The beauty and the power – and the power that is harmless...

The love that simply overflows you, unconditional, just a gift, a blessing to the whole existence... And a grace that changes not only your consciousness but even your body.

Your gestures become so meaningful, so significant, so beautiful – like roses.

Your eyes become like stars.

Your heart starts beating in tune with the universal heart.

This synchronicity is the Zen Manifesto.

And don't forget to persuade Gautam Buddha to come with you.

These are the three steps of enlightenment....

The first, Gautam Buddha comes behind you just as a shadow – but the shadow is not dark, it is luminous. There is no person in it but only presence, a tremendous presence. It is warm, you feel for the first time loved by existence itself. It is calm and cool at the same time. That's the miracle of Zen.

On the second step, you become the shadow. Your shadow is certainly dark; it is false, it has been your prison. Gautam Buddha comes in front. It is a great revolution, because your shadow immediately starts disappearing.

And the third step comes spontaneously in: freedom from oneself. You are no more, only existence is, life is, awareness is.

All these are represented by the presence of Gautam the Buddha. He was the first man in history to bring this breakthrough, to turn the horizontal consciousness into a vertical consciousness. Your roots go deep into the earth, and your branches and your flowers blossom into the sky.

This is meeting with the universe, merging into existence. A great celebration arises, and not only in you, the whole existence participates.

Nivedano...

Come back...but come back as Gautam the Buddha, with the same grace, the same beauty, the same silence, the same divine drunkenness, and sit for a few moments to remind yourself of the golden path you have traveled, the beautiful, the blissful, the ecstatic experience of reaching to the center of your being, which opens into the cosmos.

Zen is nothing but an opening into the cosmos.

You disappear, only existence remains.

This is the ultimate freedom: freedom from oneself.

This freedom becomes a great celebration. You dance with the stars, you dance with the ocean, you dance with the trees, you dance under the sky, under the stars. Suddenly the whole cosmos has become your home. You are not a foreigner, you are not a stranger, you are not an outsider. You belong to this existence. This existence belongs to you.

This is the revolution that Zen brings to humanity. This is Zen's great contribution to the world.

It is the right time for you to start celebrating life, dancing in deep synchronicity with existence – and spread this fire of Zen around the world. This is the only possibility to save humanity from committing suicide.

Okay, Maneesha?

Yes, Osho.

LET THE CHRISTIAN SHIP DROWN

BELOVED OSHO,

One day, on his way to see Ma Tzu, Tanka Tennen met an old man with a boy, and asked them where they lived. The old man answered, "Above is the sky; below is the earth!"
Tanka said, "How about if the sky crumbled away and the earth fell to pieces?"
The old man said, "Ah! Ah!"
The boy drew a deep breath, and Tanka said, "If there were no father, no child would be born."
The old man and the child entered the mountains and were seen no more.

Once, Tanka Tennen was lying on the Tenshin bridge. Lord Teikō, who was in charge of the bridge, came out and warned Tanka that he had better move, but Tanka didn't get up.
Teikō asked why he didn't listen to him. After a few moments, Tanka said, "I am a monk of nothing."
Teikō was taken aback by Tanka Tennen's response, and from then on provided him with clothing and a daily meal.
After the incident, Tanka Tennen was venerated by the whole city.

FRIENDS,

The first question:

In Thomas Merton's view:
"Zen is not a systematic explanation of life, it is not an ideology, it is not a world view, it is not a theology of revelation and salvation, it is not a mystique, it is not a way of ascetic perfection, it is not mysticism as it is understood in the West; in fact it fits no convenient category of ours. Hence all our attempts to tag it and dispose of it with labels like pantheism, quietism, illuminism, Pelagianism, must be completely incongruous.
"But the chief characteristic of Zen is that it rejects all systematic elaborations in order to get back as far as possible to the pure, unarticulated and unexplained ground of direct experience. The direct experience of what? Life itself."
Beloved Master,
Has Thomas Merton got it?

It is a very sad story about Thomas Merton. Perhaps he was one of th persons in the West who has come closest to Zen. He had the sensibilit of a poet; the others are approaching Zen from their intellect, thei mind.

Thomas Merton is approaching Zen through his heart. He feels it, bu he could not live the direct experience he is talking about. He woul have been the first Zen master in the West, but he was prevented by th Catholic church.

Thomas Merton was a Trappist monk under the control of th Vatican. The Trappist monks are the most self-torturing ascetics in Chris tianity. Perhaps that's why they are called Trappist – trapped forever.

Thomas Merton wrote beautiful poetry, and he asked again and agai to go to Japan and to live in a Zen monastery to have the direct experi ence of Zen. But permission was refused half a dozen times; again an again he was refused.

If he had really understood Zen he would not have bothered even t ask for permission. Who is the Vatican? Who is the pope? A Zen maste asking permission from unenlightened people is simply not heard of. And he followed the orders from the Vatican and from the abbot of his own monastery.

He had been reading as much as was available in English about Zen. Finally, he had a chance to go, but he did not understand the way the organized religions work. There was going to be a Catholic conference of missionaries in Bangkok, Thailand, and he asked permission to attend the conference. Deep in his heart he was going to Bangkok to attend the conference just so that from there he could enter Japan without asking anybody's permission.

But the pope and the Vatican leaders and his abbot – they were all aware of his continuously asking for permission to go to a Zen monastery.

On the last day of the conference in Bangkok, Thomas Merton spoke about Zen. And he also mentioned that he would love to go to Japan from Bangkok. That very night he was found dead. And without anybody being informed, his body was embalmed immediately, without any autopsy, without knowing the cause of his death. After you have embalmed a body there is no possibility of autopsy. There is every reason to suspect that he was poisoned to prevent him from going to a Zen monastery.

Murder has been the argument of the so-called religions. This is not a religious attitude at all. If he wanted to experience Zen, any religious man would have allowed him to go. That's what happens in Zen. No master ever rejects any disciple's interest in some other Zen monk, in some other monastery – maybe belonging to a different branch, Sōtō or Rinzai... Permission is gracefully given, and not only to those who are inquiring about going somewhere else. Even the master himself, if he feels that some other master will be more appropriate, some other path leading to the direct experience will be more fitting to the disciple, will send his own disciples to other monasteries. This is a totally different world, the world of Zen, with no competitiveness, no question of conversion.

Thomas Merton's murder shows the poverty of Catholicism and Christianity. Why were they so afraid? The fear was that Thomas Merton had already praised Zen, and although he was living in the monastery, it seemed he was wavering between Zen and Christianity. To give him a chance to go to Japan and have a direct experience under a master might have been dangerous. He might have become involved in Zen for his whole life. These so-called religions are so jealous; they don't have any compassion for individual growth, freedom.

Thomas Merton's murder is not only Thomas Merton's murder, it should make every Christian aware that Christianity is not a religion. Deep down it is more interested in gathering numbers. Numbers have their own politics. The greater the number of followers you have, the greater the power to dominate. And they are always afraid that anybody who leaves their fold is betraying.

But it is absolutely certain that Thomas Merton had already felt in his heart the immense need for Zen. Christianity was no longer satisfying. His whole life he had been a monk in the monastery, but slowly slowly, as he became aware of Zen, he could see that Christianity was not at all a religion; fictions, lies, beliefs, but not a direct experience. The very idea of Zen as a non-systematic, individualist approach to truth in a direct way – not through theology, not through any belief, not through any philosophy, but through meditation – was attracting him immensely, but it was not yet an experience.

Thomas Merton is far better than Suzuki, than Alan Watts, than Paul Reps, than Hubert Benoit, and than many others who have written about Zen. He comes the closest, because he is not speaking through the head, he is speaking through the heart of a poet.

But the heart is only just in the middle, between the head and the being. Unless you reach to the being, you don't have the experience yourself. But he was a sensitive man; he managed to state things which he had not experienced.

His statement is beautiful, but it shows clearly that he had not experienced it himself. This is his understanding – of course, far deeper than any other Western scholar of Zen. If it had really been a direct experience for him, the way he was saying, he would not have cared about anybody's permission, he would not have cared about Christianity. He would have come out of that fold – which was just a slavery and nothing else.

Because he never came out of the fold, that shows he was hanging in the middle, he was not yet certain. He had not tasted the truth. He had only heard about it, read about it, and felt that there seems to be a different approach, altogether different, from that of Christianity. But Christianity was still keeping its hold over him. He could not be a rebel, and that's where he failed, completely failed.

A man of Zen is basically rebellious. Thomas Merton was not rebellious, he was a very obedient person. Obedience is another name for slavery, a beautiful name that does not hurt you, but it is spiritual slavery. His asking six times and being refused, and still remaining in the fold, shows clearly that he was spiritually a slave. Although he was showing a deep interest in Zen, it was at the most, deeper than the mind, but not deep enough to reach to the being. He remained hanging in the middle. Perhaps now in his new life, he may either be here, or in Japan – most probably he is here amongst you – because that was his last wish before he died.

As the conference ended and he went to his bed, immediately he was poisoned. While he was dying, thinking about Zen, his last wish must have been to go to Japan, to be with a master. He had lived under Christianity his whole life, but it had not fulfilled him, it had not made him enlightened. It had only been a consolation.

Only fools can be deceived by consolations and lies and fictions. A man of such intense sensitivity as Thomas Merton could not be befooled. But a lifelong obedience turned into a spiritual slavery. He tried to sneak out from Bangkok – because there was no need to ask the abbot of the monastery, there was no need to ask the pope. He could have simply gone from Bangkok.

But these so-called religions are murderous. They must have been ready. If he showed any interest in Japan and not going back to his monastery directly from Bangkok as the conference ended...the murderers must have been already there. And because he mentioned in his last speech to the conference that he was immensely interested in Zen, and he would like to go to Japan from there, this statement became his death.

So it is not only Ayatollah Khomeini. There have been murders and murders, century after century, of people who wanted to get out of the slavery and seek and search the truth on their own; who wanted to get rid of all systems, who wanted to have a direct experience of life.

Thomas Merton's words are beautiful, but they are empty words because there is no supporting experience behind them. I will read those words again.

"Zen is not a systematic explanation of life" – but this can be said very easily by anybody reading books about Zen. It is not a systematic explanation of life; in fact, it is not an explanation at all. That makes the difference. He is denying: "Zen is not a systematic explanation of life."

I say unto you, Zen is not an explanation at all about life or existence. It is *an experience*, not an explanation. It is not an ideology.

This can be said by anyone who is reading a book on Zen. But it is stated with such certainty by so many people who have only an intellectual understanding, that it is not a great indication of whether Thomas Merton had had any experience. Zen certainly is not an ideology, it is not a world view. All these are different words for the same thing: "a systematic explanation, an ideology, a world view, a theology of revelation and salvation." He is simply being tautological, he is saying the same thing again and again in different words.

"It is not a mystique" – there he is wrong. It is, although it is not stated. That's why he thought it is not a mystique. It is the greatest mystique, but it is not said because it cannot be said. Because it is never said, he thought that it is not a mystique. These small things indicate that he's just read about it – because nowhere is it said that it is a mystique. Because no master ever indicated in words that it is a mystique, he thinks it is not a mystique. It is. It is the greatest mystique, the greatest mystery, the greatest miracle.

But to say it in words has not been the way of Zen. It attracts people, takes away their ideologies, their theologies, their religions. It leaves you absolutely fresh at the very center of your being. Without saying anything, you experience the mystique, you experience the mystery of existence and life. But because it is an experience…

In Zen they don't even use the word 'experience', they use the word 'experiencing', because the experience is not something dead and complete. It is a river flowing, flowing, alive, moving. The word 'experience' indicates that it has become complete. Anything that becomes complete becomes dead, and Zen is the most alive thing in the world; hence it cannot be said that it is an experience. We have to invent a word, 'experiencing'; instead of river, 'rivering'… That gives the clear-cut idea that a river is not static, it is moving. On the way, always on the way, moving eternally, falling into the ocean, rising into the clouds, falling in the rain on the mountains, and again into the river...moving in a circle of tremendous aliveness, never stopping anywhere.

There is no full stop in Zen, and all our words – 'experience', 'knowledge', 'understanding'...give the illusion of a full stop. We have to change our nouns into verbs – verbs come closer to life. We use the word 'life', but we should use the word 'living' – that comes closer. Moment to moment, living. 'Life' seems to be something dead; it has already completed its course, has come to an end, to the graveyard.

Zen is certainly a mystique. In fact, it is the only mystique there is. But it is not being said, it is kept a secret so that you don't go inside your being with a certain idea. You go absolutely clean and fresh. You will find the mystery, the immense mystery of life, but Zen's absolute approach is not to give you any idea what you are going to find. The reason is very scientific.

If you have any idea what you are going to find – which all the religions give you... The mind has the capacity to create an hallucination of the idea. Then the idea becomes a reality to you. Christians experience Christ, Buddhists experience Buddha, Hindus experience Krishna. It never happens to a Hindu that Christ comes, it never happens to a Christian that Mohammed comes. Strange...Mohammed comes only to those who believe in Mohammed.

Once in a while it would be good for these people to enter into somebody else's experience. In fact, it would be absolutely right to convert.... If Christ appears to a Hindu, the Hindu will become Christian; if Krishna appears to a Christian, the Christian will turn to the Hare Krishna, Hare Rama movement. But it never happens! It cannot happen because you are carrying a certain idea, so fixed that your whole mind starts creating a dream.

The mind has the capacity of dreaming, hallucinating, imagining. If you are constantly working on one single idea, sooner or later it becomes such a fixed program that when you look in silence you find suddenly Christ arising. That fulfills your idea. It is a vicious circle. Because you experience Christ arising in your mind, your belief in Christ becomes stronger.

Now it is no longer just a belief, you have experienced it also. Because it becomes stronger, there is more possibility of Christ coming closer to you. Every time Christ appears to you, he will be more solid, more alive, closer. And every time he appears, you are getting feedback for your belief system, it is becoming stronger and more fanatical. Soon you will be almost insane. You will start talking to Christ – and not only will you start talking, but he will answer.

Anybody watching you will see that you are doing both the things: you are asking the question and you are answering the question. Anybody watching you will be able to see that you are just behaving in an insane way. You are not talking to anybody but yourself. But you have gone so deep in the hallucination, with such strength and continuous feedback, that you believe it is Christ who is talking.

You can find such mad people sitting and talking in every madhouse, and you know that there is nobody. And the strangest phenomenon which the mind is capable of, is that when the person asks a question, his voice will be different. When he answers the question, his voice will be different again – booming, coming from the beyond. This whole game he is playing alone; there is nobody to answer.

In a madhouse, a madman was keeping his ear close to a wall. He was keeping his eyes down and his ear touching the wall. The superintendent came many times, but the man was completely fixed in his posture. Finally, he could not resist the temptation: "What is the matter?" he asked the fellow.

The madman said, "Shhh!"

But the superintendent said, "What are you doing?"

He said, "I am trying to listen. You can give it a try."

So the superintendent came and listened to the wall, and there was nothing to hear. He said, "I can't hear a thing."

The madman said, "Neither can I – but one never knows. I will continue till I start hearing."

If you continue till you start hearing, you are going to be completely insane. All the religions have been driving their saints, their monks, into insanity. This world is not in a mess without any reason; the religions are absolutely responsible for it.

Thomas Merton says, "It is not a way of ascetic perfection." Because he was following an ascetic way of perfection, he could see that Zen is different; it gives no discipline. The Trappist monk lives under such a strict discipline, it is unbelievable.

I have told you the story....

A man entered into one of the most prominent Trappist monasteries, and the abbot said, "Do you know our rule? For seven years you have not to say a single word. Only after seven years can you state anything you want, anything you need, anything you want to inquire about – just a small talk. Then for seven years again you have to be silent."

The man was determined to follow the discipline, so he accepted and he was shown his cell. He went into the cell and he saw that the glass was broken. So for seven years he was suffering from cold, suffering from rain – because the rain was coming directly through the window – and he could not say a single word, he had to wait for seven years.

He waited, and after seven years he went to the abbot and said, "My window is broken."

The abbot said, "That's enough. You go back. For seven years no more words. The window will be repaired."

The window was repaired, but in seven years the mattress had gone completely rotten because rain was continuously coming in, and even snowflakes were coming in. Suddenly he saw that he had not mentioned about the mattress. "My God! now seven years again..." And the mattress had gathered all kinds of cockroaches, spiders...because the window was broken, and this was a good shelter for cockroaches.

After seven years of continuous suffering with cockroaches...he again went to the abbot and said, "You repaired the window, but the mattress is absolutely rotten."

The abbot said, "Go back to your cell, a new mattress will be sent." And the people who brought the new mattress pulled out the old one and cleaned the cell, but the new mattress was bigger than the cell. They somehow forced it, and because they were forcing it, the glass of the window broke. Now again begins the same story....

Fourteen years have passed – again he is back to zero. The first day he entered, this was the situation. Seven years he has to wait again. Again the rain – and he is getting old and sick, and continuously has fever, but he cannot speak.

After seven years when he went to the abbot, the abbot said, "Shut up!" before he even spoke. "For twenty-one years I have never heard anything from you except complaints, complaints, complaints! Get out of the monastery!"

The poor fellow, after wasting twenty-one years in a Trappist monastery, was thrown out, sick, old, exhausted. Twenty-one years of continuous torture...!

Thomas Merton was living in a Trappist monastery. Obviously, he could see that Zen does not give you any discipline, it is not ascetic, and he could see what he had been doing to himself and what other Trappists were doing to themselves. It is sheer masochism – self-torture in the name of an ascetic way of life. It is not a way of life, it is a way of death! It is slow suicide, slow poisoning.

But his statement will be detected by any man who has a direct experience of Zen. He says, "It is not a way of ascetic perfection." The implication is that it is a way of perfection without asceticism. It is not a way of perfection at all.

Zen is evolution, endless evolution. Perfection is the dead end of the road, there is no more to go. In Zen there is always the infinite and the eternal available. You cannot exhaust it. In fact, as you go on the way, the way is not exhausted, slowly slowly you start dispersing and disappearing. Suddenly you find one day you are no more, only existence is.

It is not perfection at all, it is not salvation. It is dissolution, it is disappearance, it is melting like ice into the ocean.

Thomas Merton goes on, "It is not mysticism as it is understood in the West."

In the West it is understood as mysticism; that does not mean it is not mysticism. Certainly it is not the mysticism that arises out of the mind as a philosophical point of view. It is pure mysticism, not originating in the mind, but arising from your very sources of life. It blossoms into mysterious flowers releasing mysterious, absolutely unknown fragrances into existence. It is mysticism – but it is not an "ism." It is not a philosophy, it is not a creed or cult. Again and again you have to fall back towards direct experience.

He says, "In fact, it fits no convenient category of ours."

All his statements are beautiful, but something is missing. That missing link you will find only if you have the experience. Then you can compare. Otherwise Thomas Merton will look absolutely right, a man of Zen. He is not. He wanted to be, but if he had been, there would have been no need to go to Japan. I have never been to Japan.

In fact, in Japanese Zen monasteries my books are being read, prescribed in Zen universities – but I have never been to Japan. I don't need to. Buddha himself never went to Japan, Mahakashyapa was not born in Japan.

His desire to go to Japan shows that he had seen one thing clearly: that Christianity does not work. And he was searching for some new approach that worked. His statement, "In fact it fits no convenient category of ours," is true. But it is not only categories of *ours* – it does not fit into any kind of category. It is beyond categories. Neither Christian categories, nor Hindu, nor Mohammedan, nor Jaina, it does not fit into any category. It is so original, you cannot make it fit into any category. The original is always individual; it is not a category.

Do you think I fit in any category? All categories are against me! And the reason they are against me is that I don't fit with them. I have no desire to fit with anybody. I am sufficient unto myself. I don't need any religion, I don't need any philosophy, I don't need any category.

In other words: I am a category in myself.

Zen will not fit into any category because it is a category in itself. And it is such a rebellious category, such an unsystematic category, that in Zen all kinds of wildflowers are accepted as equal with the roses and with the lotuses. It does not matter whether it is a lotus or a rose or just a wildflower, the only thing that matters is flowering. All have flowered to their potential. That's where they are all equal. Otherwise their colors are different, their beauties are different, their fragrances are different – a few may not have any fragrance at all.

So they don't fit in one category, but as far as flowering is concerned, they have all flowered, blossomed, to their totality. Whatever was hidden has become a reality. What was a dream in the plant has blossomed as a reality.

Zen is a blossoming of your potential. And everybody has a different potential, so when you blossom as a Zen man you have a unique individuality. You don't fit with any category – and not only Christian categories. That's what Thomas Merton means: "In fact, it fits no convenient category of ours."

But I have to say to you, it does not fit any category at all, yours or ours or anybody else's. It is beyond the mind. All categories belong to the mind. This is the only rebellion against mind: going beyond it. This is the only revolution against the self: going into no-self, into *anatta*. This is ultimate freedom from all kinds of bondages: prisons and categories and isms and ideologies and world views and philosophies. It is an absolute freedom from all that mind can create and mind can understand. It is also free from the heart.

The heart can understand something deeper than the mind, but Zen is far deeper than the heart. The heart can be just an overnight stay. While you are going towards your being, your heart, your art, your music, your dance, your poetry, your painting, your sculpture, can be just one night's halt. But you have to go deeper. You have to reach to the very roots of your life, from where you are getting nourishment every moment, to the point where you are joined with existence, you are no longer separate.

"Hence all our attempts," says Thomas Merton, "to tag it and dispose of it with labels like pantheism, quietism, illuminism, Pelagianism, must be completely incongruous."

This is a very simple understanding which need not have any direct experience. And he comes to the point. He says, "But the chief characteristic of Zen is that it rejects all systematic elaborations in order to get back as far as possible to the pure, unarticulated and unexplained ground of direct experience. The direct experience of what? Life itself."

A beautiful statement, but empty – a plastic flower with no fragrance and with no life in it. Otherwise, why did he want to go to Japan? If he had had this direct experience he is talking about, there was no need to go to Japan, and there was no need to remain in a Trappist monastery. He should have been a man of freedom.

But he could never attain that freedom. He was longing for it, he was desiring it – and you desire only because you don't have it. If you have it, you don't desire it.

And you have asked, "Beloved Master, has Thomas Merton got it?"

Not yet – but perhaps in this life. After being murdered by the Christians...

It is a well-known fact to the people who have known the direct experience, that your last thought before you die is going to be your first thought when you are born and you grow up. As you start having intelligence, your last thought of the past life is going to suddenly pop up. It has been hiding itself inside you.

It is just like the last thought when you go to bed. Just watch what is the last thought...or perhaps it is better to create the last thought so you are clearly aware of it. For example, you simply think of zero. Go on watching the zero, so it is visual also, and the thought is inside: zero, zero, zero, zero...and sleep starts coming. And when sleep is coming, still a faraway echo, zero, zero, zero...goes on. Once the sleep settles, you forget about the word 'zero'.

Then remember in the early morning when you are feeling awake – don't open your eyes, just wait a little. Within moments, the first thought in the morning will be "zero." That will give you the idea that although you had forgotten about zero, the whole night, eight hours, it was continuously moving as an undercurrent. Otherwise, how do you find exactly that thought in the morning as the first thought?

The same happens with death, because death is nothing but a deeper sleep. The last thought, the last desire, is going to be your first thought, your first desire as you become mature enough to have thoughts. It will immediately come to your mind.

In Tibet they have a special ceremony for dying people called *Bardo*. The person is dying, and the masters of Bardo recite certain experiences that are going to happen to you: that you will be born in a certain womb of a special kind, that you will be born as an intelligent being, that your first thought will be how to find the truth, how to become a buddha... They go on repeating....

The man is dying, he is going deeper and deeper into sleep, and they go on repeating it till they feel the man is dead. They have given him the last thought. Perhaps he would not have been able to have this last thought by himself, because his last thought may be money, his last thought may be sex, his last thought may be anything that he has been desiring and has not been able to get: power, prestige, respectability.

One never knows what the last thought will be. It will be the one that you have not been able to materialize in your life and in which you have been disappointed. That will bubble up, pop up in your head, and that will drive you into a new life. That will be the determining factor for your new phase, your new journey.

The Tibetan enlightened people found that it is better not to depend on the person. It is better to create the aroma, the atmosphere in which he forgets all about money and sex, power and prestige, fame and name, and they go on repeating the Bardo in such a singing voice that it is impossible for him not to hear it.

I had one famous doctor in Jabalpur, Dr. Bharat, a Bengali doctor, but the most famous physician in that part of the country. He was the president of the Rotary Club; that's how I came to know him – because he requested me to address the Rotary Club.

So he had come to my house and taken me in his car, and had listened to me for the first time in the Rotary Club, and became very deeply interested in me. He used to come to see me once in a while. He was reading books I had suggested to him because he wanted to read something about Zen, something about Tibetan mysticism, something about Sufism, something about Hassidism – the things that I had been talking about to him.

So he came to the point of knowing about Bardo. He said, "What is Bardo?"

I said, "I will come to your clinic and give you a try."

He said, "What do you mean, you will give *me* a try?"

I said, "In fact, it is just the opposite. But let me come to your clinic."

So I went to his clinic and I told him, "Give me the chloroform."

He said, "What?"

I said, "You just give me the chloroform, and I will go on repeating: one, two, three, four, five...and you just listen at what number I stop. And when I come back, when you remove the chloroform mask, just listen to me. I will start counting at the same number where I had stopped, in reverse order."

He was a little worried. First he said, "Now we have stopped using chloroform."

I said, "You will have to do it if you want to understand Bardo."
He said, "But it is dangerous."
I said, "Don't be worried, it is not dangerous."
So I persuaded him. He put me under the mask and I started repeating the numbers: one, two, three... And I was watching inside that my voice was becoming slower and slower and slower, and that he was putting his ear close to my mouth to hear the last – it was nine. After that I could not speak, the body was completely paralyzed, my lips wouldn't move.
After ten minutes he removed the mask and he waited. As I became capable of moving my lips, he heard: "Nine, eight, seven, six, five, four, three, two, one." And as I was coming in the reverse order, my voice was becoming clearer and clearer. By the time I reached one, I was back.
I said, "This is Bardo. When you are dying, if you can manage by yourself, good; otherwise call me. Then I will give you the idea where to go, what kind of womb to find, what kind of parents will give you freedom, what kind of atmosphere to look for where soon you will become intelligent and will not remain retarded – the idea of becoming a Gautam Buddha, the idea of becoming enlightened."
But he was still alive when I left Jabalpur in 1970, so I don't know what happened to the fellow. He was old, most probably he is dead and is born somewhere. And I don't think he was capable of creating the whole program for the new journey. Bardo is programming your whole journey.

Thomas Merton must have been born in Japan or in a place where he can experience Zen without any hindrance from Christianity, without any obedience to any pope. But in the past life, when he was Thomas Merton, he was having a good contemplation about Zen that may have created the atmosphere of Bardo. And because this was his last statement in the conference...and he must have been planning it while he was being poisoned. The next morning he was to leave for Japan, he had booked for Japan – but he was not aware that Christianity will not allow you to get out of their prison so easily.
I am against all these religions for the simple reason that they have been criminals, murderers. They have been talking about peace, love, God; they have been talking great words – but they don't mean it. What

they mean can be found only in their actions, not in their words.

The second question:

Thomas Merton wrote: "Zen is one of the most mysterious of all spiritualities..."

Do you see the contradiction? Just in the first statement he was saying it is not a mystique, it is not mysticism, and now he is saying:

"Zen is one of the most mysterious of all spiritualities, being so full of impudent paradox that it is at first a real scandal to the rational spirit of the West."
Beloved Master,
But, in fact, is not Zen more rational in its irrationality – being the acknowledgement that rationality has limits and we are after the unlimited – than Christianity with its miracles, immaculate conception and resurrection?

The first thing is that Thomas Merton was not a very conscious being; he knew nothing of meditation. Without knowing meditation, you cannot be more conscious than ordinary people; everybody has a thin layer of consciousness. Hence, he forgets immediately that he has denied that Zen is a mystique, and immediately he comes to the point: "Zen is one of the most mysterious of all spiritualities."

In fact, it is simply mysterious; it has nothing to do with spiritualities. It is far beyond so-called spirituality – because what else is your spirit than your self? Hence, all spiritualities are centered on *self* realization.

Zen is not a spiritual phenomenon at all, because it is moving beyond the spirit and beyond the self. It is going into nothingness. It is melting into the blue sky.

For example, Jainism is a great spirituality. It stops at the realization of the self. Once you have realized your individuality, it stops. You become a frozen iceberg, not melting. Gautam Buddha goes beyond Mahavira. The iceberg has to melt, and once the iceberg melts, *you* are no more.

It is not even spirituality. Certainly that makes it more mysterious, but not a more mysterious spirituality. The basic approach of Gautam Buddha is that you are not, and you have to look into this nothingness.

This nothingness is the beginning of your universal synchronicity with the very heart of existence. This dissolving into the ocean of life has never been taught by anyone other than Gautam Buddha. And since Gautam Buddha, Zen masters have taken the task in their hands.

It is not a spirituality, because it has no self. It is utterly mysterious, because you are expected to dissolve yourself – which will look to the mind the hardest thing, but it is not. Once you are out of the mind, not to be is the easiest thing.

Shakespeare's statement, "To be or not to be…" All religions are in favor of the first: to be. Zen alone is there, rising high into the blue sky, declaring the phenomenon, the great mystery of *not* to be. To *be* is just an extension of your ego. Your *self* is just a polished ego and nothing else. Your self can be said to be your spiritual ego – a pious ego, very refined, very subtle, but it is nothing but ego.

Your personality is given by society, your individuality is given by your very birth. But before the birth you were not an individual, you were one with the womb of the mother. You never thought about being separate – you were not separate. You were nourished by the mother's blood, by the mother's oxygen; you were part of the mother's body. You were joined from your navel to the mother's body, and that was your very source of life. The mother was giving you life; you did not have any individuality.

So when you reach to the ultimate womb of the universe, again you will not have any individuality. Personality has to be dropped very quickly. That is only clothes given by the society to cover you, to keep you unaware of your individuality, which is more natural. Hence, all civilized cultures are against nudity. It is not just a social question; it is that they don't want you to know your individuality, they want you to think of yourself as a personality. Your clothes, your language, your education, your morality, your religion, your church-going, your prayer…they all constitute your personality. They are the clothes with which the society goes on covering you, and you forget completely about your individuality.

The first thing Zen has to do is to take away all the clothes. The second thing it has to do is to take away even the individuality and leave you in the cosmic womb, utterly one with existence. It is not spirituality, it is pure life, pure existence. But don't talk about spirituality or self-realization or salvation – they are all ego-bound.

Thomas Merton was aware of the fact that "being so full of impudent paradox..." Those paradoxes appear only to those who are trying to understand Zen from books. Zen is a direct transmission of the lamp. Without a master it is a very very rare phenomenon that somebody can become enlightened. With the master you are already moving into an energy field. You are nothing but energy, condensed energy, and the master is in tune with existence. If you get in tune with the master, indirectly you are getting in tune with existence. The moment the master sees that you are getting in tune with him, he simply moves out of the way.

That's why Buddha is reported to have said a very strange thing: "If I come on your path, immediately cut off my head." What he is saying is that the master at a certain point has to move out of the way. If he does not move out, it is the duty of the disciple to push him away and go directly into the cosmos. But no master worth his salt will ever become a hindrance.

Teachers can become hindrances – and Thomas Merton's teachers were hindrances. His abbot was prohibiting him, the pope was prohibiting him, all the senior monks in the monastery were prohibiting him. They were saying, "What is the need? You have Christ, you have Christianity, you have the greatest religion of the world. Why do you want to go to Japan, and particularly to the Zen people, who are just a small stream?"

If you are reading through books you will find they are full of paradox, but if you are studying under a master, he will dissolve the paradox. That's what I have been doing continuously. You bring the sutras which are almost without any explanation, very paradoxical, very strange, almost absurd.

My whole effort is to take that absurdity away, to take that paradox away and make things clean and clear for you, so that you can at least understand Zen not as a paradoxical system, self-contradictory, irrational, but as absolutely relevant to existence. Certainly it does not follow Aristotle's logic upon which the whole of Christianity depends.

The West finds in Aristotle the father of their whole logical mind. Aristotle is certainly a genius as far as mind is concerned, but beyond the mind he has no idea. Just as Thomas Merton was seeking to go to Japan, to have some direct experience...

Aristotle was Alexander the Great's teacher. And when Alexander was coming to conquer India, he asked his teacher, Aristotle, "Would you like me to bring some special thing for you? I can bring anything you want from India."

And what Aristotle wanted, was for Alexander to bring a sannyasin. He said, "I have heard so much about the sannyasins and their enlightenment. If you can bring an enlightened sannyasin, that will be a real gift for me. And secondly, I have heard much about the Vedas of the Hindus, their scriptures. If you can bring a set of the four Vedas with an enlightened sannyasin, that will be the greatest gift to me."

That shows that he does not understand what enlightenment is, he does not understand what sannyas is. He is asking for a contradictory thing. A sannyasin, an enlightened being, is against all scriptures – and he is asking for the Hindu scriptures also. He does not know that these are two contradictory things. But one thing is certain, that he has no experience of the inner world, otherwise he would not have asked for a sannyasin. He cannot understand what this phenomenon of enlightenment is.

Your greatest logician is absolutely unaware of his own being – to say nothing about the great being of existence – and he is still trying to figure it out through his mind. Hence his request to bring the four Vedas, so that by reading the Vedas he can understand enlightenment. The Vedas are not needed for enlightenment. You cannot understand enlightenment by reading any scripture. All that you will get will be a misunderstanding.

Thomas Merton says, "Being so full of impudent paradox" – it is not impudent paradox – "that it is at first a real scandal to the rational spirit of the West." Rational spirit? He is using the word 'spirit' in place of 'mind'. Rational *mind* seems to be relevant; rational *spirit* nobody has heard of. Either you have your rationality or you have your spirit. Both cannot exist together.

Once you have dropped your rationality, only the spirit remains, the self remains. That is the last barrier. When the last barrier also is dropped, you are no more, and existence is and life is – and this is Zen.

You are asking, "Beloved Master, but, in fact, is not Zen more rational in its irrationality...?"

No. Zen is neither rational nor irrational, because both belong to the mind. Zen is simply beyond any duality. Rational and irrational are just another duality like day and night, birth and death, darkness and light. Zen is simply beyond any dual conceptions.

Once you are beyond mind, you cannot have any duality, any trace of duality in you. You are neither rational nor irrational; you are simply here and now, without any label. All labels are gathered by the mind. You are no longer a man or a woman; you have never been born and you have never died. All that was the same stuff that dreams are made of.

You are saying that, "being the acknowledgement that rationality has limits and we are after the unlimited..." No, we are not after anything. The unlimited also becomes to the mind just the opposite of the limited – again, another duality. We are not after anything, we are just relaxing into ourselves. To go after anything is always going outward. To go after anything means to go after something which is outside you. We are not after anything; we are dropping all those processes – after this and after that, after money, after power, after prestige, after self-realization, after God. All those things are dropped. We are simply relaxing and resting into our very source.

You are also asking, "Is not Zen more rational – and we are after the unlimited – than Christianity with its miracles, immaculate conception and resurrection?"

Christianity lives on all kinds of lies. All religions live on lies, but Christianity's lies are very apparent.

Other religions have tried hard to hide their irrationalities, and sometimes you may not be able to discover where the irrationality is. For example, Jainism has no God, so the greatest lie is dissolved, and with it many other things are dissolved. There is no question of creation, and there is no question of the last judgment day; there is no question of prophets coming from God, there is no question of messiahs, messengers sent by God, and there is no question of a Jesus Christ being the only begotten of God. When there is no God, all these things disappear automatically. Jainism seems to be more solidly rooted.

Mahavira creates no miracles, does not give eyes to the blind, does not give health to sick people, does not revive the dead again into life. There are no miracles which can create doubt in your mind: "How are these things possible? These are absolutely unscientific." So Mahavira these things possible? These are absolutely unscientific." So Mahavira stands on firmer ground, and it will be very difficult to find where he is hiding his irrationality.

Most of the followers of Mahavira have never thought that there can be anything irrational in Mahavira. He seems to be very rational, far more rational than Aristotle. Aristotle's logic is simply two steps: yes-no, day-night, positive-negative. Just two polarities have been taken into account. But what about the middle ground? There are many positions between two extremes – at least there is a middle. And when there is a middle, again there is another middle – on this side, on that side. As you go on creating middles...

You see within these five fingers, one space, a second space, a third space, a fourth space – so there are nine points. But this is not exhaustive. Once you put one point between two fingers, on both sides of the middle there will be two gaps again. So it is an infinite process of dividing and dividing into smaller pieces.

Mahavira divides his logic into seven pieces. That seems to be more rational than Aristotle, because Aristotle has only two alternatives – a very poor logic. So when you study Mahavira you will be overwhelmed with his subtlety, and you will not find where to look for the loopholes.

The loopholes are there. No religion can live without loopholes – but it is far superior to Christianity. Christianity's loopholes are just there in front of everybody. Only utterly blind people can be Christians, those who cannot even see just in front of themselves.

Immaculate conception, virgin birth...and how can an intelligent person go on believing in a virgin birth? Creation of the world – and nobody asks what God had been doing before that. Was he completely unemployed...for eternity? just living with the Holy Ghost?

A strange kind of God... And suddenly, for no reason at all, six thousand years ago, he created the whole world within six days. Do you think anybody can create this whole universe within six days? And if he was so creative, then why did he remain absolutely impotent for eternity?

And if there is a beginning to existence there is bound to be an end. Things are very clear. Jesus Christ's miracles – walking on water, raising the dead – are apparently clear, but are not scientific. Resurrection...and after resurrection going directly, alive, without any vehicle, not even a horse...?

Mohammed at least had his horse going up. They just stopped in the middle for a rest at Jerusalem. Jerusalem seems to be above the clouds, a holy city. Tired after a long journey, he rested there on a rock, and then took another jump – but at least he had the horse! Jesus had not even a horse, but went directly...like a balloon, and without any gas! And after reaching paradise, he must have thrown a rope or something for his mother to hold onto, and pulled the mother also to paradise!

And people go on believing in these things! And if you remove all these things, Christianity has nothing to offer. So they go on insisting that these are real factual experiences. But the time has come when they cannot insist anymore.

Jainism is far superior, but I will tell you where its loopholes are. Its loopholes are very well hidden. It does not believe in creation. Then the question arises: the population of the world goes on growing, so from where are all these people coming? There is no sign of any life on any planet, on any star, so from where do all these people keep on coming?

At the time of Mahavira, India had only two million people. Now there are, in India alone, nine hundred million people. From where have they come? – not to say anything about the mosquitoes, because they also have souls according to Mahavira. And bedbugs, and cockroaches, and rats – just look around the world – all these have souls! From where are they coming?

Mahavira had his loophole too, so he fabricated an idea that there is a place called *nigod* – somewhere far away, just as God is far away – and this nigod is a place like a freezer, where souls are frozen from eternity, infinite souls. It cannot be a small freezer. Howsoever frozen the souls are, they will take some space, so the freezer has to be big enough to contain millions and millions and millions and trillions of souls. Then those souls start coming, one by one. Why one by one?

This nigod is an absolutely imaginary place just to answer the question: "From where are the souls coming...their number goes on growing?" If the world is uncreated, and if the same number of people had remained, there would have been no question. But every day the number of people is growing; every moment, every second, thousands of people are coming. And these are only men...what about all the other animals, all the insects...? They also have souls. According to Mahavira every living being

So finally he had to invent a lie – that there is some faraway place where souls are dormant. The top layer is released, then another layer is released. But who is doing all this work? Who is running the shop? And why have some people come first, and some are still in the freezer? Mahavira has no explanation for it.

In every religion – it does not matter what religion it is – you will find, if you search deep enough, howsoever sophisticated it is, that there will be a loophole. All religions depend on lies.

Zen is not a religion, hence it need not be dependent on lies. It is a pure search. It does not go with any prejudice or any belief in the search. It does not even say that you will find it. One never knows: you just go and see on your own whether there is something inside or not. Although anybody who has gone deep inside has always found, still Zen continues to be the only approach without any lies. Knowing perfectly well there is a hidden buddha in you, it does not tell you that you have to believe in it.

Search for yourself.

Zen gives such total freedom to you, because it does not impose any belief. Hence you cannot find any loophole in Zen. That is its beauty, that is its greatness.

The sutra:

BELOVED OSHO,

One day, on his way to see Ma Tzu, Tanka Tennen met an old man with a boy, and asked them where they lived. The old man answered, "Above is the sky; below is the earth!"

A man of Zen, certainly. He does not answer the question, "Where do you live?" He simply says, "*Above is the sky; below is the earth!*"

What is the point of living anywhere else? Everywhere the sky is above, and underneath is the earth. So wherever you live, you live between these two things: the sky and the earth. What is the point of making labels: "I live here," and "I live there"? Life exists on the earth, below the sky.

The old man certainly has an insight – but Tanka Tennen cannot accept it so easily.

Tanka said, "How about if the sky crumbled away and the earth fell to pieces?"
The old man simply said, "Ah! Ah!"

The sky crumbling and the earth falling into pieces – what to say except the last "Ah!"? But he has proved himself to be really a man of Zen – he did not argue the point. He did not ask, "How can the sky crumble? How can the earth fall into pieces?"

No, Zen is not an argument. Zen is a response, spontaneous. It does not quarrel, it simply states. He accepts what Tanka is saying, "Maybe, who knows, the sky one day crumbles, the earth falls into pieces..."

The old man says, "*Ah! Ah!* – if it happens, then this will be my response."

The boy drew a deep breath, and Tanka said,
"If there were no father, no child would be born."
The old man and the child entered the mountains
and were seen no more.

Both proved to be very extraordinary people, the old man certainly, and even the boy. When the old man said, "*Ah! Ah!*" the boy drew a deep breath. If it is going to happen, then the last breath, the last feel of life, the last dance... One breath more is not asking much.

And when *Tanka said, "If there were no father, no child would be born,"* they did not say anything. They simply disappeared into the mountains and were seen no more.

This is what I am calling freedom from oneself, the Zen Manifesto. It is a disappearance into the mountains, it is a disappearance into the ocean, it is a disappearance into the sky. Fundamentally it is a disappearance of the self. Then you are no more seen again. That old man and that young boy both proved correct.

Once, Tanka Tennen was lying on the Tenshin bridge. Lord Teikō, who was in charge of the bridge, came out and warned Tanka that he had better move, but Tanka didn't get up.

Nobody can order a man of Zen. You can kill him, but you cannot order him. You can murder him, but you cannot command him.

The man of Zen does not bother about death, because he knows his deathlessness. He does not care about who you are; lord or governor or emperor, it does not matter. You are just made of five elements: earth, water, fire, air, sky. You are made of five elements just as any beggar is: "Don't bother me."

So Tanka did not even reply, and he was lying on the bridge, which is not a place to lie down.

The lord said to him that he had better move, but Tanka Tennen did not get up and did not answer either.

Teikō asked why he didn't listen to him. After a few moments, Tanka said, "I am a monk of nothing."

"Who is there to listen? I have searched enough, I don't find anybody to listen to. I have found only nothingness. I am a man of nothingness, don't bother me. There is nobody inside me to listen to you or to follow your commandment. I have looked enough, searched enough, in every nook and corner. It is pure nothingness. I am nowhere to be found, so to whom are you talking?

"And what do you mean by saying, 'Why do you not listen to me?' Neither I am nor you are. Nobody has spoken, nobody has listened. I am a monk of nothing."

He is saying, "I am a man of Zen."

Lord Teikō was taken aback. This was a very strange man. But it was not a philosophical statement; Tennen was radiant. Because he has found, he is no more; only existence expresses itself. He is no more, so existence has taken possession of him. His peace, his silence, his grandeur, his grace, come from existence, because he has allowed. Finding that there is nobody inside, he has opened all the doors. Fresh breezes and sunrays... and sometimes the moon looks through the windows. The house is utterly absent of any ego, any self.

But a man of such nothingness has a tremendous presence. He has no personality, he has no person, he has no self, but he radiates light, he radiates joy, he radiates a dance around him of subtle energies.

Lord Teikō was taken aback by Tanka Tennen's response, and from then on provided him with clothing and a daily meal, and did not ask him to move from the bridge.

Tanka Tennen lived his whole life on that bridge. Finally Lord Teikō had to make a hut for him, because there was rain, there was too much sun, and he was just lying there naked. He had to arrange for clothes, arrange for his food. Finally, he dropped the idea of having a bridge, and made a hut in the middle of the bridge. The man made such an impact on Teikō that because of him, the whole city where he was the ruler started venerating Tanka.

He became famous as a very strange man, but a man of truth, honesty, of immense blissfulness. There was a very fine grace pouring to anybody who was receptive. That is the meaning of veneration. It should not be formal, otherwise you will not be able to understand the man of Zen.

Your veneration should be actual. That means you should be receptive to all that he is offering – not asking for anything, but simply offering. You should allow him your inner being, your inner space, to fill with his light, to fill with his dance and song. That's real veneration.

And not only in the capital…soon Tanka was known all over Japan. He was very natural, that's why Ma Tzu gave him the name Tennen. In fact, he did not give him the name, but Tanka was sitting on the statue of Manjushri, who was known as one of the most natural beings in the history of the buddhas.

Seeing Tanka sitting on the statue of Manjushri, all the monks could not believe their eyes: "What kind of monk is he? He is being disrespectful to one of the great buddhas." They asked their master, Ma Tzu, to come and see: "One stranger is sitting on top of the statue of Manjushri."

Ma Tzu came, saw Tanka, and said, "My son, Tennen. My son is very natural."

He was sitting there with such natural grace. Tanka immediately came down from the statue and said, "This is my initiation name. Now I will be called Tanka Tennen." So childlike, so natural.

He had no teachings…. People used to come to him, sit around him. Sometimes he would laugh, sometimes he would weep. And people asked, "What is the matter? Sometimes you laugh, sometimes you weep." And he always gave the same answer: "I weep for you, I laugh for myself."

And he was right, absolutely right.

Do you know my tears? I never weep in front of you, I have to weep under my blanket. I enjoy your laughter, but I know it is still not natural. It is caused by a joke.

I would love you to laugh without any cause, just out of sheer laughter. Why do you need any cause? Why do you need any excuse? Laughter is simply an expression of your health, of your nothingness. Laughter is simply coming from the very sources of existence.

The whole existence is full of laughter, but you don't hear it. In different ways it laughs, in different ways it dances, in different ways it sings songs of ecstasy.

But I feel exactly like Tanka Tennen: a sadness for you, because you have not yet become nothingnesses. So his tears were for others, his laughter was coming from his nothingness.

And don't see any contradiction – there is no contradiction. The tears are for others, because they are capable of becoming buddhas and they are delaying it. The laughter is for himself – "How strange! In this world of insanity, I have become a buddha. Can you find a greater joke?"

In this madhouse called the earth, somebody becomes a Gautam Buddha, somebody becomes a Tanka Tennen or a Ma Tzu...is it not absolutely absurd? There is no reason why.

So he is laughing at the strangeness, at the mysterious existence that to some, the blossoming comes, and to some only sadness and misery.

So his tears were actual – out of his compassion. And his laughter was also actual – out of his sheer joy, seeing that he has arrived while others are simply going in circles.

There is a special caterpillar in South Africa. It is very manlike, its behavior is very human. It always follows the leader. You will find thousands of caterpillars in a line; just as if somebody ahead of them is moving, and so they are moving.

One scientist was researching this strange behavior of leadership and followers. He had a round glass table with a raised edge like a plate, on which he put the leader. And he went on putting other caterpillars behind and behind and behind till the circle was complete. They started moving round and round – because now there was nowhere to go. And there was no way to stop, because the person ahead was moving – until they all died, just utterly exhausted. But they did not stop till they had drawn the last breath. They went on and on and on, and finally they all died, one by one. The older ones died first, then the younger ones became old, and they died, and the children became old, and they died.

After seven days that whole table was full of dead caterpillars. And the scientist who was working on them said that it is very human – that's how human beings are behaving.

Somebody is following Jesus Christ – not knowing who this fellow is. Is he sane? Have you ever wondered? All his behavior looks eccentric, his declarations fanatical. Only an insane man can make those statements – but millions and millions of people have been following him through the centuries. Twenty centuries have passed; how many millions of people have died following him? They don't know where he is going, who he is. This is the way of believers.

Zen is not for believers, it is for discoverers. It is not for retarded people who won't even take the risk of thinking whom they are following and why. Why are you a Hindu? – just because accidentally you were born in a Hindu family. That accident is deciding your destiny. Why are you a Christian?

But nobody ever wonders.

Thinking seems to be a difficult task, because it gives you a great disappointment. It takes away your lies, and suddenly you feel you are naked. It takes away your consolations, and suddenly you fall into insecurity. So it is better to keep your eyes closed, tightly closed, in case they open themselves in some moment when you are not alert enough to keep them tightly closed. This way one blind man follows another blind man, not knowing where the first one is going – and the first one is almost dead. Two thousand years have passed, and people are still following the blind – and not only the blind, but the blind who have been dead for two thousand years or five thousand years.

Zen brings you to question that to be accidental is not your destiny. To be existential is your destiny. So drop following, just stand on your own feet and look inwards. Following is always looking outwards. Look inwards and you will find eternal peace. Of course, in that eternal peace you have to disappear, but it is a sheer joy to disappear.

To be is a tension.

Not to be is a relaxation.

A haiku:

An old pine tree preaches wisdom,
and a wild bird
is crying out truth.

You just have to be alert enough and you will find the whole nature is full of wisdom, and the whole existence is crying out truth from different sources.

"An old pine tree preaches wisdom, and a wild bird is crying out truth" – a very significant haiku. You just need open eyes, receptivity, sensitivity, awareness, and this whole existence becomes your home.

Zen is concerned absolutely with your relaxedness, because only in relaxedness has one sunk deep enough into the original sources of life. There one finds such joy that who cares whether one is or is not? Joy is, life is, existence is, enlightenment is.

It is the poverty of language that we have to call a man enlightened – because when enlightenment happens, the man disappears. Then there is only enlightenment.

You cannot call Gautam Buddha an enlightened person, because the person is no longer there. Only when the person is no longer there, is there enlightenment – a completely luminous existence. From every nook and corner wisdom is flowing towards you, from every bird truth is proclaimed, from every flower beauty is proclaimed, from every mountain, from every river...thousands and thousands of glories.

The whole existence becomes a totally different phenomenon the moment you disappear. Hence, you are the only problem. If you can dissolve your problem...it means you have to dissolve yourself.

So there is no salvation for you, there is only dissolving yourself into the ultimate. And there is nothing greater, nothing more majestic, nothing more miraculous.

This dissolving is the Manifesto of Zen.

Maneesha's question:

BELOVED OSHO,

Thomas Merton wrote: "If a Christian mystic has an experience which can be phenomenologically compared with a Zen experience, does it matter that the Christian in fact believes he is personally united with God, and the Zen man interprets his experience as 'shunyata', nothingness, or the void being aware of itself? In what sense can these two experiences be called mystical?"

Beloved Master,

Why do so many Christians and admirers of Zen try to make the two fit together?

Because they cannot drop their old prison, they have become so accustomed to it. These two experiences cannot be compared. These two experiences are as far away from each other as a lie and a truth.

The God-oriented religions… Thomas Merton mentions Christianity because he is a Christian, but you can see his statement begins with an "if." Whenever there is an "if" there is no direct experience.

"If a Christian mystic" – in the first place, it is an "if." "If a Christian mystic has an experience" – no Christian mystic can have such an experience – "which can be phenomenologically compared with a Zen experience…" No, absolutely no. No Christian can ever experience phenomenologically something equal to the Zen experience, because the foundations of their search are totally different.

"Does it matter that the Christian in fact believes he is personally united…?" Yes, it does matter. To be personally united with God is a fiction. The man is living in an hallucination. It is not the experience of truth, it is the experience projected by a belief system in a particular god. There are thousands of "gods" around, not only the Christian god. So everybody can choose – they come in all sizes and all shapes. It is a commodity you can purchase from the marketplace – a Buddha, a Jesus on the cross, a Krishna playing on his flute – and you can worship them. And if you go on worshipping them you are really programming your memory continuously. Soon you will start having delusions.

A Christian or a Hindu or a Mohammedan cannot have any experience equivalent to the Zen experience; it is not a question of language only. That's what Merton is trying to do. He is saying that it is only linguistically different. They are using different language, but the experience is the same. If it was the same, why was Merton trying to go to Japan? What was the need?

A Zen master has never been known to have gone to a Christian monastery. There is no need. Merton is consoling himself and other Christians: "Don't be worried, phenomenologically your experience can be compared to the Zen experience of nothingness." No, it cannot be compared, because your experience is not of nothingness. Your experience is of a God which is filling your nothingness, which is a barrier against nothingness. Your God has to be removed. And rather than removing him, you are feeling an identity with God, you are becoming one with the God. You are hallucinating, you are dreaming with open eyes.

The Zen experience of *shunyata*, of nothingness, is not a mind projection. Only one thing can the mind not project, and that is nothingness. This has to be understood. Mind can project everything; only one thing it cannot project, nothingness, because in trying to project nothingness, the mind will have to empty itself completely. In the emptying of the mind completely, mind will disappear. Mind is nothing but thoughts put together.

We call five persons living in a house, a family. Just take those five persons out, and where is the family? 'Family' was only a collective name. We call a certain group of people a Rotary Club. Take the members out one by one, and then see whether the Rotary Club is still inside the house. There is no one.

Mind is a collective name for all your thoughts. If you go on emptying the mind to create something equal to nothingness, then God will have to be dropped; it is a thought. Then heaven and hell will be dropped; they are thoughts. Once you create a mind which has no thoughts, you have transcended mind, there is no mind anymore. You have entered into nothingness – but you will not find a God waiting there and hugging you.

And remember always, if any God hugs you it is dangerous, because that fellow, who has created this whole universe, must not be of your size. He will be huge! You will be simply killed like a mosquito! Avoid any such experience.

any such experience.

Nothingness is good. You will disappear in both the cases. In one you will be murdered, in the other you will simply disperse. But dispersing yourself is a beautiful experience; being murdered is a very ugly, torturous experience. These two experiences cannot be compared, there is no question of it at all. But it is not only Thomas Merton, many other Christians are trying to do the same.

Christianity is feeling that its moment to disappear has come; it has no reason now to remain in existence. It has lost its roots. It was perfectly okay for the uneducated, uncultured, uncivilized slaves. Now man is coming of age. Christianity was good for children to play with, a good toy. God was a toy. But when man comes of age, he does not need a toy, he needs something real.

Zen is for those who are intelligent, mature, who are no longer childish, but grown-ups. It needs daring, it needs throwing away all kinds of slaveries. And all the religions are nothing but very cunning ways to reduce humanity to indignity, humiliation and slavery. Now Christianity is trying hard somehow to survive.

Thomas Merton's statement is simply a desire somehow to keep God and God-oriented religion alive in the future also. He sees a way: if both these experiences – the experience of Zen and the experience of a Christian mystic – can be compared, they are just the same, only their language differs, then there is a possibility for Christianity and God to dominate still. But they cannot be compared. They are not only different, they are opposite to each other. One is a lie, another is a truth.

God is a fiction. Shunyata is the ultimate experience.

There is no way for Christianity to survive.

It shows certainly that Christians are aware of their death which is coming closer and closer every moment. They know their God is dead and they are keeping that God on an artificial breathing system. They are looking all over the world to see if some props can be found so that God can look as if he is still alive.

Hindus are not in such a search, because they are not so sophisticated and they are not so alert. Neither are Jainas in such a frantic search, because they are not so sophisticated and they are not so much interested. Their interest is much more in money.

what is the matter: why are Indians coming to Japan to learn technology, particularly the latest discoveries in electronics? Japan has become now the most sophisticated technological country, the richest country in the world; even America is poorer now. Japan is four times richer than America, and it is four times smaller than America. So what Japan has done is a miracle. After the destruction of the second world war, suddenly a tremendous outburst of energy.

So Indians are going to Tokyo, and the article mentions that the Japanese are going to Poona. You are all coming from Western countries or from Eastern countries which have become rich enough. From Japan, Taiwan...soon people from Korea will be here.

Indians are rushing all over the world – to America, to Britain, to Germany, to learn new technology, to be more scientific. And India still goes on claiming that it is one of the most spiritual countries. My foot! It is the most unspiritual country in the world. Gone are those days when it used to be spiritual – twenty-five centuries have passed – but the old fog remains around the mind. India is more attached to things, attached to money, attached to power, is more ambitious to have domination, prestige, respectability, than any other country.

You are the proof.

Whenever I say anything, I have the proof. You are here because you know money is not going to help, it is not going to bring your ultimate blossoming. It can buy everything, but it cannot buy buddhahood. It can buy everything, human beings included, but it cannot buy meditation.

You have to go alone on the path.

Richer countries are frustrated, utterly frustrated, because they have found money and they have found respectability. They are educated, they are sophisticated, they are intellectually far more advanced than the backward countries.

Naturally, Christianity is the only religion in the world which is becoming aware that their congregation is disappearing – they are all going to Poona!

You don't see many Indians here – very few. Very few are intelligent enough. But it is really sad. The country of Gautam Buddha is no longer interested in meditation; it is interested in bringing more technology, more riches. And most of the people who go outside to learn technology, never return – just as you would not like to return – because there they get more money.

A doctor can earn more in Germany or Japan. In America a professor can earn more, a scientist is needed more in those countries. In India he will be at the most middle class, he cannot think of being super-rich. But in Japan or Germany or America he can fulfill the ambition to become super-rich. So those who go, go forever.

There was another article a few months ago in a German magazine, asking, "What is happening? German young people simply go to Poona and then they are never seen again." It is only because of the difficulties created by the barriers of nations that you cannot stay more than three months, more than six months at the most, so you have to go and come back again. If these barriers disappear, Poona is going to become a country in itself. But it will be a foreign country to India; it will in itself be one of the most cosmopolitan worlds.

It is because of this that Christianity is more alert and is trying to survive. Hindus are perfectly asleep; although they are going to drown, they are in the same boat in which Christianity is. In the same boat Hindus are sleeping, in the same boat Jainas are sleeping, in the same boat Mohammedans are sleeping – but they are all sleeping. At least the Christian is looking all around. The boat is sinking – and he is trying somehow to save the God-oriented theology.

But it cannot be saved, it has already outlived its time. It should be more graceful in allowing itself to disappear. It is now ugly, and becoming more and more ugly. It is trying to enforce itself and pretend, "We are alive." If your God is dead you cannot be alive. You have died with your God.

I offer you resurrection.

But in resurrection you will not be Christians, you will not be Hindus, you will not be Mohammedans.

In resurrection you will be men of Zen.

Hence the Zen Manifesto. The world needs it immediately, urgently.

Now, put on the lights!

It is time for Sardar Gurudayal Singh.

Let the Christian ship drown.

You have found something alive; you can laugh and you can dance and you can celebrate.

One afternoon, Miss Pinkey Dickey, the librarian, comes into Doctor Chopoff's office with a small growth on her cheek. Doctor Chopoff examines the little blemish carefully, and then prescribes some green pills.

"There you are, Miss Dickey," says Chopoff. "If it is what I think it is, that should take care of it."

But two weeks later, Pinkey is back in the doctor's office. This time, a small wooden twig has sprouted out of the growth on her cheek.

"Hmmmm, interesting," says Doctor Chopoff. "If it is what I think it is, *these* should take care of it!" And he gives her a bottle of blue pills.

But two weeks later, Pinkey is back. This time the twig has grown into a branch with leaves and flowers on it. The doctor examines it very carefully and then says, "Hmmmm, interesting. If it is what I think it is, then these should take care of it, for sure!" And he gives Pinkey a bottle of red pills.

But one month later, Miss Pinkey Dickey is back in Doctor Chopoff's office. "Doctor!" she cries. "Look at me now!"

The doctor is shocked to see Pinkey barely able to get through the door because she now has a small tree growing out of her head.

"Hmmmm," says Chopoff. "A rare and interesting case. If it is what I think it is, these should certainly take care of it!" – and he hands her some green and purple spotted pills.

For six months, Doctor Chopoff does not hear anything from Miss Dickey. Then one day the door of his office bursts off its hinges and Pinkey Dickey comes staggering in. The doctor cannot believe his eyes. He can hardly see Pinkey underneath the huge apple tree, flowering bushes, large rocks and a bubbling waterfall coming out of her head.

"Help me, doctor!" she cries. "What *is* it?"

"Aha!" exclaims Doctor Chopoff. "*Now* I know what it is! It is a beauty spot!"

At ten o'clock in the morning, the phone rings in the office of Doctor Floss, the dentist.

"Hello!" says Floss.
"Hello!" says Wu, the Chinaman. "What time you fixee teeth for me?"
"Two-thirty," replies Floss. "Alright?"
"Yes," says Wu. "Tooth hurtee, alright! But what time you fixee?"

There is a huge explosion at the scientific laboratory, and Professor Teddy Testube, the scientist, is blown through the window and knocked unconscious. When Teddy wakes up, he is dazed and confused, but he has a sudden flash of inspiration. He decides to devote the rest of his life to the alchemy of turning regular house bricks into gold bricks.

For ten years Teddy works hard on his project until one day he gets stuck.

"Ah!" cries Teddy to Igor, his lab assistant. "Just one little answer to one last question, Igor, and we will be rich!"

But night after night Teddy's experiments are fruitless. Finally, utterly exhausted and nearly burnt out, Teddy is slumped across his workbench when Igor comes in.

"Don't give up, Professor Testube," exclaims Igor, "I have an idea! Why don't you go and see Madam Weird, the wise woman of Tibet? She will be able to answer your burning question!"

"Great idea!" shouts Teddy, jumping up. And he goes and packs his bags and leaves for Tibet the next morning.

After a long camel ride from Kathmandu, Teddy finally arrives, tired and exhausted, on the doorstep of Madam Weird's mountain retreat. The question is still burning in his mind.

But Teddy is told he must purify himself before he is granted an audience with the wise woman, so for three days, he is forced to live on a diet of Aquaguard water and raw tofu. Finally, he is admitted into Madam Weird's private bedchamber.

"Welcome, stranger," greets Madam Weird, sprawled across the huge bed in her see-through negligee.

Teddy is shocked and a little nervous, seeing such a beautiful woman way out here in the middle of nowhere.

"I can receive you today," smiles Madam Weird, "because your energy is sufficiently pure, and besides that, my husband has gone to the village for some monkey business. But I can answer one question only, and no more!"

some monkey business. But I can answer one question only, and no more!"

Perspiring, Teddy loosens his collar as he stares at her beautiful, bulging breasts bursting through her see-through negligee. There is much moving of eyeballs and raising of eyebrows, as Madam Weird beckons Teddy to come closer.

"Go ahead," she says in a throaty voice, "ask your burning question."

"Okay!" blurts out Teddy. "Tell me one thing: when will your husband be back?"

Nivedano…

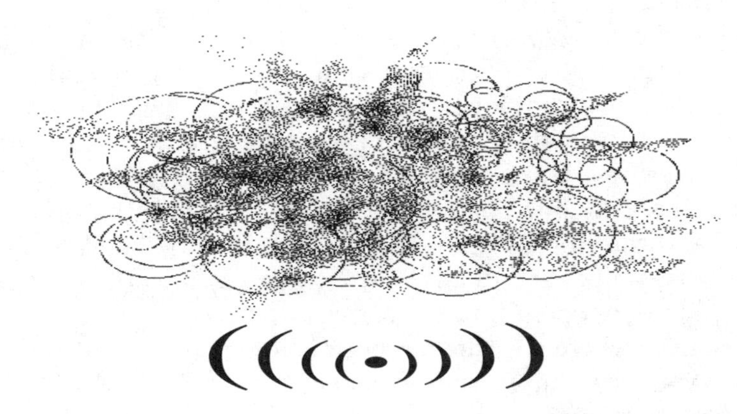

Nivedano…

Be silent.

Close your eyes…and feel your body to be completely frozen. This is the right moment to enter into your inner world. Gather all your energy, your total consciousness, and rush towards the center of your being. It is exactly two inches below your navel, inside.

A great urgency is needed, as if it is going to be your last moment.

Faster, with great intensity…

Rush faster and faster…deeper and deeper.

As you are coming closer to the center of your being, a great silence descends over you, just like soft rain falling. You can feel the coolness. The whole night is becoming silent with you.

A little closer to the center, and you are surrounded in a cloud of peace – peace that passeth understanding.

Move a little closer, and you feel a great blissfulness you have not known before, a tremendous power which is harmless, a light that is filling your very being.

You are luminous.

In this luminosity you can see the center perfectly well. Step into the center, and you will start feeling a divine drunkenness, a great ecstasy. You have heard these words – this is a direct experience.

Here you will find your original face. The face of Gautam the Buddha has been accepted in the East as a symbol of everybody's original face. Everybody is born with the potential of becoming a buddha. As you step into the center, you disappear. Only the buddha remains, only your awareness, alertness, consciousness.

Buddha has only one quality; that is the very meaning of the name "Buddha" – witnessing. Witness that you are not the body, witness that you are not the mind, and finally, witness that you are only a witness.

Suddenly a door opens into the cosmos.

You see from where your life has been coming.

You see you are no more, only existence is.

This pure nothingness, this shunyata is the only religious experience there is.

To make your witnessing deeper,
Nivedano...

Relax.
Sink into your very sources of life.
Dissolve yourself in this ocean of consciousness.

This is pure Zen.

This is the beginning of an endless journey. Gautam Buddha is reported to have said, "Ignorance has no beginning but an end. Enlightenment has a beginning but no end." You are taking the first step into enlightenment.

These are the three steps. The first step is: you will find Gautam Buddha as your shadow, but very luminous, very solid, almost tangible. You will feel a tremendous compassion surrounding you.

In the second step, Buddha will come in front of you and you will become his shadow. Your shadow of course is dark; it is only a false entity. As the buddha becomes more and more radiant in front of you, your shadow starts dissolving.

The second step is followed by the third. Your shadow has dissolved into the buddha. Only a pure witnessing buddha remains, utterly transparent, so he cannot make any shadow.

This is your pure life eternal. This life is cosmic. You have entered into the womb of existence. You are no more on the one hand; on the other hand you are all that is alive. And the whole existence is alive, throbbing. You can hear existence's heartbeat, you are so close to it.

Now gather all these experiences, the bliss, the ecstasy, the peace, the silence, the serenity, and persuade the buddha to come behind you. He has to become a constant companion to you in your acts, in your gestures, in your day-to-day affairs.

This is the first step. The second and third will follow in their own time. You have just to wait in deep trust. If the first has happened, the second is bound to happen. It is really the growth of the first. The third is the growth of the second, and the third is the final step. Once you have become enlightened, you are free from birth and death, you are free from all bondages, you are even free from yourself.

This is the ultimate freedom: freedom from oneself. And only a man who has attained the ultimate freedom can dance, and there will be no dancer but only dance; can celebrate, but now celebration will be arising from the very depths of existence itself; can laugh, but now it will be a totally different laughter – it will be existence laughing through you.

All your actions will become existential; they will have a great grace and beauty and truth and authenticity.

Nivedano...

Now come back, and bring all these experiences and the buddha following you.

With great grace, with silence, sit down for a few moments, just to remember the golden path that you have followed, and the opening into ultimate space, into nothingness, into shunyata and the great moment when you had disappeared and only existence was there.

Soon it will become your twenty-four-hour experience. Inch by inch you will be transformed into a Gautam Buddha. That is everybody's birthright.

Okay, Maneesha?

Yes, Osho.

禪
戊辰中秋

TO WAIT, TO WAIT FOR NOTHING

BELOVED OSHO,

Tanka asked Chōro, "What is the self before the empty eon?"
As Chōro was about to answer, Tanka said, "You're still noisy – go away for now."
One day, as Chōro was climbing Bol Peak, his mind opened up into enlightenment. He took a shortcut down and went back to stand by Tanka, who slapped him and said, "I thought you knew it exists."
Chōro bowed joyfully.
The next day Tanka went into the hall and said, "The sun illumines the green of the solitary peak; the moon shines in the cold of the valley stream. Don't put the wondrous secret of the ancestral teachers in your little heart." Then he got up off the seat.
Chōro came directly forward and said, "Your address today can't fool me anymore."
Tanka said, "Try to recite my address."
Chōro remained silent.
Tanka said, "I thought you had a glimpse."
Chōro then left.

FRIENDS,

It has been a long awaiting, but that is the very essence of Zen – to wait, to wait for nothing.

There is no God, there is no ultimate meaning.

Life is all there is.

Those who have found, have found nothing but that there is nothing to be found.

Zen is the ultimate manifesto of non-finding, of rejoicing without any reason, of laughing and loving and dancing without any cause.

There are believers in the world, many types of them. There are non-believers in the world; they are not in any way different, just their beliefs are negative. Somebody believes in a God, and somebody believes in a no-God, and both are as fanatic as each other.

Just the other day I was reading the manifesto of the Humanist group of intellectuals, a small, very elite group of American intellectuals. But their manifesto made me laugh. Every statement begins, "We believe…" And a belief is always ignorance. Somebody believes in God – he is ignorant. Somebody believes in no God – he is as much ignorant as the one who believes.

Each sentence of the whole manifesto begins, "We believe that there is no God." But on what grounds? Finally they give their grounds: "We believe our faith is reason. Because God is not reasonable, we will not believe in God." These are the most intellectual people of America, and it is a very prestigious thing to be accepted by the group as a member.

I am making this statement just before some of my friends in the group are going to propose my name as an honorary member in their coming meeting. It is good for me to make my situation clear to them.

In the first place, I don't become a member of any party, any organization, because every membership is a subtle slavery.

Truth can live and blossom only in freedom.

Love can blossom and be fragrant only in freedom.

Every membership is a concession and a compromise.

Sannyas is not a movement and not an organization. On the contrary, it is a declaration of independence from all organizations and all parties and all churches.

I laughed at the Humanist manifesto because finally they say, "Our faith is in reason." But if you have a faith, every faith is unreasonable. And it is so simple to see. To have faith in reason means you will not allow anything unreasonable in life.

Love is unreasonable. What is the reason of love? What is the reason of existence itself? What is the reason of reason itself? If there were no reason, would you complain to somebody? If there were no life, would there be any way to complain to some court, to some higher authority? If there is nothing, there is nothing; if there is everything, there is everything. Reason itself is unreasonable. And if one has to be vast enough, one has to include contradictions. Reason on the one side, and irreason on the other side – both have to be accepted.

The Zen Manifesto is not for anything special. It is simply for this life, this existence, this moment. It does not ask for any source, and it does not ask for any goal. Every source will make a limitation, and every goal will make another limitation, and existence is unlimited. It is not limited by reason.

So if the Humanist group wants me to accept their membership, they will have to change their manifesto. I don't believe in anything, and I don't ask for anything to have a reason. It is perfectly okay as it is. If it were not, that too is perfectly okay.

Hence, I said to you that you have to wait long for me, but it is part of the game.

Zen accepts both the presence and the absence, life and death – all the contradictions. Zen is vast enough to contain all contradictions.

Perhaps Zen is the only way that contains contradictions, and that does not disallow anything. It rejoices in everything without any conditions. It accepts everything as it is without making any demands on it. It has no commandments, "Thou shalt," or "Thou shalt not..."

Zen knows nothing about commandments.

Zen knows only a vast life which contains all kinds of contradictions in a deep harmony. The night is in harmony with the day, and life is in harmony with death, and the earth is harmony with the sky. The presence is in harmony with the absence. This immense harmony, this synchronicity is the essential Manifesto of Zen. This is the only way of life which respects and loves, and denies nothing, condemns nothing.

Every other religion, every other philosophy depends on choosing – "Condemn this, deny that, accept this, respect this..." But there is always choice. And a man who has chosen has always chosen a part, and a part is never alive, only the whole is alive. Your hand is not alive separated from you, and your eyes will not be able to see separated from you. You are an organic unity.

Zen is a declaration of the organic unity of all contradictions of life. And because existence accepts everything, who are you to choose? Who are you to judge? Zen knows no judgment. Nobody is a sinner and nobody is a saint. Both are playing a game of their choice, and both will receive their rewards accordingly.

If you have done something wrong, something wrong will happen to you. If you have been blissful to others, existence will be blissful to you...a simple arithmetic. Zen does not believe in complexities, it is a very simple acceptance of the totality that surrounds us.

These days I have been away from you, but I was aware of you, as you were aware of me. I heard your sound of joy, I heard your songs...and I was waiting for the right day to come. I was going to come yesterday, but yesterday was Sardar Gurudayal Singh's day, so I had to remain in my room just for poor Sardar's sake.

Before the sutras, a few questions.

One sannyasin has asked:

On commenting on Ten Zen Bulls, Nyogen Senzaki and Paul Reps write in the book, 'Zen Flesh, Zen Bones,' "May the reader, like the Chinese patriarch, discover the footprints of his potential self, and carrying the staff of his purpose and the wine jug of his true desire, frequent the marketplace and there enlighten others."

Beloved Osho,

What is the purpose and true desire they are indicating? Their comment seems to be contradictory to Your explanation.

I don't know what Nyogen Senzaki's and Paul Reps' inner meaning is, because their hearts are not available to me. I have also read their words and wondered that without explanation they are using words which are meaningless in themselves.

What purpose? Life has no purpose. The very use of the word 'purpose' shows that both these people, Senzaki and Paul Reps, have not understood the meaning of Zen.

Zen is rejoicing in purposelessness. What purpose is in a flower? What purpose is in the sun rising? For what purpose are you here? There seems to be no purpose to me.

I have looked deep enough in every corner of my being – there seems to be no purpose at all, and I consider it a great freedom. If there were a purpose, then you would be in bondage, then there would be a destiny you have to fulfill. Then you could be a failure.

Every purpose creates failures and successes. But if there is no purpose, nobody is a failure. Wherever you end up, that is the place you were destined to end. Wherever your boat leads you, and wherever the river moves, that is the direction. If you have any direction, you are going to be in conflict with many directions.

Don't have any direction, and don't have any desire. That does not mean repress desire. That simply means, rejoice in every desire, rejoice in every moment. Whatever is available, whatever has come across your path, love, be friendly.

Don't make any demands on existence, otherwise you will be in suffering. All those who live in misery, live in misery for the simple reason they are thinking that a certain purpose has to be fulfilled, a certain success has to be achieved, a certain ambition. And when it is not achieved – and there are more possibilities of not achieving it – you will be in misery. And even if you achieve it, it makes no difference, you will be in misery. You will be in misery because when you achieve it you will find nothing is achieved.

You have become the world's richest man, and suddenly you find you are surrounded by all kinds of junk. You cannot live if you are trying to be richer. You will be richer if you *live*.

Live each moment in as much intensity as possible, and you will be richer. But if you are living for riches, then it is always tomorrow, the day after tomorrow...and you are wasting all these valuable moments, you are becoming poorer every moment.

You are forgetting the language of living the present, and that is the only poverty.

I know of no other richness than to live each moment without bothering about the past which is no more, and without desiring of the future which is not yet. Live it! When it will come you will be able to live it too. You will be more efficient in living tomorrow if you are intensely living life today.

So I don't know what Paul Reps and Senzaki mean by "purpose." As far as Zen is concerned, there is no purpose. And I don't know what they mean by "the wine jug of his true desire."

Zen knows about the wine, but it is not of desire, it is of a silence.

It is of a desireless deepening of your life.

It is a silent song without sounds.

It is a music without instruments.

It is pure being.

At such a moment where being and non-being become equivalent, their presence and absence are synonymous. You are so present that you are almost absent, or the other way round – you are so absent that you are totally present.

Rather than Senzaki and Paul Reps, listen to your own heart. When you are no more, you are. When you are no more, you are the whole vastness of existence. When there is no desire, you are fulfilled. It is not that any desire has to be fulfilled. When there is no desire, when you have learned the art of remaining in a non-desiring moment, you are fulfilled.

When you are not doing anything, your action is perfect. Only non-doing can be perfect. Any doing is bound to be imperfect. No man is capable of doing anything perfectly. Perfection is of the imagination.

Life consists of all kinds of imperfections. You have to love the imperfect, and you have to respect the imperfect – not only in others, but in yourself too.

What Paul Reps and Senzaki are thinking of – the wine of desire – has nothing to do with Zen. Zen knows about one wine, and you have all tasted it. It is the wine that comes through the silent, meditative ecstasy of your being. It has nothing to do with desire. It has nothing to do with purpose.

Every day, whenever you reach to the point of your innermost being where everything is silent, where you cannot even say you are, a pure isness, unbounded, a tremendous drunkenness arises. I have called it divine drunkenness. That is the only wine I am acquainted with. And I don't think either Paul Reps or Senzaki understand the essence of Zen, otherwise they would not have used such wrong words.

The second question:

Many years ago I enjoyed reading Paul Reps' book, 'Zen Flesh, Zen Bones,' although it only gave me an intellectual understanding of Zen. Since You have been talking on Zen, I feel that not only have You conveyed to us the flesh and bones of Zen, but in Your silence You impart to us the very heart of Zen. Is it the Zen heart which Western intellectuals are missing, and if so, why are they missing it?

The Western intelligence has taken a certain direction; there is no reason why. The Eastern intelligence has taken a totally different direction; there also, there is no reason why. Such is the case.

The Western intellect has remained logical, rational, and has tried in every way to confine existence to reasonable terms, terms which mind can understand.

The East has taken a totally different approach. What mind can understand is a very small part, and because it is only a small part, it is going to be dead, it is going to be material. That which is beyond mind has to be understood. The East has moved into the irrational, into the mystical, into the miraculous. And certainly, the Eastern approach is far wider, far bigger. It can contain the Western approach in it, but the Western approach cannot contain the Eastern. No-mind can contain mind, but mind cannot contain no-mind. That's where the Eastern approach has reached to higher peaks.

Even a Socrates or an Aristotle has not been able to comprehend the experience of a Gautam Buddha, or the taste of a Bodhidharma, or the meaning of the gesture of a Rinzai. They have chosen a very small part – that which is available to intellect. And it is very small, hence the Western mind has been able to go into details. Because it has chosen a very small part, it can go into details. It goes on knowing more and more about less and less. Drawn to its logical conclusion, it can be said that the Western mind will finally reach to knowing more and more about nothing, because that will be the smallest part: nothing.

Albert Einstein and the neophysicists almost reached to that nothing. And they are puzzled because their minds cannot understand nothing, and they are confronting nothing. Their instruments have led them to nothing. Their analysis, their experiments have revealed to them nothing, but their minds are not ready to accept nothing. *Nothing* seems to be full of fear.

The Eastern mind has also reached nothing, but it reached nothing in a very different way. It reached nothing, dancing – not through analysis, not through logic, but through meditation. It has reached to nothingness through music, through song, through dance, through meditation. It has been a joyous experience. The nothing in the East does not create fear. It creates freedom, opens doors, destroys all boundaries. But the Western mind – it simply freaks out.

Nothing? No purpose? No God? No meaning? No destiny? Then the Western mind can only conclude suicide. But that too is meaningless. Why commit it?

So the Western intellectual lives in a very strange tragedy. All his mind can conclude is suicide, and that is what he is afraid of. So he lives halfway, wishy-washy...neither loves totally, nor dances totally, nor meditates totally. Totality is unknown, only partiality – only parts the mind can deal with easily.

The Eastern mind recognized quickly that mind is part of the body on the one hand, and on the other hand, mind is part of the education of the society. The brain is the natural part, and the mind is the part that the society has given you – the conditionings, the philosophies, the religions, the whole nurture. This small mind, which consists only of biology and sociology, cannot know the vast truth, the mysterious expanse of the ultimate.

It is absolutely needed to transcend the mind. And in a strange way, the moment you transcend the mind, you for the first time understand the mind also. Because to understand anything you have to stand apart, a little distance is needed.

A meditator can understand mind, and can understand no-mind, because he is standing apart, aloof, as a witness. He can see thoughts, and he can see the absence of thoughts, and he can understand that both are essential. Thought is for the limited, and the no-thought is for the unlimited.

Your question, that reading Paul Reps' *Zen Flesh, Zen Bones* gave you an intellectual understanding of Zen…

There is no intellectual understanding of Zen.

Zen has to be understood non-intellectually.

Zen is an experience.

It has nothing to do with reason, explanations, analytical processes. If you know what is sweet, you know you may not be able to say what it is. And if somebody asks you, "What is sweet?" you know it but you will be in trouble, you cannot say it. It is just on the tip of the tongue.

The East has not tried to approach reality philosophically, it has tried in a very different, non-intellectual, meditative way. That is the way of tasting it.

Don't ask what reality is, taste it. It is available to you; it is your very essence. Why do you go on looking in the Bibles, in the Korans, in the Gitas? Why don't you look within yourself? – it is there. And if it is not there, it is nowhere. And if it is there, it is everywhere. It is a simple experience.

One of the greatest philosophical geniuses, G.E. Moore, has written a book upon a very small, simple subject: What is good? Although he gives his book a very intellectual name, *Principia Ethica*, the meaning is the search for good: What is good, what is ethical? After two hundred and fifty pages of thick discussion, he concludes…the last sentence is that the good is indefinable. So what was all this nonsense?

One of my teachers was a student of G.E. Moore, and because he had been G.E. Moore's student, he was thought to be the authority in the university.

I had read the book before I entered his class. He opened the book…

I said, "Please, first read the last sentence."

He looked at me, puzzled. He said, "Why?"

I said, "That will decide everything. You read the last sentence, otherwise, I have the book, I can read it."

But he said, "Why are you asking that?"

I said to him, "I am not asking it for any intellectual reason, I am asking it so that you can throw the book out of the window, because the last sentence is: 'Good is indefinable.' Then why bother? Then let us do something significant. Why waste time?"

He looked at me. He told all the students to go out, and he said, "We have to come to a settlement. If you insist on reading the last sentence first, you are right, the book has to be thrown. But my whole purpose here is to teach the book."

I said, "There is nothing in it to teach."

He said, "You are right that way also, because finally, I have to come to that conclusion."

I said, "You know it, and I know it, so why waste time?"

He said, "What do you suggest? What should we do?"

I said, "What will you do after the book is finished?"

He said, "I have never thought about it."

I said, "You have been G.E. Moore's own student, and you did not ask the fellow that if you know that it is indefinable, then why waste time, why not do something significant? Then why not approach it in the Eastern way?"

The East never says anything is indefinable. It only says things are either definable or experienceable. That is the distinction the East makes clearly. If something is indefinable, it means it is experienceable.

Sweet is indefinable. How are you going to define it? The yellowness of a flower is indefinable. What are you going to say? What is yellow? Yellow is yellow – but that is tautology, that is not definition.

There are things – and those are the most valuable things – which have to be experienced. Good has to be experienced, not defined.

He said, "You are a tough student, but have mercy on me."

I said, "On one condition: if you give me one hundred percent attendance. I will never come to your class. You can go on with your indefinables; I can do something else."

He said, "I have to agree. I will give you the attendance mark whether you come or not."

I said, "That is not the question, whether I come or not. I will *not* come, and I will make it clean and clear to everybody in the class. Only idiots will come, because if something is indefinable…and you know it, and you have agreed with me.

"Nobody is going to come. You go on sitting here, reading your book, finding finally something which you knew already – that good is indefinable. Meanwhile, we could do many things which are worth doing. Even growing a rose plant, even planting a lawn, may create a little good, a little beauty, a little experience in existence. Or not doing anything, just sitting…"

I told him…just behind my university campus there was a small hillock, and there were three trees. I told him, "If you want me anytime, you can come to the hillock. In the middle tree, I sit there on top of the tree. That is when I want to experience good."

He said, "You experience good there?"

I said, "You experience good in this book which says it is indefinable; I experience it there. There, clouds are so close, and the flowers of that tree are so fragrant. And day and night nobody goes there – no traffic, no disturbance, utter silence. In that silence, perhaps someday you may know the experience of good."

What is the experience of good?

Just a feeling of well-being, a feeling of great rejoicing. Just because you are breathing, just because the blood is circulating, just because the heart is beating, just because the wind is blowing and the tree is fragrant, and the sky is clean, and a bird is on the wing.

The man was certainly intelligent. He said, "One day I am going to come with you."

I said, "Remember, the middle tree belongs to me. You can sit on the first tree or the third tree. And as far as good is concerned, it is available on all the trees. Just sit silently, and don't bring any book, and don't ask any question."

One day he came, and from the very beginning I showed him, "Go up!" So he sat on the tree. After an hour he came down. I asked him, "Did you experience something?"

He said, "Really, it is so silent here. It seems almost out of the world. And I unnecessarily wasted my time in Oxford studying with G.E. Moore what is beauty, what is good, what is silence. These trees can experience."

I said, "These trees can experience much more than is contained in any book on aesthetics, ethics, philosophy, religion."

You just have to be utterly in tune with the surroundings – when just the bamboos are giving you the definition of good, and a roseflower is defining for you what is beauty....

There is no intellectual understanding of Zen. There is an experiential understanding of Zen, that is through meditation – a taste. Something opens within you, something that has not been available to you because you were keeping your back towards it. Something, just because you look for it, suddenly comes in the mirror of your eyes, fills your very being. A tremendous dance...in small things, a beauty, a joy. But if you start defining, you start missing.

You are asking why the Western mind has been missing it. It went on a wrong track, and it is still on the wrong track.

I have told you about the Humanist manifesto. These are America's most famous intellectuals. Everything has to be defined clearly. If it is not defined, it is not acceptable. But these great intellectuals have not questioned that reason itself is undefined – what is reason? what is the purpose of it? why should it be there?

And it is a very simple thing to see, that in life there is always the opposite. If there is reason, there must be something irrational, otherwise there is no point in calling anything rational. If there is beauty, there is something that is bound to be ugly. If there is something good, then something is bound to be evil.

The moment you say, "Reason...our faith is reason," you have defined your territory. Beyond that territory, whatever exists you will not accept it – but existence accepts it. Whether you accept it or not does not matter.

There was a time when only Aristotle's logic was available – for two thousand years. Just now, this century, non-Aristotelian logic has come into existence because Aristotle's logic is very confined.

For two thousand years Euclidean geometry was the only geometry. Just within fifty years, non-Euclidean geometry has come into existence. And if you know non-Euclidean geometry, all the points of Euclidean geometry are completely erased.

All the definitions of Euclid, and all the definitions of Aristotle, are denied by modern physics, because if you listen to their definitions you cannot move into existence. Existence does not bother about Aristotle or Euclid. Existence has its own ways; it is vast enough, it is bigger than Aristotle's skull.

How much can you contain in your mind? Something will always remain beyond, and that beyond does not disappear from existence, it is there whether you accept it or not.

The East has taken a far more sane view, to accept both: the rational for the material, and the irrational for the immaterial; the rational for the outside, and the irrational for the inside. This is a saner and more balanced view, and sooner or later the West has to agree to the Eastern viewpoint.

The third question:

**You have recently referred to the "noncompetitive spirit" of the Zen masters.
Is competitiveness lacking in Zen because there is no sense of hierarchy – because the idea of hierarchy is essentially connected with the concept of a supreme being, apart from and above man?**

There is no competitive spirit. That means, no master is thought to be greater, and no master is thought to be lesser. Even the enlightened one is not thought to be higher than the unenlightened one. One is asleep, one is awake – that does not mean that the awake one is more superior than the one who is asleep. They are different states, but there is no question of superiority or inferiority. In this sense, no competitive spirit exists in Zen.

No master is trying to gather more people, more followers. On the contrary, there are cases on record where the master will look into the eyes of the disciple who has come to be with him, will shake his head and will say, "It will be better if you go to the other monastery on the other hill. Although the teaching there is different and the opposite to mine, it will be more suitable to you. And the real thing is what is more suitable for you. It is not a question that I should have more disciples and the other should have less."

Once it happened…

A disciple was thrown out by the master because for many years he had been meditating, and bringing answers, and getting beaten…and he had become habituated, and nothing was happening.

One day as he was coming in, the master closed the door. The disciple said, "I have not said anything at all."

The master said, "You should not come here at all. Go anywhere…!"

Naturally, the disciple thought, "The best place will be the master who is opposite; he teaches different things."

He went to that master. The master looked into his eyes and said, "It is better you go back to your old master; he has great mercy for you. Eighteen years he has wasted on you; I don't have that much compassion. You just go back! If he closes the door, that does not mean that he is not answering you – that is his answer. Sit down at the door, don't open your eyes, and don't move from the door. Just go back."

And the disciple went back, sat at the master's door, and closed his eyes. The whole night went by. Early in the morning the master opened the door, and the disciple was sitting there so beautifully, so peacefully, that the master who had brought a few flowers for Buddha's statue showered those flowers on the disciple's head.

The disciple opened his eyes. He said, "What are you doing? These flowers you brought for Buddha."

The master said, "That Buddha can manage without flowers today. A living buddha I have found just sitting at my door. Come in. Where have you been this long time?"

He said, "Where? I have been here eighteen years. Have you forgotten? Just yesterday you threw me out!"

He said, "I had to, because I knew immediately you would go to the opposite monastery. And I knew that the master opposite would not accept you. You are such a dodo, and only I accept dodos and make them buddhas! So there was no fear. Wherever you would have gone they would have sent you back."

There is no competitiveness, there is no condemnation. Disciples move from one teacher to another teacher with their permission – and there is no hierarchy. Gautam Buddha is not higher than Mahakashyapa, and Mahakashyapa is not higher than Bodhidharma. The very word 'hierarchy' comes from the idea of the inferior and the superior.

The world according to the buddhas is divided into two kinds of buddhas: a few are sleeping, and a few are awake – not much of a difference. One who is asleep today may wake up tomorrow. And one never knows – one who is awake today may fall asleep tomorrow. In this miraculous existence everything is possible.

It will be difficult for your reason to accept that a buddha can become again unenlightened, but I know many buddhas who are sitting here unenlightened. And many times they come to the very verge of becoming enlightened, and immediately turn away, being afraid that, "Who knows? If you go one step more, you may never come back" – and your girlfriend is waiting outside...!

Sarjano has gone somewhere for a few days. I asked Neelam, "I don't see Sarjano...?" She informed me that she had asked Sarjano, and Sarjano said, "If I am not missing him, why is he missing me?"

Sarjano, you may not miss me – I miss you. I am *my* kind of a buddha. I miss people – and even people like Sarjano! Everybody was happy when he was gone....

The sutra:

BELOVED OSHO,
Tanka asked Chōro, "What is the self before the empty eon?"

'Eon' means before the beginning of existence. Tanka is asking, "Before existence began, there was eon...?" That is only a word: 'age'; it means simply age. It would be better translated to say, 'time' – pure time existed.

Tanka asked Chōro, "What is the self before the empty eon?" Before that empty timelessness, what is the self...where have you been? You must have been somewhere – a relevant question. Existence may not have been here, you may not have been in a body, but somewhere, hiding in some corner, you must have been somewhere.

As Chōro was about to answer, Tanka said, "You are still noisy – go away for now."

Tanka was the master who asked the disciple, Chōro, "*What is the self before the empty eon?"* – before everything begins, what is the self?

And as Chōro was about to answer – because this is not a question that can be answered... To answer is to answer wrongly. There is no right answer to it – perhaps some right action. If Chōro had been a man of understanding he may have hit, slapped the master, and the master would have been happy. But it is not a question to be answered intellectually, verbally.

As Chōro was about to answer, Tanka said, "You are still noisy – go away for now. When you are silent, and there are no words in you, come back."

Only a man who has no words knows that the self can exist without boundaries. It is an experience; there is no way of proving it by argumentation. You can go into yourself and be utterly silent – no boundaries, no words, a pure isness...still, you know you are. Without knowing, without verbalizing, you experience you *are*.

This amness was there before the beginning, if there was any beginning. It is now, and it will remain forever. Even if there is an end, this amness is not going to end. And this amness has nothing to do with you. This amness is not your possession; hence, it is not the self.

Buddha is very accurate in his explanations. Perhaps no man has ever been so accurate. He describes it as no self, not as self, because to call it self will give it a line, a boundary, a territory. To destroy the territory, Buddha calls it no self. This was one of the reasons for his being misunderstood for centuries. Because who wants to attain to no self, who wants to become nothing...?

And that's exactly what you become when you reach to the very center of your being – nothing, no self. But that no-selfness is immortal, that no-selfness is pure joy, uncaused bliss.

One day, as Chōro was climbing Bol Peak, his mind opened up into enlightenment. He took a shortcut down and went back to stand by Tanka, who slapped him and said, "I thought you knew it exists."
Chōro bowed joyfully.

He didn't say anything. On this second occasion, Chōro suddenly felt a silence as he was coming up the mountain. It happens more easily in the world of Zen, because everybody is looking for silence. As he was climbing up, suddenly a moment of silence, and he found why the master had rejected him. He took a shortcut to reach the master.

Tanka looked at him, slapped him, and said, "I knew you would know it exists. It is not the self, it is not the no self; it is simply isness, and you will find it one day. I knew it, and I am happy that you have found it."

Chōro had not said a single word, but he showed his understanding: *Chōro bowed joyfully.*

Now, in any situation anywhere, this type of incident is impossible. The master slaps the disciple, and he has not said anything right or wrong. But the master does not depend on your words, he depends on your grace, on your eyes, on your face, on your very vibe. The master saw that Chōro was walking in a different way, with a different vibe, as only a buddha can walk. He did not miss the point, he immediately slapped him.

This slapping was just to check whether he was right or wrong. If Chōro had asked, "Why are you slapping me?" Tanka would have been wrong. But rather than asking anything, Chōro bowed joyfully. Not only has Tanka understood the vibe, but Chōro has also understand that slapping is not out of anger, it is out of joy.

The next day Tanka went into the hall and said, "The sun illumines the green of the solitary peak; the moon shines in the cold of the valley stream. Don't put the wondrous secret of the ancestral teachers in your little heart." Then he got up off the seat.
Chōro came directly forward and said,
"Your address today can't fool me anymore."
Tanka said, "Try to recite my address."
Chōro remained silent.
Tanka said, "I thought you had a glimpse."
Chōro then left.

What had transpired?

The next day Tanka spoke before the assembly and said, "*The sun illumines the green of the solitary peak; the moon shines in the cold of the valley stream. Don't put the wondrous secret of the ancestral teachers in your heart." Then he got up off the seat....*

What he meant was: whenever you have found the truth, spread it, don't keep it in your heart. If you keep it, it will die. Spread it wide, sow it in as many fields as possible. The more you spread it, the more it grows, the more you have it.

Chōro has become a little proud of yesterday's experience, that the master has slapped him joyfully.

Chōro came directly forward and said,
"Your address today can't fool me anymore."

He thought that he had gone beyond the understanding that is contained in the sermon of the master.

Tanka said, "Try to recite my address. If you cannot be befooled by it, please try to recite it. Let me see whether you have even heard it or not."

Chōro remained silent.
Tanka said, "I thought you had a glimpse."

Those slappings were of joy; this statement: "*I thought you had a glimpse,*" is of sadness.

The master is saying that in the first place this is impudent – "coming before the assembly and making the statement..." Secondly, "When asked to recite, if you cannot recite it, you can at least ask for forgiveness. But you remained silent like a dead lamppost."

Tanka said, "I was wrong. I thought you had a glimpse. Yesterday you had a different vibe. Today that vibe has changed."

This makes me aware of you – that whenever any recognition from the master is given to you, don't make it part of your ego. Otherwise, rather than helping, it becomes a hindrance.

The master's looking into your eyes, or his hand pointing to you, is a recognition. In his love there is a recognition. Every moment he is recognizing you with great reverence, as possible, potential buddhas. But don't become proud of it, otherwise that proudness will delay your enlightenment.

Issa wrote:

Heedless of the dew
that marks our closing day,
we bind ourselves to others.

There are few haiku poets of the caliber of Issa and Bashō. This haiku says: "Heedless of the dew that marks our closing day…" Every day so much dust is created around – so much anger, so much sadness, so much misery, so much misunderstanding.

Heedless of all this that marks our closing day, we bind ourselves to others. Our love remains unmarked, unscratched. Our hearts are just like mirrors which don't gather any dust.

That is the way of a man of Zen. Go on removing the dust, and remember your unity, your union with the whole existence. Nothing allows you to separate yourself – no anger, no desire, no failure. Nothing divides you from existence.

Every evening remove all the dust.

Go to your bed with a clean mirror, in a silent song, harmonious with existence.

Maneesha's question:

BELOVED OSHO,

Paul Reps in the foreword to his book, 'Zen Flesh, Zen Bones,' writes, "…that the one hundred and twelve techniques of 'Vigyan Bhairava Tantra' may well be the roots of Zen." Beloved Osho, do You agree with Paul Reps?

There is a possibility…the one hundred and twelve techniques of *Vigyan Bhairava Tantra* are basically one technique in different combinations. That one technique is witnessing. In different situations use witnessing, and you have created a new technique. In all those one hundred and twelve techniques, that simple *witnessing* is used.

And there is a possibility that it may not be joined directly with Shiva's book. *Vigyan Bhairava Tantra* is five thousand years old, and Gautam Buddha is only twenty-five centuries old. The gap between Shiva and Buddha is long – twenty-five centuries – and there seems to be no connecting link.

So it may not be that he has directly taken the technique of witnessing from *Vigyan Bhairava Tantra*. But whether he has taken it directly or not, there is a possibility that somehow, from somebody, he may have heard. He had moved with many masters before he became a buddha.

Before he himself found the technique of witnessing, he had moved with many masters. Somewhere he may have heard mention of *Vigyan Bhairava Tantra*, but it does not seem to have a very direct connection, because he was still searching. In fact, it was not witnessing that he was practicing when he became a buddha.

The situation is just the reverse: he became a buddha first. Then he found, "My God! It is witnessing that has made me a buddha." It was not that he was practicing witnessing, he had dropped everything. Tired of all kinds of yogas and mantras and tantras, one evening he simply dropped... He had renounced the kingdom, he had renounced everything. For six years he had been torturing himself with all kinds of methods.

That evening, he dropped all those methods, and under a tree which became known by his name, the *bodhi* tree, he slept silently. And in the morning when he opened his eyes, the last star was disappearing. And as the star disappeared – a sudden silence all around, and he became a witness. He was not doing anything special, he was just lying down underneath the tree, resting, watching the disappearing star. And as the star disappeared there was nothing to watch – only watching remained. Suddenly he found, "Whoever I have been seeking, I am it."

So it was Buddha himself who discovered that witnessing had been his path without his awareness.

But since Buddha, witnessing, or the method of *sakshin*, became a specific method of Zen.

Paul Reps' guess has a possibility, but it cannot be proved historically. And according to me, Buddha was not practicing witnessing. He found witnessing after he found that he was a buddha. So certainly it has nothing to do with *Vigyan Bhairava Tantra*, but the method is the same.

Because the method is the same, in the mind of Paul Reps, a scholarly mind, the idea may have arisen easily that Buddha's method, the Zen method, is connected with *Vigyan Bhairava Tantra*. But this connection seems to be only his guesswork. It has a possibility, but no validity.

The bamboos are asking for Sardar Gurudayal Singh's time. Put on the lights!

It is midnight at the Rotting Saint's Graveyard in Cologne. All is quiet, when suddenly, there is a rattling noise under one of the gravestones, marked Himlish Humper. Slowly, the stone begins to lift up, and the earth begins to crumble, and a bony hand reaches out into the air.

Slowly but surely, the skeleton of Himlish Humper creeps out of the ground. Himlish brushes the dust off his bones, and then knocks on the next stone marked Hector Herpes.

"Come on, Hector!" cackles Himlish. "It is time!"

Then, from under the stone marked Hector Herpes comes the sound of bones rattling, and slowly the stone lifts up and out slides the skeleton of Hector.

The two skeletons clatter and rattle as they stand up and shake hands.

"We are free!" rasps Himlish. "Let us go!"

The two guys start running and rattling down the streets of Cologne. Suddenly, Hector Herpes stops dead in his tracks. He spins around and starts rattling back towards his grave.

When he gets there he picks up the huge gravestone and carries it back to where Himlish is standing.

"What the hell are you bringing that thing for?" screeches Himlish.

"Hey!" replies Hector. "You cannot travel in Germany without your papers!"

Young Father Feever finishes his training at the Bleeding Cross Jesuit Monastery, and moves to New York as the priest of the Immaculate Conception and Miraculous Resurrection Church.

Feever soon discovers that one member of the congregation, Lucy Legs, is a prostitute, and decides to try and put her right.

Feever invites Lucy to the back of the church for an informal discussion. But when the young priest arrives, he finds Lucy sitting naked on an old tombstone, with her legs stretched wide apart.

"Ah, My God!" moans Feever, beginning to perspire. "I prayed for you last night…!"

"You idiot! There is no need for that," snaps Lucy, "I am on the telephone. But don't worry! You can have me now – just fifty dollars!"

"No! No!" cries Feever, loosening his dog collar. "You misunderstand me. I expected to find you on your knees. In fact, I think we should both start by getting down on our knees right away! Okay?"

"If that is how you want it!" smiles Lucy. "But it is a hundred dollars for doggie-style!"

In an effort to try and show the world that all Catholic cardinals are not homosexuals, Pope the Polack throws a huge ball at the Vatican. All the priests are given dancing lessons, and many glamorous women are invited to attend.

On the great night, the Vatican chapel, which has been converted for the event, is soon full of dancing couples.

At one point in the evening, Gorgeous Gloria finds herself in the arms of Cardinal Catsass, being swirled around the dance floor. Gorgeous Gloria is dressed in a skintight, off-the-shoulder dress, which highlights her figure perfectly, but many of the cardinals find the dress too revealing.

"Do you know," says Cardinal Catsass, "that I have always been a great admirer of yours, and I have always wanted to be in the same joke as you?"

"Thank you," replies Gloria.

"Yes," says Catsass. "You are also very beautiful!"

"That is very nice of you to say so," replies Gloria, wondering how she is going to get away from the old idiot.

"But I ought to tell you something," says Catsass, frowning at her strapless dress, "that I have just one thing against you."

"I know," says Gloria. "I can feel it!"

Nivedano…

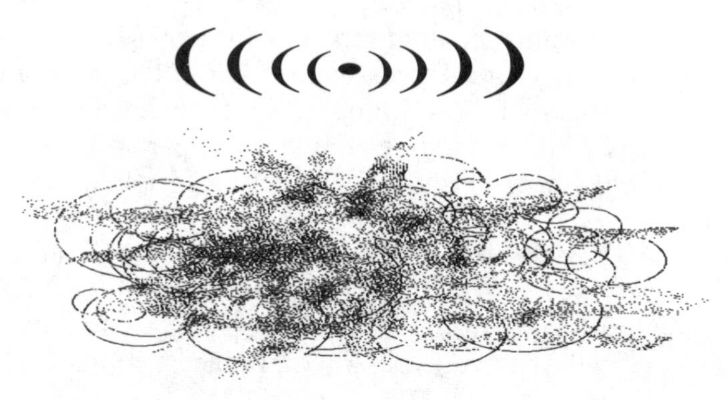

Nivedano...

Be silent...

Close your eyes, and feel your body to be completely frozen. This is the right moment to enter inwards.

Gather your energies, your total consciousness. And with an intensity, rush towards the center of your being. A deep urgency is needed, as if this is going to be your last moment of life.

Deeper and deeper...

As you are coming closer to your center, a great silence descends over you. Your heart opens up just as a lotus opens. Fragrance from the beyond surrounds you.

One step more, and you are at the very center of your being. This is the point where you are absent and present both: absent, as you have known yourself, and present, as a buddha knows himself.

This is your pure sky, your freedom, your eternity, your ecstasy.

Witness that you are not the body.

Witness that you are not the mind.

Witness that you are only the witness – a pure witness, just a mirror.

This witnessing is the only revolution that has ever happened to any man, the only revolution that has produced a line of buddhas.

Make it deeper...

Nivedano...

Relax, but remain a witness....

Gautama the Buddha Auditorium becomes an ocean of consciousness. You have just disappeared into this ocean, without boundaries.

Flowers of silence, flowers of peace, flowers of joy, have sprung up all over the place.

At this moment you are the most blessed person on the earth, because everybody is lost somewhere in the marketplace.

You are one of those chosen few who are searching the truth of your being. And it is always found, because it is always there waiting for you. It is your authenticity, it is your existence.

Zen is an existential path.

Experience your buddhahood before Nivedano calls you back.

Collect all these experiences. You have to bring them with yourself, you have to make them part of your daily life.

And remember these three things, these three steps....

First, Gautam Buddha follows you like a shadow.

Second, you become a shadow of Gautam Buddha.

And third, you disappear even as a shadow and become one with Gautam Buddha....

A pure consciousness...

A white cloud floating in the sky of ultimate freedom...

As you come back, persuade the buddha to come along with you.

Nivedano...

Come back...but slowly, peacefully, gracefully, showing your buddha nature.

Sit down for a few moments just to remember where you have been, where you are.

Has there been an experience? Can that experience remain twenty-four hours with you like a shadow?

It is your very nature, hence there is no question. It can become your very breathing, your very heartbeat.

And look...feel the presence of Buddha behind you.

If the first step is taken, the second is not far away, and the third is the easiest.

Okay, Maneesha?

Yes, Osho.

FREEDOM NOT LICENTIOUSNESS

BELOVED OSHO,

One day, Tanka said to the monks who were with him, "You should all protect your essential thing, which is not made or formed by you. So how can I teach you to do this or not to do this?

"Once, when I saw Sekitō Oshō, he taught me that I should just protect it by myself. This thing cannot be talked about. You all have your own Zazen mat; other than that, what Zen do you talk about?

"You should understand this. There is nothing which is to become buddha. Don't just go on hearing the name of buddha; you, yourselves, must see that the good devices and four infinite virtues are not from outside; don't carry them in your mind.

"What do you intend to follow? Don't use sutras. Leave the emptiness without falling into it.

"The seekers of the present day search for the Tao chaotically. Here in this place, there is no way to learn, nor any dharma to show. Even a single sip or a single bite has its own truth.

"Don't entertain thoughts and suspicions. In any place, the thing is present. If you recognize Gautam Buddha, an ordinary old man is that. You should all see, and get it, by yourselves. Don't let a blind man lead a mass of blind people into a fire cave.

"If you play a dice game in the dark night, how can you see the numbers on the dice?"

FRIENDS,

Before I answer your questions, I have to talk about a letter by Sarjano.

The other night I talked about him. He has written a very beautiful and loving letter, but as you know Sarjano, he is lying. I have no objection to it – if you are lying, lie beautifully and totally. A life without lies will be very boring.

When I told you the remark Sarjano made to Neelam: "If I don't miss him, why does he miss me?" – he was not right, he was not true. He has been missing – he may not be aware of it.

Many of you are not aware of what you are missing. Many of you are not aware of what you have forgotten. But his case can be taken as an example.

He told Neelam, "I am not coming to the discourses because they are too long. I am watching the sky, sitting on my balcony."

Do you think the sky is smaller than my discourses?

And Sarjano was not on the balcony either. He was not even in Poona. I keep myself perfectly aware of where you are. Looking at Sarjano's eyes the other day, I saw that he has been with U.G. Krishnamurti. And not only has he been with U.G. Krishnamurti, he has been taking other people there too.

There is nothing wrong in it; only one thing has to be remembered: when you are fragile in your growth, people like U.G. Krishnamurti can destroy you. These people have missed their life, and now they are living in frustration. And in frustration people start behaving like women. They start breaking things, throwing things. That's what U.G. Krishnamurti is doing.

But let him do what he wants to do. It is none of the business of anybody else to come in the way when he is throwing a disk. It is his disk. Why should you get unnecessary wounds? They are not your own.

It is a misery to say to you that many of you are carrying wounds of others, miseries of others, tragedies of others.

Have you ever looked at a simple fact – that you don't have to be miserable, it is by choice?

And if you, Sarjano, were going to U.G. Krishnamurti, you should have told Neelam without lying that you "are watching the sky." Now what has happened to the sky? The sky is still there, the balcony is still there, and what are you doing here? And particularly for you, I am going to make the discourse long. I care for my people.

Today he has written a letter in which he feels afraid that "perhaps the ghost of Rajneeshpuram will take possession of this commune also." Sarjano, it is not you speaking, it is U.G. Krishnamurti. He has never lived in a commune.

A commune gives certain responsibilities and certain freedoms. A commune is not necessarily destructive of the individual. In fact, that is the very purpose of the commune: to preserve the individual, his integrity.

A commune is not an organization, but when thousands of people are involved, somebody has to cook, and somebody has to watch on the door, and somebody has to do small things. There are people who start thinking that even doing these things is destroying their freedom. This is sheer nonsense.

A certain responsibility is not against freedom; in fact, freedom can only exist with responsible people. Somebody has to take care of the gardens, otherwise there will be no flowers.

Sarjano's trouble may be the trouble of a few other sannyasins. It has to be made clear that a commune is not dictatorial, but it is not democratic either. It gives respect to the individual. With the respect it gives the responsibility also, that you have to be aware not to trespass on anybody, and that you have to contribute to the commune.

If you are taking from the well of the commune, you have to contribute something – whatever you can do.

When you are working with friends there should be no discussion about anything, only dialogues. There should be no need to impose anything on anybody. When intelligent people are there, they can see the reason themselves. They are not to be forced.

But there are a few people who think licentiousness is freedom. Sarjano, that is your attitude.

Licentiousness is not freedom.

We are sitting here – nobody is forcing you to be silent. It is according to your intelligence that you are silent, and this gives your individuality a tremendous grace.

One of my attorneys in America was puzzled. He was not a sannyasin, and he was employed just because he was an authority of law, a dean of the faculty of law in a California university. He must have seen students his whole life, but he had never seen a master.

So he took me aside one day, and asked, "I am puzzled. Even when the magistrate comes in, it has to be announced that 'the magistrate is coming, you all stand up.' But when you come, nobody announces it. Your people are there – we can understand why they stand up. But my puzzle is, that I myself feel like standing. And when I look at the people standing, only fifty percent are sannyasins, fifty percent are other people."

As sannyasins started standing, others were too, unknowingly, without any awareness – they found themselves also standing. They may not have been in favor of me – their agreement or disagreement is not the question.

Your silence is not democratic – you have not been asked to vote to be silent. It is not dictatorial – you have not been told that you have to be silent. This is the beauty and dignity of your silence: it is arising out of you. It is not imposed from outside; it is coming from within. And when something comes from within, it has a beauty and a grace, and a tremendous aliveness. This is not the silence of a graveyard; this is the silence of a garden. It is not dead; it is throbbing with life.

Sarjano, Zen teaches revolution in a graceful way. In the name of revolution much ugliness has happened in the world. Zen wants you to understand the implications of the inner revolution, and you have to go on your own way. Zen simply makes it clear that there is nothing to be found, that there is no truth which is hidden – it is only your eyes which are closed.

Do you see the shift? All other mystery schools in the world have been teaching that the truth is hidden. If it is only a way of saying it, it can be forgiven. But the reality is, truth is not hidden. Truth is all over the place, only our eyes are closed.

And when you are going through an operation, you have to behave. Don't think that asking a certain behavior of you is necessarily slavery. Freedom can exist only according to a certain behavior pattern which you have accepted consciously, knowing all its implications.

When "yes" comes from your own being, then only is it true. If it comes out of fear, it is untrue. If it comes out of greed, it is not true. When it comes only out of understanding, without fear, without greed, without punishment, then you act according to your inner truth.

It is a miracle that thousands of people can live here without any conflict, without any fight, without any violence. The whole world can live with such peace and silence if freedom is not misunderstood as licentiousness.

Freedom is a greater responsibility, it gives you dignity and pride. It makes you aware that you are living in a meaningful way. There is no other meaning to be found.

When I said to you yesterday there is no meaning in life, there is no ultimate goal, you can misunderstand me. What I was really saying is that there is no meaning in life; hence you are free to create it. There is no goal in life, no fixed fatality; then your hands are free to paint, to sculpt, to love, to live. But now you have to depend only on one thing, and that is your own inner light.

Zen is the awakening of the inner light. And in that awakening, all moralities follow on their own accord.

People have asked me, "Zen looks beautiful, but where is the morality?" Because all the religions of the world teach you morality, they have created an idea that unless a morality is taught, forced, disciplined, you are going to be immoral. Your immorality is taken for granted.

The truth is different. If you simply awaken into your consciousness and act according to that awareness, your life is going to be moral, virtuous. Without being dragged by religions, forced by people, without creating any guilt, Zen gives you a tremendous freedom. But the freedom is as great as is your responsibility – if you drop responsibility you also drop your freedom.

Most of the people in the world have lived in slavery because of a simple psychological fact: slavery is cozy, freedom is an open sky. Slavery is the security of the cage. The bird in the cage need not worry about food, need not worry about enemies, need not worry about changes of seasons, but he has sold his freedom for all this security.

Zen's effort is to take you out of your cages. Those cages have beautiful names: Christianity, Hinduism, Jainism, Buddhism. The effort of Zen is – it does not matter what kind and what shape of cage you are living in, but don't live in a cage. And the whole universe is available to you. It has not to be searched for, it is already there throbbing in your heart. Just be more conscious of your interiority, and you will start growing up.

Very few people grow up, most people only grow old. Growing up makes one a buddha. And the lowest has the potential to become the buddha. But never become a Buddhist – that is a cage. Never belong to any organization. Never belong to any system of belief or morality. Just belong only to your own freedom, and freedom certainly brings immense responsibility. For everything you do you are responsible. There is nobody else to take the responsibility. That's why people have agreed to believe in all kinds of lies.

God is a lie, but it helps people to make him responsible. He made the world – if he has made us the way we are, he is responsible. They have believed in prophets, in messiahs, just to give them their responsibility. And all your messiahs, your Christs, your Krishnas, ask you only one thing: "Believe in me and I will take care of your spiritual life."

There are millions of Christians, and they believe in Jesus and they believe in God, but their spirituality has not blossomed. Nor has it blossomed in other religions. Something is fundamentally wrong. Zen makes it a point to make you aware of that wrong. Giving up responsibility felt good – the burden is gone. But with the responsibility gone, your freedom has also disappeared. And a man who doesn't know freedom, knows nothing of life, knows nothing of love, knows nothing of creativity, knows nothing of this immense universe.

When I say there is no meaning, I mean you have to create meaning. It is not there ready-made, on sale. When I say there is no goal, I simply mean you have to learn to live without goals. A man lives only to the point, to the depth...who has no goals, no sources, who is alone in this vast universe, without any guidance.

All scriptures are unholy, because they all pretend to be your guidance, your guides. But you don't need guides. You need awareness, and every guide will want you to be blind. It is easier for the guide if people are blind, because they don't ask questions, they don't create doubt. They are ready to be slaves if security is given to them, and that's what all religions are giving you: security in afterlife, security in heaven.

Just the other day I was watching a film about Jesus, and I love the man. Unless I love anybody, I don't criticize him, I don't feel he is worth criticizing. Watching the film, there were a few points....

In one part, a rich man, a young man who had just inherited almost an empire, came to Jesus and asked him, "I would love to follow you, but what are the conditions?"

Jesus said to him, "The first thing to do is, go and distribute all that you possess to the poor."

The man said, "All?"

Jesus said, "Yes. Give everything and come to me."

The man was standing, he hesitated, and a giggle went through the crowd. And as the rich man disappeared into the crowd to hide his face, Jesus made his famous statement: "A camel may pass through the eye of the needle, but a rich man cannot pass through the gates of God."

In this way, poverty has been praised. And when you praise poverty you destroy the art of creating wealth, the art of creating more comforts, and you console the poor in his misery and in his poverty. And the man, the young man who has come, you ask too much of him too early. A master should not be in a hurry. He has just inherited an empire, and you ask him to distribute all...!

And he asked, "All? Do you mean all?"

If Jesus had said to him, "Distribute a part of it," and as he would have come closer, "Distribute a little more," as he would have become more intimate and more understanding, his whole empire would have been distributed. It is Jesus who is preventing him. He has come and he is ready, but asking too much when the time is not ripe shows a hurriedness.

I would not have asked him for anything. If he had come, he would have been welcome, and by and by, you would have helped him to disperse his empire.

In fact, before a person becomes alert and aware, you should not ask such impossible things. But all the religions have been asking impossible, unnatural things. That man must have gone with a guilt, with a feeling of inferiority that he did not have the guts. Now you have created a wound in him. Who is going to heal him?

People have looked at Jesus as if he is a healer. I say unto you, he has created more wounds in humanity than any other man. But those wounds are very psychological; they are not on your body, they are on your mind. And all the religions have done that.

All the religions have condemned women because they have the body of a woman. Nobody has bothered that without a woman's body there would be no possibility of procreation. Even the so-called God had to use a woman. Strange! Why did he have to make poor Mary pregnant? And both were condemned: the husband, the wife. The name of Jesus' father is not mentioned much at all. But as I was watching the whole story, he seems to have been far more human, far more understanding than even your God. God at least could have managed nine months; there was no need to create this scandal of Jesus not being the son of his own father. The same God gives the commandment: "You should not commit adultery" – and he himself commits it. Jesus is the proof of God's adultery.

But these fictions are consoling – a God who comes when it is needed. Strange...that he was needed in Judea, in Israel, and he was not needed anywhere else. And Judea is a small place...nothing beautiful about it. God chooses a poor carpenter's wife – and he is thought to be omnipotent...he knows all. So he must have known that this boy was going to be crucified at the age of thirty-three.

Knowing all this, still all the religions have been condemning women. And all their *tirthankaras*, and all their *avataras*, incarnations...all are born of women. And still, the mother of all your godmen is condemned. In the trinity of Christianity there is no place for the woman. In fact, around the world the woman has been treated as if she is just a commodity to be used.

But why have women accepted it? For the same reason you have accepted other kinds of slaveries: security; the husband will take care. Ancient Indian scriptures say, "When a woman is a child, the father should take care; when a woman is young, the husband should take care; when a woman is old, the son should take care." But because of this security and care, you are destroying the woman's freedom. And the woman has agreed – just as other people have agreed – to all kinds of slavery. The reason simply is, their consciousness is missing.

The whole effort of Zen is to bring you to your own consciousness, and then there is no need of any scripture, and there is no need of any guide. You have your own light and you can live accordingly, intensely, joyfully, dancingly. But people go on trying to find some guide.

For what has Sarjano been going to U.G. Krishnamurti? Perhaps *he* may give him the truth.

Nobody can give you the truth.

Truth is already enshrined in you.

You have to discover it.

The first question one of the sannyasins has asked:

In his book, 'The Way of Zen,' Alan Watts writes, "One must not forget the social context of Zen. It is primarily a way of liberation for those who have mastered the discipline of social convention, of the conditioning of the individual by the group. Zen is a medicine for the ill effects of this conditioning, for the mental paralysis and anxiety which come from extensive self-consciousness."

Beloved Master, first, I don't see any need to master social conventions to be ready for the way of Zen. On the contrary, trying to master dead, old rules shows stupidity.

Why not drop them immediately?

Second, do You see Zen as a medicine for the ill effect of conditioning?

Whenever you are reading a book, remember the man who is writing it, because those words are not coming from the sky, they are coming from an individual mind.

Alan Watts was a trained Christian missionary. That training continues to affect his effort to understand Zen. And finally, when he came a little closer to Zen, the Christian church expelled him. That brought a crisis in that man's life. He was not yet a man of Zen, and he had lost his credibility as a Christian. Under this stress he started drinking wine, became an alcoholic and died because of alcoholism. If you know this man you will understand why he is saying what he is saying.

His statement that "One must not forget the social context of Zen," is simply saying something about himself – that if he had not forgotten the social context and remained a docile Christian, things would have been better. His interest in Zen, rather than bringing him freedom, brought him catastrophe. But Zen is not responsible for it; he could not go the whole way.

He tried somehow to make a Christian context for Zen. Neither did Christians like it, nor the men of Zen. They don't need any Christian context, they don't need any social context. It is an individual rebellion. Whether you are a Hindu or a Mohammedan or a Christian does not matter. Whatever load you are carrying, drop it. Whatever the name of the load, just drop it.

Zen is a deprogramming.

You are all programmed – as a Christian, as a Catholic, as a Hindu, as a Mohammedan…everybody is programmed. Zen is a deprogramming. So it does not matter what kind of program you bring; what kind of cage you have lived in does not matter. The cage has to be broken and the bird has to be released. There is no social context of Zen. Zen is the most intimate and the most individualistic rebellion against the collective mass and its pressure.

Alan Watts is not right. His understanding of Zen is absolutely intellectual. He says, "It is primarily a way of liberation for those who have mastered the discipline of social convention." All nonsense. It has nothing to do with social convention. There is no need to master something which you have to drop finally. There is no point in wasting time. In other words, he is saying, "First, get into a cage, become a slave of a certain conventionality, a certain religion, a certain belief system, and then try to be free of it."

He is simply showing his mind, unconsciously. He was encaged, and for years trained as a Christian priest. You can expel a Christian, but it is very difficult for the Christian to expel the Christianity that has gone deep into his bones, into his blood. He could not expel it, hence his advice for others who may follow: "It is primarily a way of liberation for those who have mastered the discipline of social convention, of the conditioning of the individual by the group." Absolutely no.

It does not matter whether you are conditioned this way or that way. Conditioned fifty percent, sixty percent, or one hundred percent – it does not matter. From any point freedom is available. And you will *have* to drop it, so the less you are conditioned the better, because you will be dropping a small load. It is better if your cage is very small. But if you have a palace and an empire, then it is very difficult to drop it.

When Jesus asked the fishermen to drop their jobs and "come follow me," they really dropped. There was nothing much to be dropped – just a fisherman's net, a rotten net. A good bargain: dropping this net and following this man, you will enter into the kingdom of God. But when he asked the rich young man to drop everything and "come and follow me," the rich man hesitated and disappeared into the crowd. The less you have, as far as conditioning is concerned, the easier it is to drop it.

And he is asking that first you should be conditioned by the group, and master the discipline of social convention. Strange... Do you have to become first a soldier just to get retired from the army? If you don't want to fight, you don't have to become a soldier. Why not be fresh? But he was not fresh.

He was contaminated by Christianity, and he hopes – according to his programming – that everybody first should be conditioned, chained, handcuffed, put into a jail, so that he can enjoy freedom one day. A strange way of experiencing freedom!

When you are free there is no need of being conditioned by any group, by any belief. There is no need. As you are, you are already too conditioned. Society does not allow their children to grow like the lilies in the field, pure, uncontaminated. They pollute them with all their conditionings, centuries old. The older the conditioning, the more precious it is thought to be.

And contradictorily...the second statement he makes: "Zen is a medicine for the ill effects of this conditioning."

Zen is not a medicine. Zen is the explosion of health. Medicine is needed only by sick people, but health is needed by everyone – more health, a more juicy life. Zen is not a medicine, Zen is the inner explosion of your wholeness, your health, your ultimate immortality.

The questioner has said, "Beloved Master, first, I don't see any need to master social conventions to be ready for the way of Zen" – you are right. "On the contrary, trying to master dead, old rules shows stupidity" – you are again right. "Why not drop them immediately?" That's what Zen is asking you: "Why not drop it immediately? Why go part by part?"

I have told you a story in Ramakrishna's life....

A man had gathered ten thousand golden rupees. And at that time, the rupee was really gold; the word 'rupee' simply means gold. And this was his desire – that one day when they were ten thousand, he would offer them to Ramakrishna, of course, to gain virtue in the other life. When small donations are given and people are getting great virtues… for ten thousand gold pieces you can purchase even God's own house!

He went, dropped his bags of golden coins, and told Ramakrishna, "I want to offer them to you. Please accept them."

Ramakrishna was a strange man. Ordinarily, a traditional sannyasin would not have accepted. He would have said, "I have renounced the world, I cannot accept." But Ramakrishna was not a conventional type. He said, "Okay, I accept. Now do me a favor."

The man said, "I am at your feet. Whatever you want."

"Take all these coins to the Ganges" – which was just behind the temple where Ramakrishna lived – "and drop all the coins into the Ganges."

The man could not believe it. "What kind of…ten thousand gold pieces?" But now he cannot say that this is not right, he has already lost possession of them. Now they belong to Ramakrishna, and Ramakrishna is saying, "Go and drop them. Just do me a favor."

Hesitantly, reluctantly, the man went. Hours passed. Ramakrishna said, "What happened to that man? He should have come back within five minutes."

So Ramakrishna sent a sannyasin to look for him….

The man had gathered a big crowd. He was first checking each golden coin on a stone, and then he would throw them one by one. And people were jumping into the Ganges and collecting, and it had become a great show, and the man was enjoying.

When informed, Ramakrishna said, "That man is an idiot. Just tell him: when you are collecting something you can count them, but when you are throwing, what is the point of wasting time? Just drop the whole load."

Ramakrishna was, in a simple way, indicating that when you are dropping your conditioning, your mental conceptions, your beliefs, don't drop by and by. They are all interconnected; drop them all. If you cannot drop them all in a single moment, you will not be able to drop them at all. Either now, or never.

Secondly, the questioner has asked, "Do you see Zen as a medicine for the ill effect of conditioning?"

I don't see Zen as a medicine, because a medicine sooner or later becomes useless. When your cold is over, you don't go carrying on with the Greek aspirin!

Mukta keeps them for everybody; she has taken the responsibility. By being Greek she has to carry Greek aspirins. And everybody knows, so whenever somebody needs one, they look for Mukta.

If Zen is a medicine, when you are cured, what will you do with Zen? You will have to throw it away, or give it to the Lions Club. But Zen cannot be thrown away, nor can it be given to the Lions Club. In the first place, there is not a single lion.

Zen is your very nature; there is no way of throwing it away. All that you can do with Zen is two things: you can remember, or you can forget. This is the only possibility. If you forget your nature, your buddhahood... this is the only sin in the world of Zen: forgetfulness.

Gautam Buddha's last words on the earth have to be remembered: *sammasati*. *Sammasati* means right remembrance. His whole life is condensed into a single word, *remembrance*, as if on dying, he is condensing all his teachings, all his scriptures into a single word. Nobody has uttered a more significant word when dying. His last message, his whole message: sammasati, remember. And when you remember, there is no way to throw your consciousness away.

Zen is not a meditation. Zen is exactly sammasati – remembrance of your ultimateness, remembrance of your immortality, remembrance of your divineness, of your sacredness. Remembering it, and rejoicing it, and dancing out of joy that you are rooted, so deeply rooted in existence that there is no way for you to be worried, to be concerned.

Existence is within you and without you – it is one whole.

The second question:

In the whole history of human consciousness, You are the first to give the utmost respect to women and to make available all the opportunities to grow into enlightenment. But why were Zen masters consciously ignoring women for centuries? There are only a few instances of women being enlightened,

**but not being Zen masters!
Is it true that woman by nature is not much interested in the growth of her consciousness? Could You please include this great matter of the better half in Your Zen Manifesto?**

It is just unfortunate that all the religions found a simple way of enslaving people, and that was celibacy. Either you become a celibate and go into the monastery or if you don't become celibate, guilt is created in you. You know that you are not doing what is expected of you. And it is not much different inside the monastery either; they are suffering from the same trouble.

Sexuality is a natural phenomenon. If religions had accepted sexuality as a natural phenomenon as you accept breathing, the world would have been totally different; the woman would have been respected just as the man is. Because of this question of celibacy, all the religions have created a thick background against women. First, the celibate has to be afraid of the woman. That does not change his sexuality, he simply becomes homosexual.

Just now, one of the bishops of England who is third in the hierarchy... There is a possibility he may become the archbishop soon; there is only one man in between him and the archbishop. He has come with a declaration that celibacy only means that you should not make love to women, it does not include homosexuality. A great idea. But it is not that he is the pioneer founder of a new truth – homosexuality was born in the monasteries of all the religions. It was bound to happen if you keep men and women apart. Then women become lesbians, and men become homosexuals.

Now even a few countries allow homosexual marriages, lesbian marriages. They think it is a very progressive step. There are thousands of lesbian couples married by the church, but only in America. This year there is going to be a new kind of man born in America: through artificial insemination, because those women couples, howsoever they love each other, howsoever they *eat* each other, they cannot produce a child. But hospitals are available – and a man is nothing but an injection...!

There are idiots, also, who are trying to find some way to have a child born through a man. Because if this goes on, and lesbian couples go on and they can have children, what about homosexuals? Those poor fellows...! Some artificial womb has to be invented – it is already invented – then homosexuals can also have children. Then the heterosexuals will look very traditional, out of date. Progressive people...!

All this nonsense happened because of a single ill idea, sick idea: celibacy. So religions became afraid of women, and the monks who followed, they became afraid. Even a man of the courage of Gautam Buddha, for twenty years continuously, did not allow any woman to be initiated. And when finally he allowed – he had to allow, because the woman who came to ask him to be initiated was no ordinary woman.

Gautam Buddha's mother died immediately after giving birth to him. This woman was Gautam Buddha's mother's younger sister. She did not get married, just to be able to take care of this small child. Now that woman was standing in front of him, asking him to be initiated. He had rejected her for twenty years continuously. That day he hesitated. This woman had sacrificed her whole life...without her he would not have been alive. She was more than a mother to him and he could not refuse.

So under such compulsion, he initiated the first woman, but with a very sad announcement. He said to the ten thousand monks who always moved with him, "My religion was going to last five thousand years. Now that I have started initiating women, it will last only five hundred years."

Such fear – that the woman is going to destroy, that the women and the men together are going to forget all about meditation. Once in a while...and it is very natural....

Meditation is not natural. Meditation is something which only a very evolved consciousness can manage. But reproduction, all kinds of animals are doing perfectly well without any guidance. Only man needs guidance. Now there are great discussions all over the world about how to teach children sex. Strange, no bird teaches sex, no animals have any classes, guidelines.

I have heard about a small boy who found a book, *How to Make Love*. He was standing on the head of a small girl and reading the instructions, because it said, "You should be on top of the girl" – so he stood on the head of the girl. And he said, "Now it does not say anything, and I don't enjoy it very much."

And the girl said, "Neither do I enjoy it. Get down, I'm getting a headache!"

Only man needs to be taught sex. This is what religions have done – they have made sex something sinister. They have created a China Wall against knowing it. And even a man like Gautam Buddha or Mahavira or other Zen masters remained content with the cultural programming. The cultural programming was: celibacy is a must.

Nobody is celibate; nobody has ever been. Because to be celibate you need to change your whole biology, your whole physiology. How can you change? You don't even know that sex does not exist in your genitals, it exists in your head. The triggering point is in your brain. Unless that point is operated on, you cannot be celibate. However long you stand on your head, that is not going to change. It simply makes it stronger. So the fear that the woman may attract people and may distract them from their meditation, from their discipline, condemned the woman.

And why was she not accepted? Because she could not manage. Her sexuality is more open than man's sexuality. Every month she has to go through a certain period, the menstrual period. Now she cannot hide it. That shows that she cannot be celibate.

Only recently, scientists have come to the conclusion that just as women have their monthly periods, men also have them. If you want to check it, you should make a diary, and just go on writing. Whenever you feel sexual, make a note, a dot. And you will be surprised that there are a few days in every month when you are more sexual than other days. And they are the same days every month – that is your menstrual period. But your menstrual period is not so visible, it is just cerebral; the mind gives more signals.

If you take note you can find it yourself. There are a few days you are not interested in sex at all, in fact, you are disgusted with it. And if every man and woman keeps a diary, it will be very helpful.

Don't approach a woman on certain days. Don't approach your husband on certain days – those days he is disgusted. Those days you can send him free to any holiday spot...don't be worried! Those days he is not going to be interested in any woman. In fact, these disgusting days have created all your religions. All your religious philosophers must have had more menstrual periods in a month than ordinary, normal people have. They seem to be so much concerned with sex. Ordinary people are not so much concerned.

And as one grows up, my own understanding is, just as at the age of fourteen one becomes interested in sex, if he is allowed – without guilt, without inhibition – to live his sex intensely, he will be spent out by the age of forty-two. But it does not happen. People are not spent out even in their grave. They are still thinking about women.

Do you think about what people do in the graves? If you are compassionate, make holes in graves and always put a *Playboy* magazine, or a *Playgirl* magazine, and the dead will be so happy. That is what they are doing all the time.

It has been counted that in every three minutes a man thinks once about sex. In every three minutes? You can make a diary...and you may be surprised that you are not the average. You may think four times, five times – but this is the average. Every woman thinks one time in seven minutes. That disparity creates all the trouble. When *you* are thinking of sex, she is not thinking of sex.

In an intelligent society people simply should make a mark on the board – "I am ready." If the other is ready, he will come. If he is not ready, he makes a cross – "This is not the right time for me." There is no need for any fight, there is no need for pretending that you have a headache, that you are too tired, that the office is too much. Just be plain – that there are moments you are interested, and there are moments you are not interested. Nothing can be done about it; there is no way to change this process.

But these people found a clue. In condemning sex you can make the whole of humanity enslaved. Everybody becomes a sinner, everybody becomes guilty. Everybody thinks that he is not the right person. And according to me, I have not come across any wrong person; everybody is right. Maybe in that moment that is his right to be miserable, to throw things, to shout. And you know...every day in gibberish... From where does that gibberish come? Do you think it comes from outside? Suddenly you burst, you allow it. It has been roaming inside you; you allow it freedom. Just remember one thing: throw out your gibberish and keep your hands up so nobody else's gibberish falls on you.

The woman has not been accepted because she cannot pretend to be celibate. Unless sex is accepted as natural, women will never be liberated. Liberation of womankind is the acceptance of sex as a natural phenomenon. Man is not superior in any way, nor is the woman inferior; both are natural beings. Both are different, and they should be different. They should assert their own individuality. They should not imitate man. But you see, the man allows himself to imitate women, but he does not allow women to imitate him.

Would you like your wife to grow a beard? a mustache? Just think... your wife with a mustache, My God...! Without a mustache she is so beautiful. With a mustache, you will not be able to stand her anymore.

But why are you shaving your mustache? You are imitating women. A man without a mustache is just like a man without a nose. I cannot conceive how you go on imitating.

Now women are trying to imitate. They dress in the same clothes as men – in blue jeans – and they smoke the cigarette in the same way, and make spirals of smoke. And they think this is liberation! This is not liberation; this is stupidity.

The right point has not been discussed by the intelligentsia, whether they are men or women. The right thing to discuss is: treat sex as a natural phenomenon; accept it. Don't make much fuss about celibacy. All celibacy is fraud. And don't make celibacy a stepping-stone to meditation; it is not.

In fact, love can be a stepping-stone to meditation. And that is where I differ from the whole human past.

I want love and meditation to merge.

I want men and women both to be enlightened, to be awakened. There is no difference in the consciousness. All the differences are in the skin, in the bones, not in your awareness. There is no feminine awareness, and there is no masculine awareness. And it is awareness that makes a man or a woman enlightened.

I am opening the doors which have been closed for centuries.

The sutra:

BELOVED OSHO,

One day, Tanka said to the monks who were with him, "You should all protect your essential thing, which is not made or formed by you. So how can I teach you to do this or not to do this?"

Zen takes tremendous leaps into the unknown. Now this statement means: "How can anybody decide what is right and what is wrong? How can anybody decide what is moral and what is immoral?"

It is all social convenience.

It is moral for everybody in the world to eat in the night – it is immoral for the Jainas. It is all social convenience.

What Tanka is saying is, "I would not say anything non-essential, and all that is made by you or decided by you is non-essential. Only one thing in you is essential which is not made by you or formed by you – that is your very being. You should all protect your essential being." Protect from whom? – from all those who are forcing non-essential things on you. "You are a Christian, you are a Hindu, you have to do this, you have to do that."

Protect your essential being. And the definition of the essential being is: that part of you which is not made by you. Just go inside and look at the center of your being from where radiates all your life. It is not made by you, and it is not made by anyone else. It exists in its own right. This essence is Zen. Everything else is commentary.

He must have been asked about what is real, what is unreal, what is right, what is wrong. And he must have been answering, "How can I teach you to do this or not to do this? Only remember one thing: the essential being is not manufactured by anyone. And if you can remember it, and you can live in the light of it, then whatever you do is right. There is no need to decide what is right and what is wrong. No morality is needed at all."

Zen is absolutely amoral. It leaves you absolutely free to live according to your own awareness. Whatever your insight feels is right, do it – even if the whole world says it is wrong, it is not wrong. Live according to your own light, not according to the lights of others.

There are many who would like to sell you a lamp. They are all around. All kinds of lamps are being sold, but nobody bothers that you are blind, the lamp is not of much use. The only real thing is to bring your light from its dormancy into activity. Only that light will decide your life, your actions. And once you have found that light you are not worried about anything. You don't feel guilty about anything. You don't think about choosing to do this, or not to do this; you simply do whatever seems right. The right response comes out of a right awareness; hence Zen has no morality, but it has a far higher sense of consciousness. It does not need morality.

A blind man needs a staff to find his way. But if your eyes are right, you don't need a staff, it will be an unnecessary burden.

Zen gives you eyes and takes away all staffs. It gives you your inner awakening and takes away all moral concepts. Hence, I call it the greatest rebellion in the world. It makes you for the first time free from the society, from the collective, from the masses, from the religions; you simply *are*.

And existence looks far more green when your eyes are open; looks more light, looks more miraculous, more majestic, when your inner light starts spreading around the cosmos.

"Once, when I saw Sekitō Oshō, he taught me that I should just protect it by myself."

Tanka is remembering the moment when Sekitō threw him from the window of a two-story house, and jumped upon him. He had many many fractures, but Tanka was not concerned. He was sitting on his chest and asking, "Have you got it?" And it seems Tanka got it, because since then he never asked any question. Since then he himself started a small monastery, teaching the same as Sekitō.

He says, "*Once, when I saw Sekitō Oshō, he taught me that I should just protect it by myself.*" There is no need for anybody to protect it, there is no need for anybody to guide it, to indicate it. You are enough unto yourself.

Let this be the declaration of the Zen Manifesto:

You are enough unto yourself.

You are the whole universe.

"This thing cannot be talked about. You all have your Zazen mat; other than that, what Zen do you talk about?"

The Zazen mat is the mat given to every Zen disciple to sit upon. And

Zazen simply means sitting and doing nothing. Just sitting and doing nothing, slowly slowly, the traffic in the mind disappears. Slowly slowly, all turmoil within you settles down. At that moment the disciple gives the mat back to the master, bows down. Nothing is said.

When you go to a Zen master, he simply gives you a mat to sit on, and – "Don't bother me because there is nothing to say. Just sitting silently you will find it. And when you have found, please don't forget to return the mat, because other disciples will be coming."

Once it happened when Rinzai became enlightened.... And rather than returning the mat, he folded it and started to sneak out of the door. The master said, "Hey! Rinzai! Bring that mat back. It does not look right for an enlightened man to steal a mat from a poor master."

Rinzai said, "I thought now that I have become enlightened, somebody will come to me and I would have to supply a mat. So to begin with...but you are such a particular guy, you will not leave me even the mat..."

Rinzai had to give the mat back and touch the feet of the master. And then the master gave him many mats.

He said, "Don't be worried, but don't steal. That does not look right. When you have become a buddha then stealing is not right. Before you have become a buddha you can do anything."

So I want you to be aware. Whatever you want to do, do it quickly, because soon you will become buddhas. And then don't harass me – "I forgot to do this, now what to do?" I don't take any responsibility.

I don't even have mats. You have to bring your own mat. So even if you take it away, there is no problem.

"This thing cannot be talked about. You all have your own Zazen mat; other than that, what Zen do you talk about?"

Zazen is Zen. Sitting silently, doing nothing, an explosion comes to you. Your own nature blossoms, your buddhahood comes to its ultimate peak.

"You should understand this. There is nothing which is to become buddha. Don't just go on hearing the name of buddha; you, yourselves, must see that the good devices and four infinite virtues are not from outside; don't carry them in your mind.

"What do you intend to follow? Don't use sutras.
Leave the emptiness without falling into it.
"The seekers of the present day search for the Tao chaotically. Here in this place, there is no way to learn, nor any dharma to show."

Tanka is one of the most significant Zen masters. He will not bother about any essentials – what to say about the non-essentials. No sutras, no philosophies, just the Zazen mat. In that Zazen mat everything is contained. Just sit down and look inside. You don't have to follow anybody, you don't have to recite any sutra. You don't even have to remember anything outside you. Just be a pillar of remembrance: *sammasati.*

You are not going to become buddhas; you are buddhas, you simply don't accept it...once in a while you accept.

People write me letters, "When in front of you, it seems to be that really I am a buddha. But when I go out and see the rickshaw wallahs, I forget all about the buddha, and I start haggling about the price."

"In your presence," people have been writing to me, "we feel perfect." You are perfect. Just in my presence you become aware of it. Because I go on beating on your head that you are a buddha, finally, just being tired, you accept – "Okay, I am a buddha." But outside the gate you think it is still time, you can go to a movie.

Buddhas don't go to a movie.

It happened once....

One friend was driving me in Bombay, and just as a joke he stopped his car and he asked me, "Would you like to come into the bistro?"

I said, "Perfectly right."

He was not really expecting that...he became afraid. He said, "No, no, I was just..."

I said, "No. Just come on behind me." The poor fellow had to come. And when they saw me, many people recognized me. The naked girl who was dancing, touched my feet. I said, "Don't stop the dance."

The manager came with a special seat for me to sit. He said, "What can I do?"

I said, "Why make so much fuss about it? I am just an ordinary buddha. Just bring ice cream."

My friend was perspiring in the air-conditioned place. When we went out, he said, "I am never going to drive you anywhere."

I said, "I did not start the joke. You asked me, and when I do anything I do it completely."

Later on he said to me that everybody condemned him for taking me into such places. I said, "Are there more such places? Once in a while take me to such places, because buddhas have not been visiting…so it has become conventional. We have to drop the convention."

My buddhas are going to visit bistros, and discos, and they are going to do every kind of thing. And you need not be worried. That is your worry: that you cannot do both things, you cannot dance in a disco and be a buddha.

I tell you, whether you dance or not, you are a buddha. You can dance joyfully in a disco, and still you don't lose your buddhahood. You cannot lose it; there is no way of losing it.

Tanka is right. To a man of awareness the whole existence is *dharma*, the whole existence – *"Even a single sip or a single bite has its own truth."*

The man who has come home is not to be a beggar. This has been the past. I want to change it completely.

Zen has taken a few steps, but hesitantly. I tell you, whether you want it or not, you *are* a buddha, you are not going to *become* a buddha. It is your very essentiality. And once this is recognized, the whole life becomes sacred, nothing is denied. This is the new man I want to introduce into the world – the new buddha. This manifesto is for the new buddhas.

Ukō wrote a small haiku, but let it sink deep in you.

Silencing the glitter
of the stars –
night rain.

He must have been sitting in his small hut looking at the night stars glittering, and then suddenly…the night rain silencing all the glitter of the stars. Why has he written this?

In this is contained the whole manifesto.

The stars are there, they are shining; the rain comes, the clouds come, and the stars disappear, but they are still there. The clouds or the rain cannot take them away.

Your buddhahood is just your inner glitter, your inner luminosity. Rain comes, and clouds come, but they all pass away. Your interiority remains untouched. Your glitter is not the glitter of the stars that can be taken away, or that can be erased even for a moment. Your glitter and your silence is so deeply rooted in you that there is no way to avoid it.

You have been avoiding. Everybody has been trying to avoid the buddha, but you will not succeed, I promise you. Sooner or later you will get tired of hiding, of running away from yourself. Sooner or later you will sit down – a Zazen mat or no mat – silently, peacefully, and suddenly the explosion. And this is what you have been looking for all your many lives.

Maneesha's question:

BELOVED OSHO,

Is there any truth to what Alan Watts states when he writes: "One must not forget the social context of Zen. It is primarily a way of liberation for those who have mastered the disciplines of social convention, of the conditioning of the individual by the group."

Maneesha, there is no truth in it. Alan Watts is one of the important people who have introduced Zen to the West. But they carried it intellectually, they themselves were not men of Zen.

He goes on to say that Zen must specifically be set against the context of Confucianism, with its accent on what is proper, on ritual.

It is absurd. Zen is a revolt against Confucianism. There is no need to think of it in the context of Confucianism.

Confucianism is an intellectual approach towards the world, a logical approach. Confucius is the same to the East as Aristotle is to the West, but Zen is against logic. Zen contains contradictions.

Zen has to be experienced on its own. No context is needed.

Conversely, Alan Watts says again, "Zen might be very

dangerous medicine in a social context where convention is weak, or, at the other extreme, where there is a spirit of open revolt against convention ready to exploit Zen for destructive purposes."

As I have told you already, Alan Watts remains a Christian. And from the Christian point of view he goes on thinking about Zen: "What will be the consequences of it if the social order is very fragile in some place? Zen can be destructive."

He is afraid. First the social order should be consolidated. Zen is, according to him, for very mature people, otherwise it may lead to licentiousness. But his fear is his own; he himself became a licentious person.

It is not true. If Zen reveals your liberation, you cannot fall into irresponsibility; that is impossible, even if your social order is fragile, not strong enough. He is worried that it may be a "dangerous medicine in a social context where convention is weak." No, it is not a medicine at all. And secondly, where convention is weak, it is easier for Zen to blossom. It is the solid convention which prevents Zen, like a rock.

He is also afraid – "at the other extreme, where there is a spirit of open revolt against convention ready to exploit Zen for destructive purposes."

There is no possibility of exploiting Zen, because Zen is not only revolt, basically it is silence, basically it is stillness. Essentially it is opening of your consciousness. In this opening of your hidden, dormant buddhahood, there is no danger that you will become dangerous to the society, that you may become a curse to the society. It is not possible, simply because Zen stills you, calms you down.

It is a very different revolution. Alan Watts cannot think about it. He is worried that a communist who is against society may use Zen, but it is not easy to use Zen. The communist, by learning Zen, will become silent; his revolution will become responsible, it will have more dimensions and more integrity, and will add more blissfulness to the society. Zen cannot be exploited in any possible way.

But the fear is that of a Christian. All the religions will be afraid in the same way. But Zen, wherever it has existed, has always brought peace, love, joy. That cannot be said about Christianity, although Jesus talks about love.

I told Anando, who was sitting by my side watching a film on Jesus where he says, "Don't think that I bring peace to the world, I bring the sword." That sword has been used by Christianity. More people have been killed by Christians than by any other religion. And Alan Watts does not seem to be aware of the crimes of Christianity. Zen, in not a single situation, has been a curse to man. It has always been a blessing because it is coming out of your blissfulness, it is coming out of your laughter.

It brings me to Sardar Gurudayal Singh's moment....

At two o'clock on a Sunday morning, on the little Greek island of Crete, the phone rings at the bedside of Doctor Siffolis.

"Ah, Doctor!" croaks the voice of old Mrs. Helluvamess. "I am sick! And I have to go to Bishop Kretin's church service today. Can you give me something for a headache?" Doctor Siffolis clambers out of his bed and walks over to the house nextdoor to give the old lady an aspirin.

"Now, shut up and go to sleep – you old hypochondriac!" shouts Doctor Siffolis, and he goes back to bed.

An hour later, the phone rings again. "Ah! Doctor!" wheezes Mrs. Helluvamess. "Can you give me something for stomachache?"

Siffolis drags himself out of bed and takes the old lady a bottle of prune juice. "Now go to sleep!" says the doctor – "and leave me alone!"

But half an hour later, there is a pounding on his door. "Ah, Doctor!" wails the old lady. "Can you give me something for my bladder?"

"Go away – you pest!" shouts Siffolis. "Just let me get some peace!"

There is a muffled groan at the door, a loud thump, and then silence. Worried by the silence, Doctor Siffolis gets up and goes to investigate. Sure enough, there on the doorstep, as dead as a dodo, lies the body of old Mrs. Helluvamess. But as the doctor reaches down to drag her body inside, he has a heart attack and collapses, dead as a dodo.

Two days later, Bishop Kretin leads a double funeral at the little cemetery of the Holy Orthodox Church of the Blessed Bleeding Virgin. With old Mrs. Metaxa, the last remaining member of his faithful flock, Kretin buries the bodies of old Mrs. Helluvamess and Doctor Siffolis, side by side.

That night, six feet beneath the ground in the churchyard, there is a sudden knock on the side of Doctor Siffolis's coffin. "Ah, Doctor!" comes a ghastly voice. "Holy shit!" cries the doctor. "What is it now?"

"Ah, Doctor!" croaks the old woman. "Can you give me something for worms?"

Little Albert is cruising around the house in his pajamas looking for some excitement, so he decides to go to his six-year-old sister's room.

"Hey, Susie!" shouts Albert, knocking on her bedroom door, "what is happening, Baby?"

"You cannot come in!" cries Susie. "I am in my nightgown, and Mommie says it is naughty for boys to see girls in their nighties."

"Okay," says Little Albert, as he walks away. "Have it your way."

A few seconds later, Susie calls out, "You can come in now. I have taken it off."

Father Famine, the Christian Catholic, is making a missionary tour of all his stations in Africa. He arrives at the small outpost at Ogaboga where Chief Bonga, the village leader very proudly shows the old missionary around.

"Tell me," asks Father Famine, "do you think that our Catholic Christian religion has made any progress here in your village?"

"I am completely certain it has," replies Chief Bonga enthusiastically. "These days we eat only fishermen on Fridays."

Nivedano...

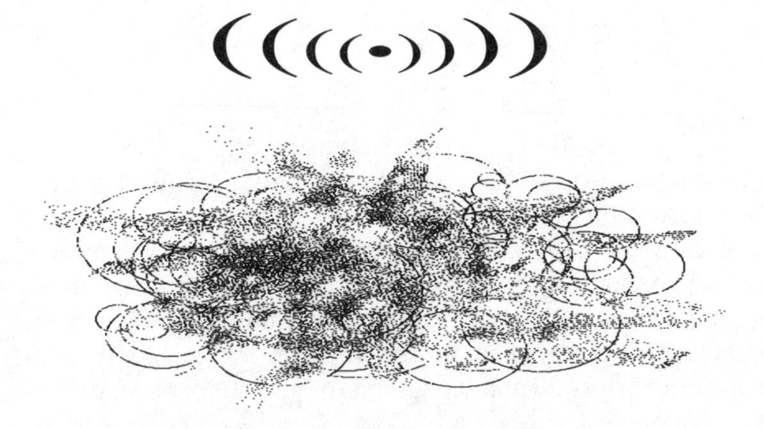

Nivedano...

Be silent...

Close your eyes...and feel your bodies to be completely frozen.

This is the right moment to enter inwards.

Gather all your energies, your total consciousness, and rush towards your center of being, which is exactly two inches below the navel, inside you.

A deep urgency is needed to reach – as if this is your last moment.

Faster and faster...

Deeper and deeper...

As you start coming closer to the center of your being, a great silence descends over you, and a great light fills your whole being – a light without source. You are this light. Another name for this light is buddha.

Relax into this light, witnessing three things: first, you are not the body; second, you are not the mind; third, you are only this witnessing consciousness.

Nivedano...

Relax... Let go... Melt, just as ice melts into the ocean.

A pure consciousness fills Gautama the Buddha Auditorium.

All separations are lost. You are at ease with existence.

This at-easeness with existence goes on growing to the moment when it becomes a constant awareness twenty-four hours, waking or asleep.

Flowers are showering on you, blessings from the whole existence.

Existence always rejoices in the meditator, because the meditator brings existence to its ultimate expression, and to its ultimate beauty.

At this moment you are the buddha – you have always been. These are the three steps that will help you to remember.

The first step is: the buddha comes as a shadow to you, following you.

The second step: you become the shadow following the buddha.

And the third step: even as a shadow you disappear into the buddha. You become just a pure light, an awareness, infinite and eternal.

You have always been this, just you had forgotten. Remember – *sammasati*.

Nivedano...

Come back, but come back with the awareness.

Come back followed by the buddha.

Sit for a few moments, silently, just to remember to what space you have been, what beauty you have experienced, what silence, what splendor, because this is your essential being.

Except this, everything will be taken away from you. But your essential being cannot be taken away even by death.

And we are here only to learn that which cannot be destroyed even by death – the immortal, the eternal.

It is only a question of remembrance, a forgotten language remembered again.

And keep on remembering all the day along. Act the way a conscious person acts. Doing ordinary things: chopping wood or carrying water from the well, do it as if the buddha is doing it himself.

And what I am saying to you is not a philosophical statement, it is the experience of thousands of buddhas.

To find the essential in you is the Manifesto of Zen.

Okay, Maneesha?

Yes, Osho.

THE SKY OF COMPLETION

BELOVED OSHO,

Once, Hotetsu – a disciple of Ma Tzu – and Tanka Tennen, were on a Zen tour visiting various Zen masters to ask questions. One day, Hotetsu saw fish in a pond and motioned to them with his hand.
Tanka said, "Tennen."
The following day, Hotetsu asked Tanka, "What is the meaning of what you said yesterday?"
Tanka threw his body to the ground and lay there, face down.

On his last day, Tanka said to his disciples, "Prepare a bath for me – I am now going."
Then he put on his straw hat, held a stick in his hand, put on his sandals and took a step forward.
But before his foot touched the ground, he had died.

FRIENDS,

First, a few questions. Somebody has asked:

I heard You say that we sometimes carry other people's wounds. What does this mean? Is another person's wound simply their thought pattern that we adopt? If we can so easily accept someone else's wound then why is it so difficult to accept our own buddhahood?

It is a very complicated question, but if you are ready to understand I am willing to answer. Everybody is carrying other people's wounds. In the first place, you are living in a sick society where people are angry, full of hate, enjoy to hurt – that is the superficial level which can be understood easily. But there are subtle levels, there are so-called religious saints who are creating feelings of guilt in you, who are condemning you to be a sinner. They are giving you an idea which will create misery around you.

And the older the idea is, people accept it more easily. Everybody around the world is saying, "We are living in sin...all these people cannot be wrong." I am alone in declaring to you that you have chosen to live in misery; it is your choice. You can drop it immediately and dance in joy, in blissfulness.

But the wound is deep. And one becomes very much familiar with one's misery. One clings to it as if it gives you a certain coziness, but it only gives you a life of hell. But your hell is supported by everybody. If you are miserable everybody is sympathetic to you. Have you ever gone into the matter? When you are miserable, those who are sympathetic to you are nursing your misery. Have you ever seen anybody sympathetic to you when you are dancing with joy? When you are blissful, people are jealous, not sympathetic.

According to me, the whole foundation of life has to be changed. People should be sympathetic only when there is pleasure and joy and rejoicing, because by your sympathy you are nourishing. Nourish people's joy, don't nourish their sadness and their misery. Be compassionate when they are miserable. Make it clear that this misery is chosen by yourself.

On a deeper level...perhaps the questioner has not asked me to go that deep, but the answer will remain incomplete if I don't go deep enough.

The very idea of reincarnation, which has arisen in all the Eastern religions, is that the self goes on moving from one body to another body, from one life to another life. This idea does not exist in the religions that have arisen out of Judaism, Christianity and Mohammedanism. But now even psychiatrists are finding that it seems to be true. People can remember their past lives; the idea of reincarnation is gaining ground.

But I want to say one thing to you: the whole idea of reincarnation is a misconception. It is true that when a person dies his being becomes part of the whole. Whether he was a sinner or a saint does not matter, but he had also something called the mind, the memory. In the past the information was not available to explain memory as a bundle of thoughts and thought waves, but now it is easier.

And that's where, on many points, I find Gautam Buddha far ahead of his time. He is the only man who would have agreed with my explanation. He has given hints, but he could not provide any evidence for it; there was nothing available to say. He has said that when a person dies, his memory travels into a new womb – not the self. And we now can understand it, that when you are dying, you will leave memories all around in the air. And if you have been miserable, all your miseries will find some location; they will enter into some other memory system. Either they will enter totally into a single womb – that's how somebody remembers one's past. It is not your past; it was somebody else's mind that you have inherited.

Most people don't remember because they have not got the whole lump, the whole heritage of a single individual's memory system. They may have got fragments from here and there, and those fragments create your misery system. All those people who have died on the earth have died in misery. Very few people have died in joy. Very few people have died with the realization of no-mind. They don't leave a trace behind. They don't burden anybody else with their memory. They simply disperse into the universe. They don't have any mind and they don't have any memory system. They have already dissolved it in their meditations. That's why the enlightened person is never born.

But the unenlightened people go on throwing out, with every death, all kinds of misery patterns. Just as riches attract more riches, misery attracts more misery. If you are miserable, then from miles, misery will travel to you – you are the right vehicle. And this is a very invisible phenomenon, like radio waves. They are traveling around you; you don't hear them. Once you have the right instrument to receive them, immediately they become available. Even before the radio was there, they were traveling by your side.

There is no incarnation, but misery incarnates. Wounds of millions of people are moving around you, just in search of somebody who is willing to be miserable. Of course, the blissful does not leave any trace. The man of awakening dies the way a bird moves into the sky, without making a track or a path. The sky remains empty. Blissfulness moves without making any trace. That's why you don't get any inheritance from the buddhas; they simply disappear. And all kinds of idiots and retarded people go on reincarnating in their memories and it becomes every day thicker and thicker.

Today, perhaps, it has come to the point to be understood and to be dissolved; otherwise it is too thick to allow you to live, to allow you to laugh.

Your own consciousness has no wounds.

Your own consciousness knows nothing of misery.

Your own consciousness is innocent, utterly blissful. To bring you in touch with your own consciousness, every effort is being made to detract you from the mind. The mind contains all your misery, all your wounds. And it goes on creating wounds in such a way that, unless you are aware, you will not even find how it creates them.

Just today, Anando told me Zareen used to be very happy when she came to the ashram from her house. Seeing the beauty and the freedom and the joy of the commune, she finally moved, took a revolutionary step in her life – left the home and became part of the commune. But since then, she has not been seen so joyous.

I said, "Anando, tell Zareen clearly what has happened: If you are aware, you will understand very clearly."

She used to come to the commune from her house which was dark and dismal and miserable. In a free open sky it was a joy. But since she moved to the commune...deep inside, the mind made the commune her house. And all the misery of her house has started erupting, and now she has nowhere to go. Once she understands it – that the misery is created by a concept that she has carried, and although she has moved spaces, she has not moved the concept... Once in a while the idea must come to her – "It is better to go home." But it won't make any change. In the first place the home will be more dark, more miserable, and the husband will look more of a stranger than he has ever been. But one thing will be good: then she can come to the commune and be happy.

But why not simply understand the point, and be happy wherever you are? And going back to the home is not just in your hands. As far as I know, your husband is not going to accept you back. He has told it to a sannyasin.

Don't keep the past burdening you. You have come into an open space, now learn the ways of freedom and love and friendliness. And you all have the capacity; there is no question of being miserable for any reason. No reason is valid to make anyone miserable. In fact, we have to search for a valid reason to be miserable. Otherwise people will ask, "Are you mad? Without any reason and you are miserable?" So somehow you go on inventing reasons. But remember, those are only invented reasons. Nobody asks you when you are happy, "Why are you happy?" There is no reason to be happy. Happiness is our nature. To be joyful needs no reason, no cause.

This commune has to be a commune of understanding, awareness, looking into one's own mind patterns and remembering that they are not yours. You are simply the watcher, and the watcher is outside the mind.

I teach you the watcher.

The only way to get out of misery patterns, whether ancient or new, is witnessing. I say it is the only way, because nobody has escaped from the mind without becoming a witness. Just witness, and suddenly you will start laughing at your own misery. All our miseries are so superficial – and most fundamentally, they are all borrowed.

And everybody is giving his misery to everybody else he comes in contact with. People are talking continuously about their miseries, about their troubles, about their conflicts. Have you ever heard anybody talking about his joyous moments? About his dances and songs? About his silences and blissfulness? No, nobody talks about these things. People go on sharing all their wounds, and whenever you are talking about your misery to somebody, without your knowing, you are transferring a miserable pattern. The person may be thinking that he is only listening to you, but he is also catching the vibe of misery, the wounds.

When I said that you carry other people's wounds, my statement meant that your own consciousness has no wounds. If everybody becomes alert, meditative, there will be no wounds in the world. They will simply disappear. They will not find any house, any shelter. This is possible. If it is possible for me, it is possible for everybody.

And in your question you also ask why "we can so easily accept someone else's wound," and why it is "so difficult to accept our own buddhahood."

You can accept somebody's wounds because you also have wounds. You understand the language of wounds, miseries, sufferings.

And you ask why we cannot accept the idea of being a buddha.

In the first place, you rarely come across a buddha. Very rarely does a buddha exist in the world, so even if you meet him you will not understand his language. Most probably you will misunderstand him. You know misery, and he is talking about bliss. You know wounds, and he is talking about eternal health. You know only death, and he is talking about eternity.

In the first place, it is difficult to find a buddha. In the second place, it is difficult to understand his language because it is not your language. Otherwise, this must be the simplest thing in the world – to understand one's buddhahood. It is so obvious. Your very being is already a buddha, but you have forgotten the path to your inner being. You have traveled long on many paths, but they all lead outside. And slowly, slowly you have forgotten that there is a small space within you which you have not explored.

Meditation is nothing but an exploration of your ignored inner space. That small space will suddenly remind you that you are a buddha. And unless it becomes a mindfulness in you that you are a buddha... It is not a concept; nobody can convince you that you are a buddha...you cannot be otherwise.

If you simply go in, the very experience of the interior space explodes in the recognition and remembrance of your buddhahood. It is not a philosophy, it is an existential experience.

The second question:

What is the relationship between Zorba and Zen?

The whole past of humanity has tried to keep them separate, and this has been an unfortunate experiment. The Zorba has remained incomplete, just superficial. And Zen has remained incomplete; it has only the inner world, and the outer is missing.

My Manifesto of Zen is that Zorba and Zen are not antagonistic to each other. The Zorba can melt into Zen, and only then will both be complete.

The man who has lived outside has lived very superficially, and the man who does not know anything about the inner, knows nothing about the existential, about the eternal. And on the other hand, the man who knows something of the inner starts thinking that the outer is illusory.

Nothing is illusory.

The outer and the inner are part of one existence.

I want Zorbas to be buddhas and vice versa. And unless this becomes possible, there will not be many buddhas, and there will not be many Zorbas either. In the completion of Zorba and Zen, a tremendous quality comes to your life: you relish every moment of the outside world, every flower of the outside world. And you relish simultaneously the inner freedom, the inner joy, the inner drunkenness. There is no question of any division. But humanity has lived in a divided way, and that has been a catastrophe.

It is time for Zorba to start meditating, and it is time for the people who are meditators not to allow themselves to escape from the world. They have to come to the world with all their juice, with all their ecstasy ...to share.

It seems very difficult to understand, because the whole tradition of the world goes against it. But I don't see any difficulty.

In myself I have joined Zorba and Zen together; hence I don't see any difficulty. I am in the world, and yet I am not of the world.

I rejoice in the birds, the flowers, the trees.

I rejoice in myself, in my silence, and I don't see there is any difference. The inner and the outer slowly have become melted into one whole. And unless your inner and outer become one whole, you will remain incomplete – and incompletion is misery.

Only in completion is there bliss.

Only in completion have you come home.

You have come to existence without any conflict, in tremendous ease, relaxed.

The Zorba in the past has been tense and worried that perhaps he is not the right person. And the man of Zen has been with the tension that he has to avoid this, he has to avoid that – that he has to become a recluse far away in the mountains. But the very fear of the world shows your misunderstanding.

The world has not to be feared, it has to be loved.

We are the world.

There is no question of escaping from anything. Every moment everything has to be enjoyed without any guilt, without any inhibition. But all the religions have been against it.

I proclaim with this manifesto a totally new sky for religious consciousness: the sky of completion, the joining of the inner and the outer, of the material and the spiritual, of Zorba and the buddha.

The third question:

I understand from listening to You that although Mahavira and Buddha were enlightened, they still retained something of their former Hindu conditioning which colored their expression of truth.
In the therapies here, through Your discourses, are You cleansing our minds from all conditioning so that we emerge as buddhas who are absolutely free of conditionings?

It is unfortunate, but it is true that even a Buddha or a Mahavira remained within the conditioning of their social structure. That is a flaw in their enlightenment. It is not as high as it can be; some weights go on dragging them down.

My effort here is to destroy all conditioning – Hindu, Mohammedan,

Christian, Jewish... It does not matter what kind of conditioning you are carrying, I want you to drop it. It is a weight.

And through all the therapies, I am trying to do something else which the West has not understood yet. Through therapies they try to bring you to normal humanity. Their psychoanalysis brings people to what they call sanity.

My therapies here, and all the psychoanalytic methods used, have a different purpose. It is not to make you into normal, average, so-called sane people, it is to cleanse you of all traps, all theories, all religions, all kinds of conditionings. All these therapies here are deprogramming you, and leaving you free without any program.

The negative part is being done by the therapies – they destroy your programming. And the positive part is done by meditation. As your minds are deprogrammed there is a danger, because you have become accustomed to live according to a pattern, a life-style. If it is taken away you will immediately jump into another life-style, into another prison. You cannot live alone.

Therapies are doing the negative part, and meditation is giving you the joy of living in freedom, the joy of living in awareness – not according to any scripture, and not according to anybody, but according to your own light.

The day you start living according to your own light, your buddhahood is far more complete than even Gautam Buddha's. He is a good pioneer. He started a process, but in the beginning perhaps it was impossible to do it completely. After twenty-five centuries it is possible now to complete the process of Gautam Buddha, and not to create buddhas as against Zorbas, but to transform the Zorba into a buddha, make the Zorba the foundation of the temple of the buddha.

Man is not to be divided, and man has to be given the total freedom of being himself. But this is possible only when, first, therapies cleanse you of all the garbage that society has forced upon you, and when meditation takes you inwards so you don't have to look into any scripture for guidance.

The scripture is within you.

And you don't have to borrow light, the light is burning always inside you, the inner flame. Once you have found your inner flame, you have found the whole universe in its completion.

You are the complete man.
The new man has to be the complete man.

A little biographical note:

When Tanka was eighty, he went to Mount Tanka and made a hut which attracted hundreds of seekers. Within three years a big monastery had grown.

The sutra:

BELOVED OSHO,
Once Hotetsu – a disciple of Ma Tzu – and Tanka Tennen, were on a Zen tour visiting various Zen masters to ask questions.

It is part of the Zen world that even masters go on traveling to different monasteries to ask questions. Questions are asked all over the world, but not the way it is being done in Zen.

Masters who have arrived, who know the answer, just playfully go on traveling from monastery to monastery to ask questions to see whether this master is just a pretender. And out of their questions, a whole beautiful tradition has arisen: masters pulling each other's legs, and after finding that both know it, rejoicing in it like children dancing on the beach.

Hotetsu – a disciple of Ma Tzu – and Tanka Tennen, were on such a tour to ask Zen masters questions, and both were already enlightened.

One day, Hotetsu saw fish in a pond and motioned to them with his hand. Tanka said, "Tennen."

The word *tennen* has been given to Tanka because he was one of the most natural, simple, innocent persons.

When Hotetsu saw fish in a pond and motioned to them with his hand, Tanka simply said, "Tennen" – it is natural; don't feel embarrassed. A great buddha playing with the fish…don't be worried. Tanka said. "It is natural."

The following day, Hotetsu asked Tanka, "What is the meaning of what you said yesterday?"
Tanka threw his body to the ground and lay there, face down.

What is he saying? "A fish is born out of the water, lives in the water, disappears in the water – it is natural. And now if you ask me again, 'What is the meaning of what you said yesterday?'..."

Zen masters are not recorded to repeat their answers, they respond: *Tanka threw his body to the ground and lay there, face down.* He is saying, "I am also a fish made of the earth, and one day I will disappear into the earth. I am not anything more special than a fish."

On his last day, Tanka said to his disciples,
"Prepare a bath for me – I am now going."
Then he put on his straw hat, held a stick in his hand,
put on his sandals and took a step forward.
But before his foot touched the ground, he had died.

What a way of dying! – with such clarity. Death is coming – be prepared for a journey. And the people who saw him standing with one foot up, could not see that that foot was indicating towards the invisible. He had left the body, and the consciousness had become part of the cosmos.

But a man of meditation becomes aware to leave the body when the time is ripe, or when the body is trying to get rid of his consciousness. A Zen man dies consciously, hence his death is not a death but an entry into immortality.

And Tanka Tennen would be the right figure – with his straw hat on, holding his stick in his hand, putting on his sandals, and taking a step forward... But before his foot touched the ground, he died, standing, ready for the eternal journey. This shows an intense awareness of one's being. And it also shows that the man is free of the mind.

Only a man free of mind has the clarity to see things as they are going to happen. And he is always ready, even for death. Most of the people are not found ready for death. If you ask them, "Are you ready for death?" they will say, "Wait, there are so many things to do." Only a man of meditation is always ready. He has done everything in each moment with such totality, with such completion, that he will not ask death to wait.

Tanka ordered his disciples to prepare a bath. They had no idea why he was asking for a bath. They had no idea why he was putting on his straw hat. Where was he going? He did not say anything. The only thing he said was, "Prepare a bath for me – I am now going." Going where? Going into nowhere, going into the cosmos: "Enough I have lived in the body. Now I am going to dissolve like ice dissolves in the ocean" – a beautiful way of dying.

Zen is both a beautiful way of living, and a beautiful way of dying.

A haiku:

Autumn wind.
The strength of the lotus in a single
flower.

There is a strong autumn wind, but that does not make the lotus flower freak out, although it is very fragile. The strength of the lotus in a single flower...a small stem.

Such is life. Any moment the strong autumn wind – and the lotus flower is gone. But go the way the lotus flower goes, without any misery, without any fear, without any concern. Existence is our home. Whether we are in the body or not in the body, it does not matter; in fact, not to be in the body gives you a tremendous space. You are everywhere. Once you used to be somewhere.

Now if you ask about Tennen's address, it will be "care of nowhere," or "care of everywhere" – both mean the same thing. But he died so naturally, just as he lived.

A question from Maneesha:

BELOVED OSHO,

If I understand him rightly, Hubert Benoit seems to think that one does not need a master to learn how to let go. He writes, "I have need of a master to learn some movements that I wish to make with my limbs, but I have no need to learn how to decontract my muscles. I have need of a professor of philosophy, or of poetry, in order to learn how to think in the truest or most beautiful way; I have no need of such a person if I wish to learn not to think."
Would You please comment?

Maneesha, the content of Hubert Benoit's statement is absolutely true, but in practice it does not happen so. It is true that if you want to learn philosophy you need a professor, but if you don't want to learn you don't need a professor. He has forgotten one thing, and that is: you have already learned a philosophy; now what to do with that philosophy? You will need a professor to help you to get rid of that philosophy. In practice, nobody is unconditioned, hence, somebody is needed to indicate that your mind is conditioned, and a conditioned mind cannot know the truth.

So in content, he is right, but in practice, he is just philosophizing. He understands Zen intellectually, and perhaps he has written the most complete treatise on Zen, but what he is writing, he himself has not practiced.

Practice is a totally different phenomenon from learning. You will have to be told how to relax, although you don't need to be told. But if you don't need – according to this man who has written extensively on Zen… If nobody needs to relax, if nobody needs to be told to relax, why are people tense? If nobody needs to be told to unlearn, then why are there not innocent people? In practice, things take a totally different standpoint.

I will agree with him philosophically, but I know practically – you have to be told how to relax. You have to be told how to unlearn. You need a master. In reality, there is no need, because you are the buddha. But who is going to remind you? You have forgotten it for so long that you have become accustomed to the idea that you are not the buddha.

Maneesha, even beautiful things can be said, but only with intellectual understanding. It is not Hubert Benoit's experience. His intellectual grasp is clear, but his existential experience is missing.

Now, it is time for Sardar Gurudayal Singh.

After so much philosophy, one needs to laugh….

It is a bright Monday morning in downtown Santa Banana, California. Getting ready for his first patients to arrive, is the neo-specialist in super-surgery, Doctor Decapitate. Doctor Decapitate looks around at his modern, high-tech, computerized, chromium-plated office, pushes a button, and in walks his first patient, Porky Poke.

"Doc!" cries Porky, his head wrapped in bandages.

"Ah! Don't tell me!" shouts Doctor Decapitate. "It is your head!"

"That is fantastic!" cries Porky. "How did you know?"

"I could tell immediately," replies Doctor Decapitate. "I have been in this business for thirty years!" Then the doctor fiddles with some switches and buttons on his computer, and cries, "There is no doubt about it – you have a splitting migraine headache."

"That is incredible!" says Porky. "I have had it all my life. Can you cure me?"

"Okay," says Decapitate, consulting his computer screen, "this may sound a little drastic, but there is only one way I can help. I will have to remove your left testicle."

"My God! My left ball?" cries Porky. "Well, okay. I will do anything to stop this headache!"

So one week later, Porky Poke waddles out of Decapitate's private surgery, missing his left nut, but feeling like a new man.

"It is gone!" cries Porky, trying to dance, but finding his movements painfully restricted. "My migraine is gone!"

To celebrate the occasion, Porky goes directly to Moishe Finkelstein's Tailoring Boutique to get a whole new wardrobe of clothes.

Moishe takes one look at Porky and says, "You must be a size forty-two jacket."

"That's right!" exclaims Porky. "How did you know?"

"I could tell immediately," replied Moishe, "I have been in this business for thirty years. And you wear a size thirty-six pants – with a thirty-four inch leg."

"Amazing!" shouts Porky. "That is incredible. You are absolutely right!"

"Of course I am right," replies Moishe. "I have been doing this all my life. And you take a size nine and a half shoe."

"Unbelievable!" cries Porky. "That is exactly right."

"And," says Moishe, "you wear a size four underwear."

"No!" replies Porky. "You are wrong. I wear a size three."

"That is not possible," snaps Moishe, taking a closer look. "You wear a size *four* underwear."

"Ah no, I don't!" says Porky. "All my life I have worn size *three!*"

"Okay," says Moishe, "you can wear a size three – but it is going to give you a terrible migraine!"

One afternoon, on the little Greek island of Crete, Bishop Kretin is visiting old Mrs. Metaxa, his last remaining church member.

"Oh, dear," cries old lady Metaxa, fanning herself and feeling faint. "I am so worried, Your Holiness. All our congregation are gone. There is only me and you left – what are we going to do?"

"Don't worry, my child," replies Kretin, pouring the old lady a cup of tea. "Nothing can happen to us. God is taking care."

Just then there is the smell of smoke in the room, and a voice from downstairs cries – "Fire! Fire! Everyone run for your lives!"

Freaked out, the bishop and old Mrs. Metaxa get up and run for the window as huge flames suddenly engulf the apartment. They get out on the window ledge ten stories up, and hang there by their fingertips, calling for help.

At that moment, Old Saint Plato, the Greek Orthodox angel, appears before the two good Christians dangling in the air, as the flames burn closer.

"I can help you out of your trouble," announces the ancient angel. "I can grant you one wish each – you can choose wherever you would like to be!"

Immediately Mrs. Metaxa cries out, "Ah! I wish I was relaxing peacefully at the church of the Blessed Bleeding Virgin!"

"Okay," says Old Saint Plato, shaking his head. "If that is what you want!" And, POOF! – a new gravestone appears in the churchyard, inscribed: "Rest in Peace – Mrs. Metaxa."

Then, Saint Plato turns to Bishop Kretin. "And what about you, bishop? Where would you like to be?"

Just at that moment, a bird flies over and shits right in Bishop Kretin's eye. "Ah!" cries Kretin, "bloody hell!"

One afternoon in the Solly Saperstein Salesroom of Salami Sandwiches, the phone rings.

"This is Solly," says Solly, as he picks up the phone.

"Hello," says the voice on the other end. "Is that you, Solly?"

"Yes," says Solly, "this is Solly."

"It does not sound like Solly," says the other voice.

"Well," replies Solly, "this is me, alright – Solly Saperstein here!"

"Are you *sure* you are Solly?" says the voice.

"Sure I am sure!" replies Solly, looking in the mirror. "It is *me* – this is *Solly!*"

"Hm," says the voice, "I want to speak to Solly – Solly Saperstein, please."

"Hey!" cries Solly. "It is *me*, you idiot! This *is* Solly!"

"Really?" asks the voice. "Is this *really* Solly?"

"*Yes! Christ!*" cries Solly. "*This is Solly!*"

"Well, listen Solly," says the other voice, "this is Moishe. Lend me one hundred dollars, will you?"

"Okay," says Solly, "I will tell Solly when he comes in!"

Nivedano...

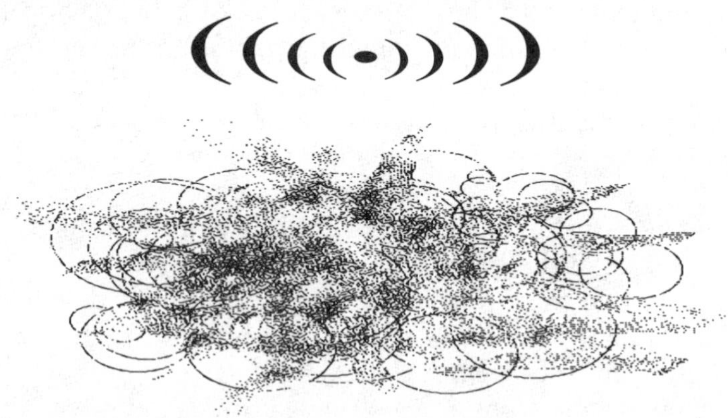

Nivedano...

Be silent...

Close your eyes...and feel your bodies to be completely frozen. This is the right moment to enter inwards.

Gather all your energies...gather all your consciousness. And rush towards the center of your being, which is just two inches below your navel inside your body, with an urgency as if this may be the last moment of your life.

Deeper and deeper... Faster and faster...

As you are coming closer to the center of your being, a great silence will descend over you, and a great light, just like a flame, will arise from the very center of your being. This flame, this fire, is your eternal nature. This is your original face.

The only thing that needs to go deeper and deeper into the center is witnessing.

Witness, you are not the body.

Witness, you are not the mind.

Witness, you are only a witness, a pure awareness, symbolized by Gautam Buddha.

This moment you are the buddha. Next moment, it depends on your remembrance. You can remember and never forget it. It is up to you to live a miserable life of the mind, or to live a blissful, peaceful, rejoicing of no-mind.

Witnessing is the secret.

Make it deeper...

Nivedano...

Relax...and just disappear.

This moment you are melting, and Gautama the Buddha Auditorium is becoming an ocean of pure consciousness....

This is the art of both life and death. If you can live with this consciousness, your whole life will become a path of roses, and your death will be the crescendo of your dance.

Sadness, misery, are man manufactured.

Bliss, joy, are your natural potentialities.

Meditation is just to know your potential.

Before Nivedano calls you back, gather all the light, all the joy, all the peace, all the silence – the whole truth of this moment.

And persuade the buddha, the flame, to follow you. It will come along, it has to come; it is your very nature.

These are the three steps: first, the buddha, the flame of light, follows you like a shadow; second step, the flame is ahead of you, you become a shadow; and the third step, even your shadow disappears, only the flame, the flame of awareness remains. Gautam Buddha is simply a symbol, a metaphor.

Nivedano...

Come back...but come with grace and peace and silence.

And for a few seconds sit just to remember where you have been, what space you have entered in. And feel the flame behind you, the warmth, the love, the compassion. The buddha is standing behind you.

The day is not far away when you will be standing behind the buddha. And once you are behind the buddha, just a shadow, it does not take much time for the shadow to disappear and become part of the buddha.

The buddha is only a symbol of pure awareness. Don't take it literally.

This awareness, this silence, this peace, makes you the most blessed people on the earth at this moment.

You can remain twenty-four hours in this blissfulness. It is up to you. Don't get into old patterns of misery. It takes a little while to get rid of them, but once you have some inner light within you, they start disappearing on their own.

Except meditation, there is no other religion.

Okay, Maneesha?

Yes, Osho.

福

CHAOS – THE VERY NATURE OF EXISTENCE

BELOVED OSHO,

Sekishitsu was a disciple of Chōshi.
On a visit to Sekitō, the monk, Sekishitsu, became enlightened.
After his enlightenment, Sekishitsu went back to his master, Chōshi.
Chōshi had also been a disciple of Sekitō.
Chōshi said, "Did you reach Sekitō?"
Sekishitsu replied, "Yes, I did, but was not introduced."
Chōshi said, "Who did you receive precepts from?"
Sekishitsu replied, "Not from him."
Chōshi then said, "If you were like that there,
what will you be here?"
Sekishitsu said, "Not much difference."
Chōshi said, "That is too much."
Sekishitsu said, "My tongue has no color yet."
Chōshi replied, "You noisy novice – go away!" and Sekishitsu
immediately went away.

FRIENDS,

First the questions from sannyasins.

The first question:

From what I heard You say last night about reincarnation, I understand that even individuality is superficial. Reincarnation was a consolation for me, that "my essence" or "soul" would continue. But now I understand that nothing of me will continue. In witnessing, do we all "plug in" to the same witnessing energy? Don't I even have my own witness?

The ultimate truth hurts very much.

Finally, everything is gone, including me and you. What remains is a pure consciousness.

It is not that you are plugged into it, you are no more.

The dispersion is so intimate and so ultimate that first your personality has to disappear, then your individuality has to disappear, then what remains is pure existence. It makes one feel a little worried and concerned, because you don't know the experience of not being.

Just think for a moment.... Before this life you were not. Was there any trouble? Any anxiety?

After this life you will not be again. What is the fear? There will be silence and peace, in the same space where anxiety, tensions and anguishes flourished. They all will have melted just the way a dewdrop disappears into the ocean.

Hence, Zen does not teach you self-realization. Self-realization is a much lower goal. Zen teaches you the ultimate: no-self realization, or realizing that disappearing into the whole is the final peace.

Your very being is an anxiety. At whatever level you are, some anxiety will remain. You *are* anxiety, and if you want anxiety to disappear, you have to be ready to disappear yourself.

The second question:

In my witnessing I have experienced nothing – by that, I mean that there was nothing discernable other than the simple state

of conscious waiting. I have witnessed events of the mind, body and emotions, and I have observed out-of-the-body experiences, but I don't have the clarity to understand the nature of these things.
What is the nature of no-mind apart from mind? Is it a receptive, passive mind as opposed to an active mind? Or is it truly non-mind? And how does consciousness receive and recognize information if it has no mind-brain to perceive it?

You have asked too many questions in one question.

The first thing to remember is that when I say witness, in the beginning you witness things of the body, of the mind, of the heart, emotions, thoughts...layer upon layer you go on witnessing. And finally, you find just a pure mirror, the witness itself. I call it a pure mirror because it is witnessing nothing. This nothingness is your very nature.

Out of this nothingness arises everything, and into this nothingness dissolves everything. And if you are ready to be nothing – even while you are alive – your life will have a flavor of peace, silence, and grace.

All your educational systems and all your cultural beliefs, force you to be ambitious, to be somebody. But to be somebody means creating anxieties in a silent pool, ripples and waves. The greater the ambition, the more tidal is the wave of anxiety. You can become almost insane desiring. Trying to be somebody, you are trying the impossible, because basically you are nobody.

Zen has an absolutely unique perception into the nothingness of everyone. It does not teach you any ambition, it does not teach you to be someone else. It simply wants you to know that in the deepest part of your being you are still nothing, you are still carrying the original purity which is not even contaminated by an idea of "I."

So while you are witnessing, you say, "I have experienced nothing." If you have experienced nothing, you should not be there. Experiencing nothing means you are not, nothing *is* – simply waves in the water, coming and going.

It is not that *you* witness nothing. You are creating another small "I," but it contains the whole world of ambitions. Experiencing nothing simply means you are not. And there comes a tremendous joy, because the whole energy that was involved in anxieties and desires and tensions, is released in a dance, in a blissfulness, in a silence, in a tremendous insight, but it does not belong to any "I" – a pure white cloud without any roots, floating in freedom, without any reason and without any direction. The whole existence has become its home. It no longer separates itself. This inseparation is the ultimate blossoming of buddhahood. To know that you are not is the greatest knowing.

You ask in your question if there is no one who perceives all this. That no one is not yet no one if it perceives anything. When there is nothing left, there is no perceiver, everything is dissolved into existence.

Zen is the only existential religion in the world. Every religion thrives on your desire to be separate, to be individual, to be special, to be self-realized, to be a saint. Those are all cowardly desires.

Zen is a brave step.

It cannot be transcended by anything more courageous.

A quantum leap into nothing and silence....

If you start asking who is silent, you are not silent. If you start asking who is perceiving all this, who is witnessing, you have not yet come to the nothingness I am indicating to you.

And it is such a small thing to understand what you have gained by being – troubles. Zen shows you the way of non-being, the way out of all troubles, the way of silence.

Meditation comes to its flowering when there is nobody. This flower of nobodiness, of nothingness, is the ultimate expression of existential heights. Otherwise, you remain a small someone, somebody, confined. Why not be the whole? When it is possible to drop into the ocean, why remain a dewdrop and be afraid of many kinds of death, of the sun which will evaporate you...?

Why not take a small jump into the ocean and disappear? Why not be the ocean itself? It is another way of saying it. When I say, "Be nothing," I am simply saying, "Why not be everything?"

Disappear into the existence. You will blossom into flowers, you will fly with the birds; you will become clouds, you will be oceans, you will be rivers, but you will not be somebody special with an "I." The "I" is the trouble, the only trouble, and then it creates many troubles around it.

The whole experience of Zen is the experience of getting into a state of no-I, no-self, and then there is no question – nobody is to ask, and nobody is to answer.

The third question:

It has been said that duality is the nature of mind. But by saying "mind" does that mean only the analytical processes which occur mainly in the left brain? Does that mean that activity such as music, beauty, wholeness and synthesis also arise from an inevitable intrinsic dualism of the mind itself?

Everything that arises out of the mind is bound to be dual. It may be arising from the right side of the mind or the left side of the mind, it does not matter.

There is a music which does not rise from the mind. That music is absolutely soundless, and is heard only by those who have come to be nothing. There is a beauty known, there is a dance experienced only by those who have gone beyond the duality of the mind. Meditation can be defined as going beyond the duality of the mind.

Whatever comes out of the mind is going to be ordinary; it may be music, it may be mathematics. One arises from the right side, one arises from the left side – that does not matter. Your music and your mathematics, your philosophy and your poetry, all are very superficial.

But there is something in you which is never heard, never can be said, never can be conveyed, but can only be lived. This nothingness I am talking about is a living experience of being no one. Out of that nothingness, a life arises full of music, but the music is soundless; full of beauty, but the beauty is formless; full of joy, but the joy is indefinable; full of dance, but there is no movement.

A meditator knows something that mind is not capable of knowing about. The mind only knows the superficial, and the superficial is always dual; it is divided for and against.

Nothingness is non-dual, it is not divided. It is just pure silence, but a very alive silence. And if out of that silence anything happens, that has a beauty and a truth which anything created by the mind cannot be compared with.

A man of silence – he may not even do anything, but just his silence is a blessing to the whole existence. His silence is a music only heard by those who have gone deeper and beyond the mind.

The sutra:

BELOVED OSHO,
Sekishitsu was a disciple of Chōshi.
On a visit to Sekitō, the monk, Sekishitsu, became enlightened.
After his enlightenment, Sekishitsu went back to his master, Chōshi.
Chōshi had also been a disciple of Sekitō.
Chōshi said, "Did you reach Sekitō?"
Sekishitsu replied, "Yes, I did, but was not introduced."
Chōshi said, "Who did you receive precepts from?"
Sekishitsu replied, "Not from him."

Do you see the mysterious way Sekishitsu is replying? When asked, *"Did you reach Sekitō?"* he said, *"Yes, I did, but was not introduced,* because neither has he a form nor have I a form. Neither has he a name nor have I a name. There is no possibility of introduction."

Chōshi said, *"Who did you receive precepts from?"* – then from whom have you received the teachings?

Sekishitsu replied, *"Not from him* – I have received, but I have received from a nothingness. To me, my master was not a man of words. We met beyond the words. We looked into each other's eyes and something transpired. But he has not said a single word; that is why I cannot say that I have received any teachings from him. Of course, being with him I have become enlightened."

Sekishitsu became enlightened just by seeing Sekitō. Nothing was verbally said to him; neither did he become a disciple, nor did he become initiated. Just watching Sekitō...just seeing that pillar of silence, that nothingness – and he simply disappeared as a being, himself; he became a nothing. And without saying a word, he left Sekitō and went back to his master, Chōshi.

Chōshi became enlightened also in the company of Sekitō. That is why he is interested in asking what has happened: *"Did you reach Sekitō?* – because you look as if you have not only reached him, but you have found him. You have penetrated his being; you are carrying his fragrance. What is the matter? *Did you reach Sekitō?"*

Sekishitsu replied, "Yes, I did, but was not introduced. Nothing was said by him, and nothing was said by me."

Chōshi said, "Then from whom did you receive the precepts? You seem to have realized the purity of consciousness. You cannot deceive me; I can see you are no more. How did it happen? Who told you the precepts – the techniques, the methods, the disciplines?"

Sekishitsu replied, again in a roundabout way, *"Not from him."*

Chōshi then said, "If you were like that there, what will you be here? If you have not received the teachings, the disciplines, the precepts from a great master, Sekitō, what kind of person are you going to be here? *If you were like that there, what will you be here?"*

Sekishitsu said, "Not much difference. I will be the same. Neither time makes any difference, nor space makes any difference. I was no one there, I will be no one here."

Sekishitsu said, "Not much difference."

Chōshi could not understand this roundabout way of talking; he was a simple man of Zen. He said, *"That is too much* if you are going to be the same here too. Here you have to follow the precepts; here you have to meditate. Here you have to enter into the world of Zen."

But Chōshi was not a great master of Zen, he was a man of Zen. He has understood nothingness, but he was not capable of conveying it. He said, *"That is too much* if you are not going to be any different here."

Sekishitsu said, "My tongue has no color yet." He is saying, "Don't be worried. I am as pure as a child. I have not been programmed by anyone. I am a tabula rasa, a clean slate. My tongue has no color yet."

Chōshi replied, "You noisy novice" – because according to Chōshi, this young man was just a novice. He could not penetrate and see in this novice the transformation that had happened in the companionship of Sekitō.

He was an ordinary man of Zen who had followed precepts, principles, step by step. He could not understand this quantum leap – a pure jump. That was too much. He thought, "This man is too noisy. I am asking simple questions; he goes on in a roundabout way. Go *away!" And Sekishitsu immediately went away.*

This anecdote is very strange. Its strangeness is that it is not necessary that a man of Zen will be able to understand another man of Zen. Of course, a master will be able to understand all kinds of Zen people, but a master is multidimensional, and a man of Zen is only one-dimensional. He has followed a certain path, and he thinks only by following that path does one reach to the nothingness he has reached.

If one has to reach nothingness, any path will do. There are as many paths as there are people to travel. But to understand that, a great master is needed.

There have been enlightened people, but still they could not understand other enlightened people for the simple reason that they have followed a certain path and the other fellow has not followed that particular path. They have become too conditioned by the path. They cannot see that when you are going into nothingness, every path is the right path.

When you are going somewhere, every path is not the right path, but when you are going nowhere, every path is the right path. But to understand that every path finally leads into nothingness, needs a multidimensional consciousness.

There are masters, and there are mystics, and this is the difference: the mystic can understand only one-dimensionally; the master has a wider view, a bird's-eye view. He can look from above and see that all paths are leading to nowhere.

Chōshi could not understand Sekishitsu. Sekishitsu left him immediately; this was not the right place for him. He had already gone beyond the paths and the precepts and the scriptures.

Kyorai wrote:

Immobile haze.
Moon, spring, sleep.

He is saying this is what life is: "Immobile haze. Moon, spring, sleep" – simple, no complication.

A sannyasin lives a life of such simplicity: the moon, the spring, the sleep – and he is fulfilled. A little immobile haze, and then arises the moon, then comes the spring – there are flowers – and then the sleep.

If you can conceive life in such simple terms – a little dance, a little love, a little playfulness, a little laughter, a little music, and then comes the eternal sleep, life becomes just a small drama. Soon the drama will be over. The acceptance that the drama will be over, that we are just players in a game which is not going to last forever – we will have to vacate the place for other players – then life becomes very simple, without any complexity and without any competition. One lives silently, peacefully, and prepares himself for the eternal peace, the eternal silence, the eternal sleep.

Maneesha's question:

BELOVED OSHO,

Fritjof Capra contends that, "Modern physics goes far beyond technology. The way – or Tao – of physics can be a path with a heart, a way to spiritual realization."
Do You agree?

Maneesha, the question is not of agreeing or not agreeing, because all agreements and disagreements are of the mind. I know that Capra is simply guessing. He is a man who knows modern physics and a little bit of the philosophy of Tao. And it is a very small thing to create a physics of Tao, or a Tao of physics, because the word *Tao* simply means the way, and modern physics certainly has gone beyond technology. It has moved beyond the boundaries of mind, and is in a tremendous chaos. As far as mind was concerned, things were clear. But now, modern physics has come to a point where mind cannot make any sense. Capra himself, being a physicist, started learning about Tao in the effort to understand the chaos that modern physics has entered into, and that perhaps Tao may help.

But he is not a man of Tao, he is still an intellectual trying to make some definitions, trying to make something out of the chaos. He is still thinking of spiritual realization, and there is no spiritual realization because there is no spirit as such.

There is a dispersion into nothingness. You cannot call it realization. It can be called *de*realization, but it cannot be called realization. Nothing is realized. Even that which was there is no more – only silence prevails.

I know the chaos of existence is ultimate. Every effort to bring it into a system is bound to fail. Philosophies have failed, science has failed. More efforts will be made, but I can predict with absolute authority that no system is going to explain this vast existence. It is bound to remain a mystery.

Religions have tried in their own way, but failed. Philosophies have failed. Science came with great systematic logic, and in the beginning of this century science was absolutely certain that it was going to succeed and explain away the whole mystery of existence, bring it down to rationalization. But on the contrary, the opposite has happened.

As science has approached deeper into reality, all its old concepts have become invalid. Now Aristotelian logic is no longer logic, and Euclidean geometry is no longer geometry. Now, science is at a point where everything again has become mysterious – no explanation, and no reason. But the effort continues.

My approach is totally different. I want you to know that chaos is the very nature of existence, you cannot make it a cosmos. You cannot make it a system, either by Tao or by Zen. You cannot make it an explained system where everything is knowable.

I have always divided existence into three segments: the known, the unknown, and the unknowable.

That which is unknown will become known tomorrow.

That which is known today was unknown yesterday. But the known and the unknown are a very superficial part. Beyond both is the unknowable. That unknowable is a chaos; it is irrational, illogical. There is no way to bring it into explanations, no way to make a science of it, or a philosophy of it. This chaos I have called nothingness. You can enter into it, you can be one with it, you can rejoice in it, but don't try to conceptualize it.

So it is not a question, Maneesha, of my agreement or disagreement with Fritjof Capra. I know existence is a chaos, and will remain always a chaos. All efforts of man are bound to fail in systematizing it. It is not a system; it is not mechanics. Hence, I always have loved Gautam Buddha's statement. Asked, "What is truth?" he replied in a very strange way. He said, "Whatever works." He did not define truth, he simply said, "Whatever works is true."

And more than that, even today we don't know. We don't know what electricity is, we only know how it works; we don't know what it is. There is no way to know it, and there is no need.

Let existence function.

Use it, love it, rejoice in it. There is no need to systematize it; all systems are bound to fail.

Zen is not a system, it is a path towards the chaos.

Go dancingly in without bothering and worrying what it is.

Rejoice in it!

What is the point in thinking what is music?

Love it, listen to it, create it.

What is the point of finding the definition of dance?

Dance!

But still very few people are of the age, mature enough to recognize this immense chaos without fear, and to use it as much as you can. Love it, live it, and drop the childish idea that you have to understand it. What are you going to do by understanding it? And in the first place, understanding is not possible.

Mind is too small, and existence is too vast – without any boundaries. There is no possibility that there will ever be a system which explains everything. And that will be a very fatal day if some system explains everything – life will lose all joy.

People are trying to explain everything. Then love becomes just chemistry, biology, hormones. Do you ever think about love as hormones, as biology, as chemistry? And the moment you think about chemistry, biology, hormones, love loses all mystery. And certainly love is more than chemistry, biology, or hormones can explain. They may explain sex, but they cannot explain love.

Love need not be sexual. In fact, at the highest point even sexuality transforms into love...love unexplained, irrational, a chaos. You can experience it, but you cannot explain it.

It is time for Sardar Gurudayal Singh....

It is a sunny afternoon in the rose garden of the Vatican in Rome. Pope the Polack is deep in discussion with a smart-looking gentleman in a three-piece suit, carrying a black briefcase.

"I am prepared to offer you one million dollars!" exclaims Herman Hoover, the businessman.

"No way," says the papal fruitcake. "One *billion* dollars, and no less!"

"Okay," says Herman, "our last offer – five hundred million dollars!"

"No way!" cries the Polack, stomping his foot. "Six hundred million! One dollar for every Catholic or the deal is off!"

"Holy shit! Let us forget the whole thing," shouts Herman. And the businessman walks off in frustration.

Meanwhile, old Mario the gardener, pops his head over the rosebushes and calls out to the pope. "Hey-a, Your Holiness!" says Mario. "That-a guy wanted to give you so much-a money. Why did-a you refuse?"

"You don't understand," says the Polack. "You don't know what that guy wanted me to do."

"So?" asks Mario. "What-a did he want?"

"Well," says the pope, "he wants us to change the end of the Lord's Prayer."

"Really?" asks Mario. "But-a, at the end-a we always say-a, *Amen*."

"I know," snaps the Polack pope. "But this guy wants us all to say, *Coca-Cola!*"

It is that fateful night in old Jerusalem town. Upstairs at the downtown MacDonald's burger house, Jesus is host at his famous farewell dinner party.

Ronald MacDonald, the clown, is running around giving everyone party hats and whistles, trying to get the serious saints to laugh.

But Jesus has been looking moody all night when suddenly, he puts down his wineglass and shouts across the smoke-filled room, "Peter!" he cries, pointing his finger. "Peter! Tonight, you are going to betray me!"

"Ah no, Lord!" calls back Peter, turning pale, "I would never betray you!"

"Okay, Peter," says Jesus, "I was just checking up on you. Come over here and eat some bread and drink some wine with me."

So they eat bread and drink some wine. And then Jesus says, "Okay, Peter, you can go."

Then Jesus looks around the room again, and calls John, his beloved disciple.

"John!" shouts Jesus. "John! Tonight you are going to betray me!"

"Ah no, Lord!" replies John, falling off his seat in shock. "I would never betray you. It is just not possible!"

"Okay, John," replies Jesus. "Don't get excited! I was just checking. Come over here and drink wine and eat some bread with me!"

As the evening progresses, one by one, Jesus calls his apostles to him, eating some bread and drinking wine with each of them.

Finally, his wandering eye rests on Judas, who has been sitting in the corner for the past hour, making out with Mary Magdelena.

"Judas!" shouts Jesus.

"Yes, Lord!" replies Judas, straightening his shirt.

"Judas!" cries Jesus. "Come here! I want you!"

"Yes, Lord," says Judas, jumping up and standing nervously in front of Jesus. "Judas!" says Jesus. "Tonight, you are going to betray me!"

"Ah, *Jesus Christ!*" cries Judas. "Why do you always pick on *me* when you get drunk?"

Sexy Miss Thornbum, the primary school teacher, wiggles into the classroom one morning.

"Now, children," she announces, "today, we are going to start a whole new and exciting subject called Sex Education!"

There is a loud cheering from the boys, and excited squealing from the girls as Miss Thornbum claps her hands to restore order.

"Settle down, children!" shouts Miss Thornbum. "Soon, you little boys will be getting interested in some little girls, and some of you little girls will have your little eyes on some little boys."

Suddenly, Little Albert interrupts. "Hey, Miss Thornbum!" he shouts. "And for us Little guys who are already screwing – can we go out and play football?"

Nivedano...

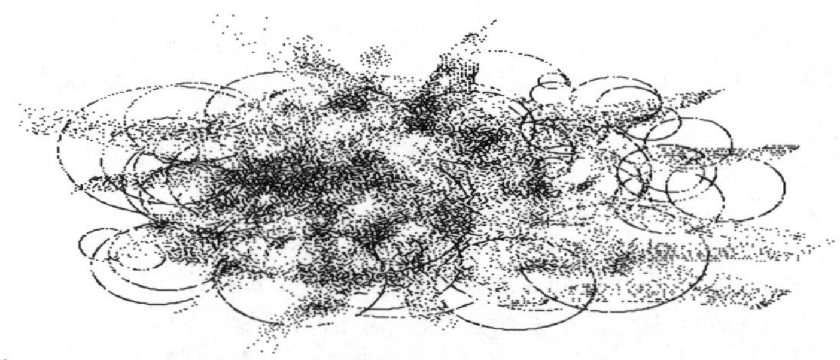

Nivedano...

Be silent....

Close your eyes...and feel your bodies to be completely frozen.

This is the right moment to enter in.

Gather all your energies, all your consciousness, and rush towards the inner center of your being. It is exactly two inches below the navel, inside you. In Japan they call it *hara*.

Rush towards this hara with absolute urgency as if this is going to be your last moment.

Faster and faster...

Deeper and deeper...

As you start coming close to the hara, a great silence descends over you. And inside, the whole interior becomes luminous.

At the very center there is a flame, the eternal flame of life. This eternal flame of light is your very source, and is also going to be your goal.

As you come closer and closer to the flame, everything becomes peaceful inside, but a peace that is alive, a silence that is a music, and an experience which allows you to become a witness.

Witness that you are not the body.

Witness that you are not the mind.

Witness that you are only a witness, a pure witness and nothing else.

Deepening into this witnessing, one disappears into the ultimate chaos of existence. That is the greatest bliss.

Make the witnessing deeper and deeper.

Nivedano...

Relax...

Just remain a witness and melt like ice melting into the ocean.

Let this Gautama the Buddha Auditorium become an ocean of consciousness.

You are no more, only a consciousness pervading, prevailing.

You are drowned into the ocean.

This is the most refreshing experience, and the most transforming experience. This experience makes buddhas out of you.

A buddha is one who has come to be at ease with existence.

These three steps may be significant for you....

First, the flame follows you. The flame is represented symbolically by the buddha. In the East the face of the buddha has become a symbol of our ultimate nature.

In the first step you will find the buddha following you.

In the second step, you will find yourself following the buddha as a shadow.

In the third step, even the shadow disappears, only the luminous buddha remains. And this luminosity is eternal and immortal, can be experienced but cannot be explained.

Those who have experienced it, their life has become a light, a joy, a bliss, and a blessing for all those who have come into their contact. In other words, their life becomes a love, a song, a dance, for no reason at all.

This great experiment is being done here.

You are the most fortunate people in the world this moment, because everybody is busy in the mundane – you are looking for the sacred and the ultimate.

Before Nivedano calls you back, collect all this experience, this silence, this peace, these flowers that are showering on you – this music, and this luminosity. And persuade the buddha to come with you, to become part of your everyday existence.

Nivedano...

Come back, but with the same grace, the same silence, the same beauty.

Sit for a few moments just to remember what space you entered into, what golden path you have followed.

And it is not a question just to do meditation at some time of the day. Meditation has to become your very breathing.

Whatever you have been in these silent moments, you can be twenty-four hours...an undercurrent of joy, peace, love, compassion.

In whatever you are doing, you can do it as if you are a buddha. The "as if" will disappear soon, because fundamentally you are buddhas. It is not something that you have to achieve, it is something that you have forgotten and you have to remember it – *sammasati*.

Okay, Maneesha?

Yes, Osho.

MIND ONLY THINKS, MEDITATION LIVES

BELOVED OSHO,

Gyōzan said to Sekishitsu,
"Tell me what to believe in and what to rely on?"
Sekishitsu gestured across the sky above, three times with his hand, and said, "There is no such thing."
Gyōzan asked, "What do you say about reading sutras?"
Sekishitsu replied, "All the sutras are out of the question. Doing things that are given by others is dualism of mind and matter. And if you are in the dualism of subject and object, various views arise. But this is blind wisdom, so it is not yet the Tao.
"If others don't give you anything, there is not a single thing. That's why Bodhidharma said, 'Originally, there is not a single thing.'
"You see, when a baby comes out of the womb, does he read sutras or not? At that time, the baby doesn't know whether such a thing as buddha nature exists or not. As he grows up and learns various views, he appears to the world and says, 'I do well and I understand.' But he doesn't know it is rubbish and delusion.
"Of the sixteen ways or phases of doing, a baby's way is the best. The time of a baby's gurgle is compared to a seeker when he leaves the mind of dividing and choosing. That's why a baby is praised. But if you take this comparison and say, 'The baby is the way,' people of the present days will understand it wrongly."

FRIENDS,

First, the questions from the sannyasins.

The first question:

I heard You say that the center of our buddhahood is at the 'hara' point inside the body. Is there also a sleeping buddha energy in our hearts and in the third eye? Do we all have the same potential of remembering, each one with his or her unique expression of creativity? Please comment.

The *hara* center is the source of all your energy. It can grow just like a tree grows from the roots into different branches.

According to a different calculation of Patanjali, the energy can be divided into seven centers, but the original source remains the hara. From the hara it can go up.

The seventh center is in the head, and the sixth center is what you call the third eye. The fifth center is in our throat, and the fourth center is exactly in the middle: the heart. Below the heart there are three centers, above the heart there are three centers. But all these seven centers grow like a tree from the original source of the hara. That's why, in Japanese, suicide is called *hara-kiri*. People don't cut their throats, they don't cut their heads. They simply pierce a small knife into the hara center – just exactly two inches below the navel – and the person dies. And you will not know at all that somebody has committed suicide. Just the energy is released from the body, the source is opened.

I am trying to take you to the very original source. From there, it is up to you to bring your energy into any center you want.

Between the first center, the hara, and the seventh center in the head, the energy can move just like the energy moves into different branches of a tree – from the roots to the uppermost flowering. The hara is the source. When it blossoms, it reaches suddenly to the seventh center, piercing your heart, your throat, and at the seventh center it blossoms as a lotus. Man is also a flowering tree.

These are different ways of looking at things. Patanjali's yoga is one of the ways; Zen is a totally different approach. To me, Zen seems to be more scientific, while Patanjali seems to be more intellectual and philosophical. Zen begins from the very source.

The buddha is not lying anywhere else other than in the hara; he is not lying in the heart. The energy can be brought to the heart, then the expression will be love. The energy can be brought to the third eye, then you will be able to see things which are not ordinarily visible – auras of people, auras of things, a certain kind of X-ray energy that goes deeper into things. If the same energy moves into the seventh center, according to Patanjali, *samadhi* is attained – you become enlightened.

But these are different calculations. Rather than talking about samadhi, I would rather encourage you to enter into the source of energy from where everything is going to happen. I don't like to talk about the flowers much, because that talk will remain simply conceptual. My approach is more pragmatic.

I want you to experience your sleeping energy. And the moment you reach there, it awakens. It sleeps only if you are not there. If your awareness reaches to the source, it wakes up, and in its waking is the buddhahood. In its waking you become for the first time part of existence: no ego, no self, a pure nothingness.

People are afraid of the word 'nothingness'. In the second question that fear is clear.

The second question is:

**Though You have infused the sutras with life and humor,
for me, Zen remains the stark beauty of the desert,
and I long for something else.
Why can't I drop the idea that my way is not via emptiness,
but fullness? I still carry this longing for some kind of union,
a melting outwards rather than dissolving
into nothingness inside.**

With whom are you going to melt outside? You don't know even who you are. And who has told you that Zen is a "stark beauty of the desert"? Zen is perhaps the most beautiful path, full of flowers, songs, joy and laughter.

But the idea of nothingness creates a certain fear of dissolving into a desert. It is just your mind that makes the difference between emptiness and fullness. In realizing either, you will be realizing the other too, because they are two aspects of one thing, of one phenomenon which can either be called nothingness, or can be called fullness.

Zen has chosen rightly to call it nothingness, because fullness can give you misunderstandings. The moment you think of fullness you start imagining. The moment you think of melting into someone outside, immediately a God, a paradise, a heaven, and all kinds of imaginations arise. And those imaginations will prevent you from going anywhere.

I am not helping your imagination at all. I am trying to uproot your imagination in every possible way. I want to leave you without images, in utter silence, in nothingness, because that is the only way to attain fullness.

When the dewdrop disappears in the ocean, it is not that it becomes nothing. Yes, it becomes nothing but it also becomes the ocean. In its disappearing as a dewdrop, on the other side it is also becoming the whole ocean. So the fullness and nothingness are not two things, only two concepts of the mind, but in reality, only two ways of saying one thing. Emptiness, or nothingness, is better because it does not allow any imagination to arise.

Fullness is dangerous. If rightly used there is no problem. Fullness will also dissolve God, and paradise, and heaven and hell, and incarnation. But mind is capable of using the idea of fullness in a way that it cannot use the word 'nothingness'. To prevent the mind from using the word 'fullness' and preventing you from realizing the reality, from Gautam Buddha onwards the word 'nothingness' has been chosen. But nothingness is not absence; nothingness is not dead. Nothingness is fullness, but so full that you cannot define it, and you cannot make a limit or a boundary to it.

Unbounded fullness and nothingness, in experience, mean exactly the same. But for the beginner, the word 'fullness' is dangerous – and everybody is a beginner.

Begin with something which is less capable of taking you astray from reality. Fullness can be used only by a master who knows that nothingness and fullness are synonymous. But for the beginner it is dangerous, because for him fullness means something *opposed to* nothingness. If 'fullness' is synonymous with 'nothingness', then there is no problem. Then the desert becomes the ocean, then there is only beauty and song and dance.

Nothingness gives the idea to the mind that everything will be lost. You will be lost, but the truth is, the moment everything is lost, including you, you have gained the whole universe – all the stars within you, and the vast universe inside your heart. It is not losing anything, so don't be worried about *nothing*.

The questioner goes on:

Is this just my refusal to grow up? Am I fooling myself? Are we all to embrace the Zen Manifesto no matter what 'type' we feel we are?

There is no question of type. All types are just superficial. At the innermost core there is only one existence. The Zen Manifesto is not for a particular type, it is for all – for men and for women, and for black and white, and for Hindu and Mohammedan, and for Christian and Buddhist. It does not matter what kind of conditioning you have been brought up in, Zen is simply a technique of entering into your *veryness*. The entrance is so deep that nothing remains, and all is found.

Gurdjieff has written a book, *All and Nothing*. I would like to withdraw the word 'and', because all is nothing; there is no question of *and*. Whatever type you are – introvert, extrovert – it does not matter, you are all part of the same existence. And when you relax into existence, all your differences disappear, only oneness remains. You can call that oneness whatever you like, but basically it is nothingness. You can give it any color, you can call it by any name, but don't start calling it by another name from the beginning, because that can take you astray. Somebody may think that he can call it God, then he will start worshipping a God which is man manufactured.

For the beginner, *nothing* is the most secure path to avoid the mind playing games. *Nothing* is beyond the reaches of the mind, so it cannot play games with it. But anything else you name it, mind is capable of playing games with it.

The whole effort of meditation is not to allow the mind to play games. It has been playing games for centuries. One has to come to the point of seeing all the games of the mind: all the gods, all the messiahs, all the prophets, all the religions, all the philosophies.

Existence is available to a silent being, not to the learned, not to the well informed, not to the scholar. It is available to the innocent, and meditation is a way of becoming innocent again. Getting back your childhood, being reborn, knowing nothing, a silence, a joy, a blissfulness arises which is indestructible, which is eternal.

The third question:

The other night I heard You say there is no reincarnation, no soul, no spirit after death, only pure consciousness, pure silence.
Is it then so, that part of us, of our own consciousness, is aware of that endless silence, of being part of the whole?

All your questions arise out of your mind, and I am trying to take you beyond the mind. Beyond the mind there is no question, there is nobody to ask. But if you start thinking about meditation, that is not meditation. If you start thinking, "What happens when awareness witnesses the wholeness of existence?" – if you start thinking, you are moving inside the mind in a circle, in a vicious circle, you may find some answer, but that answer is not the truth.

You have to go beyond thinking, beyond questioning.

Just be silent and you will know.

You are not, only the universe is.

You are just a ripple in the river, arisen in a certain moment and dissolved back again, but not for a single moment separate from the river. This whole existence is nothing but a vast ocean in which all kinds of ripples, tidal waves, arise and disappear, and the ocean remains.

That which remains is your authentic reality. That which comes and goes is just a dream, or just a phenomenal, illusory reality. For a moment the tidal wave can think, "I am separate from the ocean." But you know, however the wave may be tidal, it is not separate from the ocean. Even when it is thinking it is separate – and it looks separate – deep down it is part of the ocean.

I am taking you deep down into the ocean. In that ocean nobody is separate. Suddenly a tremendous joy arises that you are eternal, that you are oceanic, that you have always been and you will always be...but not those small personalities that you have taken again and again. This time you stop taking personalities and simply become the whole.

The *whole* feels more cozy than nothingness, but they are simply two ways of saying the same thing. The whole appears cozy, it seems you are becoming more than you were before. And *nothing* seems dangerous – you are becoming even less than you were before. You were at least something, now you are becoming nothing. But becoming whole, you have to become nothing. Becoming part of this vast existence, you have to relax the separateness, the individuality.

The questioner goes on asking:

Does the dewdrop still feel or experience some aliveness inside, when first it melts into the ocean?

The dewdrop disappearing into the ocean feels for the first time a vast life. Only the boundaries that were making it a small dewdrop have disappeared. The dewdrop is still there, but it is no longer a dewdrop, it has become the ocean.

I have told you about Kabir, one of the most important mystics of the East....

When he became enlightened he wrote down a small statement: "The dewdrop has disappeared into the ocean – *Bund samani samund mein.*" But before dying, he called his son Kamal, and told him, "Please correct it. It was my first experience, now I know better. The dewdrop has not entered into the ocean; on the contrary, the ocean has entered into the dewdrop. So write it down that the ocean has entered into the dewdrop."

Both mean the same, but one is the experience of the beginner. The dewdrop disappearing into the ocean feels like you are going into a vast nothingness. But once you have reached into that vastness, when you are no more, suddenly that vastness is you. There will be no self, no sense of *I*, but a sense of totality, of wholeness.

It is difficult to bring it into language. That difficulty is shown in Kabir's changing the statement. In fact, no statement is right. Whether you say the dewdrop has entered into the ocean, or you say the ocean has entered into the dewdrop, you are still talking of two things: the dew-drop and the ocean.

If I had been present there, I would have said, "It is better to cancel both. Whatever has happened has happened, nothing can be said about it. One thing is certain, there is no more separation. So what has entered into what does not matter. There have been two, now there are not two."

The sutra:

BELOVED OSHO,
Gyōzan said to Sekishitsu,
"Tell me what to believe in and what to rely on?"
Sekishitsu gestured across the sky above, three times with his hand,
and said, "There is no such thing in which you can believe,
on which you can rely. *There is no such thing."*

What does he mean by gesturing three times to the sky?

Existence is just a vast sky with no end and no beginning, no boundary. There is nothing to believe and nothing to rely on. One has just to disappear. All belief is man manufactured, and all reliance, relying on a God or relying on a Christ, is out of your own fear. But there is nothing to rely on, and there is no security.

Don't cling with anything. Everything that you cling to is your own imagination. Your gods are your imagination, and your philosophies are your imagination. Existence has no gods, and existence has no philosophies – just a pure silence, but a silence which is musical, a silence which is a dance; a silence which blossoms into many flowers, and into many fragrances; a silence which manifests into immense varieties; a silence which is multidimensional. Just relax into it. Don't try to believe or trust, because all belief and trust is clinging.

Sekishitsu gestured across the sky above, three times with his hand, and said, "There is no such thing... You just please drop the very idea of relying on anything, or believing in anything. Just relax. This whole existence is yours. Why do you want to cling to a special part? It is all the same – the same sky, the same silence, the same purity, same innocence."

Gyōzan asked, "What do you say about reading sutras?"

Man wants something. His mind is always finding some way to avoid the nothingness or the wholeness of existence.

Gyōzan immediately asked, "If there is nothing to believe and nothing to rely upon, what do you say about reading sutras?"

Sekishitsu replied, "All the sutras are out of the question.
Doing things that are given by others is dualism of mind and matter.
And if you are in the dualism of subject and object, various views arise. But this is blind wisdom, so it is not yet the Tao.
"If others don't give you anything, there is not a single thing..."

Have you ever thought about it? – that all that you know has been given to you by others. If you put that aside to sort out what is yours, you will find a pure emptiness is yours, everything else has been given to you by others. Then who are you? – a pure emptiness hidden behind all those words and beliefs and religions which have been given to you.

"If others don't give you anything, there is not a single thing. That's why Bodhidharma said, 'Originally, there is not a single thing.'"

Bodhidharma's statement is of tremendous value. There is not a single thing separate from the whole. All separation, all dualism, is the game of the mind. As the mind becomes silent, all that game disappears, all those players are no longer there.

What happens when you wake up in the morning to your dreams? In the dreams have you ever doubted that what you are seeing is not true? Nobody in a dream can doubt. Whatever appears in the dream, appears to be the right thing at the moment. Only in the morning when you wake up, suddenly do you realize that all the night you have been dreaming of things which were not true, which were just mind creations, flowers in the sky – Bodhidharma's statement, "*Originally, there is not a single thing.*"

"You see, when a baby comes out of the womb, does he read sutras or not? At that time, the baby does not know whether such a thing as buddha nature exists or not. As he grows up and learns various views, he appears to the world and says, 'I do well and I understand.' But he doesn't know it is rubbish and delusion.
"Of the sixteen ways or phases of doing, a baby's way is the best. The time of a baby's gurgle is compared to a seeker when he leaves the mind of dividing and choosing. That's why a baby is praised.

But if you take this comparison and say, 'The baby is the way,' people of the present days will understand it wrongly."

And that is true even today.

When I am saying to you, "Be nothing," I am saying in other words, "Be just a newborn baby, a pure consciousness, undivided into knowing and not knowing. The baby's consciousness is pure. It knows nothing, it does not even know that it is."

You must have heard small babies talk about themselves as separate persons. They may say, "*The baby* is hungry. *The baby* is thirsty." The "I" takes a little time to grow. It takes at least three to four years for society to create an ego so the baby starts saying "I" – instead of saying, "The baby" is hungry, "I" am hungry. And the moment the baby says, "I am hungry," he is no longer a baby. He has entered into the world, he has graduated, in a way.

But according to Zen, once again you have to become just like the baby. This second childhood is the greatest revolution possible.

Jesus is right when he says, "Unless you are born again, you will not understand the truth." He had been traveling for seventeen years in the East, and he had gathered much. And that was really the problem why Jews could not accept him. He was talking a language that was not theirs. He was making interpretations of the old Jewish tradition in a way that had never been heard and that he had brought from the East.

And at that time the whole of the East was full of the vibrations of Gautam Buddha. Just five hundred years had passed since Gautam Buddha was alive, yet his vibrations were in the atmosphere. And there are possibilities that Jesus did not only visit India and Tibet. There is a place in Japan which also proclaims that he visited there. In the Bible these seventeen years are completely missing. They don't listen to any other argument, because that would be disturbing to whatever they have managed up to now as their Holy Bible.

Jesus was much influenced by Buddha's teachings. This teaching, "Unless you are born again," has the flavor of Gautam Buddha who was continuously teaching that you have to drop everything that has been told to you, you have to forget everything that has been programmed in you. Gautam Buddha brings to the world the first deprogramming philosophy. And when you are deprogrammed completely, who are you? – just a pure nothingness, just a silence. All words were borrowed, all sutras were given to you, all religions were forced on your mind. You are not a Christian, and you are not a Hindu, and you are not a Mohammedan. You were born just as pure consciousness.

You have to attain that pure consciousness again. This is rebirth. And this rebirth brings the buddha, the pure consciousness, the consciousness which knows no boundaries; hence, it cannot call itself "I." A consciousness which has become one with the whole has nothing to say.

Buddha, when he became enlightened, for seven days remained silent, wondering whether to say it or not. "Because in every possible way," he thought, "it will be misunderstood. It is better to be silent." But a compassionate heart could not be at ease in silence, seeing that "Everybody needs this exploration, this excursion into himself. I know the way, if I remain silent it will be criminal. But if I say anything, then too, I will not be absolutely right in saying it, because that which is beyond the word cannot be brought into the word."

So after seven days, compassion took over, and finally he tried. For forty-two years he went on saying to people, and always making it clear – "What I am saying, don't take it literally. I want you to experience it. Only then will you understand the meaning of it – not by hearing me, but by experiencing it. Only by tasting it, will you know the sweetness of it."

Bonchō wrote:

River.
One long line
through snowy fields.

Life is just a river, a long river – a long line through snowy fields. And then what happens? Each river, small or big, dissolves into the ocean, finds its way without any guide, without any sutras, without any masters. It may go astray, zigzag, but finally it reaches to the ocean. And that reaching to the ocean is *becoming* the ocean. That is the rebirth. That's what we mean by meditation. That's what we mean by the Zen Manifesto.

Every river is destined to disappear one day into the ocean. Go dancingly, go joyfully. There is no need to be worried, there is no need to be hurried. The ocean is waiting – you can take your time, but take your time with joy, not with tensions and anxieties. Rejoice and dance and sing and love, and finally you are going to disappear into the ocean. The ocean is always waiting for you.

Even though you are far away from the ocean you are part of it, always reaching, always coming closer to the ocean. Everybody is going to become a buddha today or tomorrow – and there are only seven days in a week, so you can choose...!

Maneesha's question:

BELOVED OSHO,

Wilhelm Reich says, in his book, 'Listen, Little Man,' that he found that man reaches out with his life energy when he feels well and loving; that he retracts that energy when he is afraid. Reich says that he found that this life energy – which he termed "orgone" – is "found in the atmosphere," outside the body. He says he succeeded in seeing it and devised apparatus which magnified it. Is what he observed so?

Maneesha, Wilhelm Reich was one of the unique intelligences born in this century. What he has found has been known to the East as *aura*.

You must have seen around the statues of Buddha or Mahavira or Krishna – a round aura around the head. That round aura is a reality. What Wilhelm Reich said was authentically true, but the people to whom he said it were not the right people to understand it. They thought he was mad because he described life as an energy surrounding the body. It is exactly true.

Life is an energy that surrounds your body. Not only your body, but flowers, trees...everything has its own aura. And that aura, that energy surrounding you shrinks and expands, in different situations.

Any situation where your energy shrinks, should be thought bad, sick. And every situation where your energy expands, should be respected and loved. In love your energy reaches out, you become more alive. And when you are in fear, your energy shrinks, you become less alive.

Now, poor Wilhelm Reich was thought by Americans to be mad, because he was not only magnifying that energy – he had found a few exercises in which that energy magnifies – he was even catching that energy in boxes, big boxes in which a man could enter. And if the man was sick he would come out whole and healthy. Naturally such a man should be thought mad. He was selling those boxes, empty boxes – but they were not empty. He had found ways to collect the energy which is available in the atmosphere. Around a tree you can find that energy showering, but with your bare eyes you cannot see it.

After he was declared mad and imprisoned, another man in the Soviet Union even managed to photograph it. And now it has become a recognized psychology in the Soviet Union, that life has an aura. And the man, Kirlian, has developed a certain sensitive plate to photograph it.

He would photograph the hand, and the hand would come with an aura around it. In a very strange way his photographs even showed if a man would be sick within six months: "Right now he does not show any pattern of sickness, but his aura is shrinking at a certain point…" And if at a certain point the aura is shrinking, maybe the person will become deaf, or blind if the aura around the eyes is shrinking. And all his photographs proved to be right. When he said, "This man is in danger of losing his eyesight," there was no visible sign, there was no reason to believe it, but within six months that man became blind.

Now in Soviet psychology, Kirlian photography is recognized by the government. It is spreading into other countries also.

A man can be cured before he becomes sick. Kirlian photography is very predictive. It shows, at least six months ahead, what is going to happen.

In the East, it has been known for centuries that before your death – six months before – you stop being able to see the tip of your nose. Because your eyes start turning upwards, they cannot see the tip of your own nose. The moment you recognize you cannot see the tip of your nose means that within six months your energy will shrink, go back to its source. And the aura, without any photographic technology, has been recognized by yoga for five thousand years. But now, it can be accepted on scientific grounds.

Wilhelm Reich was a unique genius. He could manage to see and feel what is not ordinarily possible.

But if you are very meditative, you will start seeing the auras of people, even your own aura. You will see your own hand with the light rays around it, radiating. And when you are healthy you will feel your aura expanding. When you are sick you will feel your aura shrinking – something is shrinking within you.

When you are by the side of a sick person, you will have a strange feeling that he somehow makes you feel sick, because the sick person exploits the auras of the other without his knowing. He needs more life, so whoever has life and comes around him – he takes his life.

And you know by experience, without understanding, that there are people you want to avoid, because meeting them you feel sick, meeting them you feel that something has been taken away from you. And there are people you want to meet, because meeting them you feel an expanding, you feel more alive.

Wilhelm Reich was right, but unfortunately the masses never accept their own geniuses; on the contrary, they condemn them. Because if Wilhelm Reich is right, then everybody else is almost blind. And in anger he wrote the book, *Listen, Little Man.* But that book is beautiful, and his anger can be forgiven because he was mistreated by "the little man," by the masses. He was first thought to be mad, then forced into a madhouse, and he died in a madhouse.

In the East, he would have become a Gautam Buddha. He had the quality, the insight. But a wrong society, a society of very little men, of very small people...small-minded, who cannot conceive the vast, who cannot conceive the mysterious.

The whole atmosphere is full of life. And if you understand your own sources of life, you will be suddenly aware that birds are alive, trees are alive, grasses are alive – everywhere there is life! And you can dance with this life, you can start having a dialogue with the atmosphere. Of course, people will think you are mad, because people are still the same. The same people crucified Jesus, the same people forced Wilhelm Reich into a madhouse, the same people poisoned Socrates...but those little people are in the majority.

Wilhelm Reich's anger is right, but still I would say, rather than anger, the little man needs compassion. He was angry because they misbehaved with him, they destroyed his whole life. Rather than understanding him – he would have opened a new door to experiencing, to loving, to living – they destroyed the man completely. Obviously, he became angry.

In the East, the same little men are there, but the Eastern genius has never been angry with them. Rather than being angry, it has shown compassion, it has felt compassion for their blindness, and it has tried in every way to bring light to them, a little understanding to their hearts.

It is time for Sardar Gurudayal Singh....

The Reverend Rump is very excited one afternoon when a new organ is delivered to his church. A large crowd of people gathers outside the church to watch as the organ is slowly lifted out of the delivery truck.

Suddenly, one of the delivery men lets go of a rope and the organ starts to fall on top of the Reverend Rump, who is standing beneath it. But at the last moment, Hamish MacTavish pushes the vicar aside and stops the organ before it smashes on the ground.

"Bless you, my son," gasps Reverend Rump, picking himself up. "You saved me! When you come to church next Sunday, you can come and play on this new church organ!"

"Ah!" sighs Hamish. "There is no need for me to go to church, Vicar."

"Really, my son?" asks Rump. "Why not?"

"You see, Vicar," replies Hamish, "I have a church of my own at home."

"Really?" asks the vicar. "What do you mean?"

"Well," explains Hamish. "It is like this. My whole family lives in one room, so we have a three-level bed. The kids are on the top level, singing all day like little angels. Then, on the middle level, there is my mother-in-law. She is preaching day and night, dealing out the Ten Commandments and the wrath of God. Then, on the bottom level, there is me and my wife – playing on *my* organ!"

Swimming casually in the warm sea waters off the coast of Africa, are four huge sharks – Jaws, Toothy, Munch, and Little Belch. The conversation naturally turns to their favorite joy – eating.

"The best food in the world is found just near Australia," says Jaws, the biggest shark. "The menu is full of young, sporting people with tender muscles and skin well toasted by the sun."

"Ah, that is okay," replies Toothy, the big white shark, "but an even better delicacy can be found off the Canary Islands. The beaches are packed with fat, oily German tourists. Just like butter melting on your tongue!"

"Not bad," interrupts Munch, the oldest shark. "In my long years of gobbling, I find the summer waters off Miami Beach to be the ultimate in dining pleasure. The place is filled with politicians with their giant livers soaked in rum or wine – and no backbones!"

Then, old Munch turns to the youngster of the group, Little Belch. He hears a strange sound coming from Belch's stomach, and asks, "Hey, kid! What is that noise coming out of your belly? Where have you been eating?"

"Ah!" groans Belch, "I have got indigestion. I went for lunch yesterday off the beach at Goa – and the strange people I ate there will not stop singing and dancing!"

Mrs. Nora Bone gets a midnight telephone call from her son, Billy, who just got married that afternoon and is staying at the Swelling Sausage Honeymoon Hotel.

"Mom," sobs Billy, tearfully down the phone, "we are having some problems in the bedroom!"

"What kind of problems, Billy?" asks Nora Bone, anxiously.

"Well, Mom," moans Billy, "Nellie is lying there on the bed, naked and breathing hard.... And, well...Gee, Mom – I don't know what to do!"

"It is quite simple, Billy," snaps Nora Bone, in her best motherly voice, "you just take down your pants and put the hardest part of your body in the place where Nellie, your wife, you know...where she wee-wees!"

"Ah, I get it!" cries Billy. "Gee, thanks, Mom!" – and he puts down the phone.

Mrs. Nora Bone sighs deeply, shakes her head and goes back to bed. But fifteen minutes later, the phone rings again. This time it is Nellie Bone, her new daughter-in-law.

"What is the matter now?" snaps Mrs. Nora Bone.

"It is your son, Billy!" cries Nellie. "He has got his head stuck down the toilet!"

Nivedano...

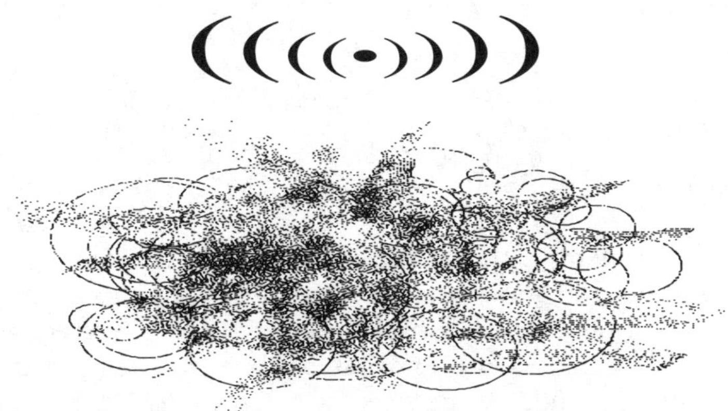

Nivedano...

Be silent...

Close your eyes...and feel your bodies to be completely frozen.

This is the right moment to enter in.

Gather all your energies, your total consciousness, and rush towards the center of your being, just two inches below the navel inside you – the hara center – with an urgency as if this is the last moment of your life.

Faster and faster...

Deeper and deeper...

As you are coming close to the center of your being, a great silence descends over you, and a peace that you have never known, and a light fills your whole interior.

From the very center you can do one thing which is not possible otherwise – witnessing.

Witness that you are not the body.

Witness that you are not the mind.

Witness that you are only a witnessing consciousness, a pure consciousness, eternal, immortal.

This is your being and everybody's being.

To deepen this witnessing,
Nivedano...

Relax...but remember the source of hara – the very source of your life – and flowers will start showering on you.

You are melting into a consciousness which is vaster than you. Gautama the Buddha Auditorium has become an ocean of consciousness. Ten thousand buddhas are no longer ten thousand, but a single, a non-dual, pure consciousness without any ripples in it.

This is your buddha nature. Out of this buddha nature arises all ecstasy, all blessings, all blissfulness.

This is only an experiment – it has to become your very life. You have to be a buddha around the clock, alert, aware, compassionate, loving, rejoicing in life, expanding life, making it a dance.

Zen is not a renunciation, it is a rejoicing.

It is the manifesto of dance and celebration.

Collect all these experiences which are happening inside you, you have to bring them to your everyday life. And ask the flame, which is symbolized by the face of Gautam Buddha, to come behind you. The face of Gautam Buddha is everybody's original face. It will come behind you. It has been waiting for you to request it.

First, it will come following you. Soon you will find you are following it. And at the third stage, the final stage, you will disappear, only the buddha remains.

The buddha is your nothingness, and it is your fullness. It is your wholeness. You can call it any name, but remember it is universal. It has nothing to do with you and me.

Nivedano...

Come back...but come back as buddhas – silent, peacefully, with a grace, and a beauty.

Just for a few moments, remember where you have been, the space that you entered, the center than you touched, the flame that you have seen.

Slowly slowly, meditation becomes your very life, your very heartbeat. That day is the most blessed day when you don't have to meditate – you are meditation. Your very being, whatever you are doing or not doing, is silent, peaceful, loving, alert and aware of its eternity.

This experience is the only sacred experience. This experience brings back again your childhood, a pure silent consciousness, rejoicing in everything that it does. The whole universe becomes a celebration and life is no longer a misery. Every moment existence is available for you to rejoice, sing, dance, love, and expand your life energies.

Mind only thinks, meditation lives.

Mind is a very small thing.

Meditation is as vast as the whole universe.

I teach you the vastness, I teach you universality, I teach you eternity.

You are not what you appear in the mirror, you are much more. You are vast, as vast as the whole universe.

This declaration is the Zen Manifesto.

Okay, Maneesha?

Yes, Osho.

INSCAPE – THE ULTIMATE ANNIHILATION

BELOVED OSHO,

A monk asked Daiten, a disciple of Sekitō,
"How is it when one meets the person-in-there?"
Daiten replied, "The person is not in there anymore."
The monk asked, "What is 'in there'?"
Daiten said, "Don't ask that question."
The monk then asked, "In the ocean of misery, the waves are deep.
With what can we make a boat?"
Daiten replied, "Make a boat with wood."
The monk said, "If we do, can we go across the ocean?"
Daiten replied, "The blind are still blind; the dumb are still dumb."

On another occasion a monk from Korea came to see Daiten. When the monk unrolled the sitting mat to make a bow, Daiten said, "Before you leave your country, get the single phrase!"
The monk had no answer.
Daiten then came forward and said, "If you ask about the single phrase here, I will answer with two phrases."

FRIENDS,

First, the questions from the sannyasins.

The first question:

Apparently sex was used by some Zen masters – for example, Ikkyū – as a way to transform energy. However, in no translation to date does evidence of this appear. It seems disciples excluded from their records about their master any mention of sex, for fear that their master would be misunderstood. Would You like to comment?

It is a long story....

Zen has moved from one country to another country, from one climate to another climate. It was born in India.

Hinduism, as such, in its early stages, was very natural, very existential. It had no taboos about sex, its seers and saints had wives. Celibacy was not an imposition, it came on its own accord through the natural experience of sex. Hinduism in its early stages was a very natural, very existential approach – almost like Zen.

But then there was another tradition which is represented by Jainism. It is a very puzzling question, and historians are almost silent, because nobody wants to stir any controversy. It is left to me to create all kinds of controversies.

Jainism is not a part of Hinduism; it is far more ancient than Hinduism. In the excavations at Mohenjo Daro and Harappa – both places now are in Pakistan – great cities have been found in ruins, and there is a possibility that those cities had naked statues like Mahavira. And the symbol of the swastika, which is the symbol of Jainism, is also found in those excavations. It is a possibility that those cities existed long before Hinduism entered this country. Hinduism is not a native philosophy to this country.

The people who lived in Harappa and Mohenjo Daro – it is unclear how they were destroyed. But either through natural catastrophe or by invasion, something happened that those two cities were destroyed seven times. On seven layers excavations have revealed new older cities, and with an absolute indication that they were not primitive, not tribal. They were as advanced as a modern city.

Their roads were sixty feet wide, as wide as in any modern city. That indicates those people must have invented vehicles, otherwise there was no need for such big roads. And they had a very strange method of piping water into houses. They had great reservoirs built on a height so the water could flow, without any mechanism, towards the city. They had swimming pools, and strangely enough, they had attached bathrooms, which shows a very high culture.

Jainism has never indicated that it belongs to Hinduism. Its whole approach is different. Most probably Jainism comes from Harappa and Mohenjo Daro culture, which was destroyed either by natural catastrophe or by invaders from Mongolia.

All the Aryans – and Hindus are the main source of the Aryans – the Europeans, the Slavs, and the English people, all come from Mongolia. Their origin is the same place in the center of Mongolia. They had to leave that place because of overpopulation. They spread in all directions, and one branch came down to India. It seems the branch that came down to India invaded the natives, completely erased the natives. Perhaps a small section remained which became almost synonymous with it.

Jainism has nothing in common with Hinduism. Its language is different, its conception about the world is different, it has no God. It does not have any yoga system, it does not have any Tantra. It is absolutely against sex, it is repressive of sex. But this repressive tradition of Jainism influenced the whole of India.

Of course, their saints looked far more deeply holy than the Hindu saints who were married, who had children. And not only children, but they were allowed to have concubines. These saints were just householders and lived in the forests, they had all the possessions that anybody can have. In fact, they had more possessions than ordinary people, because thousands of disciples brought presents to them. Each seer had become almost a university in himself. Around him thrived hundreds of teachers, disciples, visitors. But compared to the Jaina saint, these Hindu saints looked very ordinary.

Because of this comparison, Hinduism also became contaminated with the idea of repression of sex. Otherwise, you can see beautiful statues of men and women in deep embrace, in different postures even in the temples in Khajuraho, in Konarak, in Puri. Such beautiful sculpture you cannot find anywhere else. These temples were Hindu. Of course, sex was accepted by the Hindus – not only accepted, but a system of transforming the sexual energy, Tantra, was developed by the Hindu saints.

Jainism has remained a very small current, but very influential. It is one of the very important things to understand: the more miserable your saint, the holier he seems. If the saint is happy, joyous, loves life, and enjoys everything that existence allows him, you cannot think of him as very holy. To be holy, one has to be miserable.

In short, pleasure in any direction is condemned. Jaina saints looked more saintly, more holy, and Hindus felt that they had to change – and by and by, they did change, but not consciously. They started respecting the repressed person. Tantra became taboo, and Hindus became completely disoriented from their own sources. It happened again when Christianity came, and Hindus became even more repressed.

Gautam Buddha is the original source of Zen. He was born into a Hindu family, but he lived a very different life than is possible for ordinary people. From his very childhood he was allowed everything that he wanted; he was kept surrounded by beautiful girls; he was married. His whole life up to the age of twenty-nine years was wrapped in pleasure, in dancing, in music, in women, in wine, because the astrologers had predicted that this boy either would become a great saint or would become a great conqueror of the world.

And of course, his father was concerned and worried – he did not want him to become a saint. He was his only son, and he wanted him to become a world conqueror. He asked the astrologers how to prevent him from becoming a saint. Those idiots advised that he should be surrounded with pleasure: "Don't let him know that there is misery. Don't let him know that there is sickness, old age, death. Don't let him know at all about these things. Just let him be drowned in music, in dancing, surrounded by beautiful girls. Make three palaces in different places for different seasons: a cooler place when it is summer, and a warmer place when it is winter..."

And the father followed all the instructions of all those so-called wise men; in fact, their advice made him a saint. Twenty-nine years of continuous luxury – he became fed up. And suddenly, when he saw one sick man, it was a shock, because for twenty-nine years he had been kept unaware of sickness, old age, or death. And when he saw these things... how long can you prevent?

Even twenty-nine years must have been very difficult for the father to manage him not to see a flower dying, or a pale leaf falling from the tree. In the night, the garden had to be cleaned of all dead flowers, dead leaves. Gautam Buddha should not know that there was something like an ending.

But this created exactly the situation in which he became first, exhausted, bored...so many beautiful women. By the age of twenty-nine years, he became as old as a man cannot experience in three hundred years. In twenty-nine years he saw everything of luxury, of sex, of licentiousness. And when he suddenly came to know old age, and saw the body of a dead man being carried, he was shocked. He would not have been shocked if from the very beginning he had known that people become old – it is natural. These twenty-nine years of protection proved dangerous.

When he saw the dead man, he inquired of his charioteer, "What has happened to this man?"

The charioteer said, "I am not allowed...in fact, the whole city has been told that you are passing by this road, so no old man, no sick man, no dead man, should be allowed on this path. How he has entered...but I cannot be untruthful, he is dead."

And the second question immediately was, "Is the same going to happen to me?"

And the charioteer said, "I don't want to say it, but the truth is, it happens to all. Nobody is an exception."

And just then he saw a sannyasin in orange robes. He asked, "What kind of man is this, and what kind of uniform...?"

The charioteer said to him, "This man is in search of the eternal. He has become aware that this life is momentary, made of the same stuff as dreams are made of. Hence he has started a search to see whether there is something inside him which will survive even death, or if there is nothing. He is an inquirer."

Gautam Buddha was going to inaugurate the annual festival of youth. He told the charioteer, "Take me back home. I am no longer interested in the festival. I have been cheated. For twenty-nine years I have not been allowed to know the truth."

That very night he escaped from the house. And because he was bored and fed up, those who followed him after his enlightenment obviously thought that sex was dangerous because it keeps you attached to the world. Naturally those who followed Gautam Buddha became escapists.

For Buddha it was right, it was not an escape; it was simply getting out of the prison. But for others, it was not getting out of the prison. They had not even lived in the prison, they did not know the prison, they had not explored the prison. It had not come to their consciousness that it was a bondage. They simply followed Gautam Buddha. For them, sex became repressive, pleasure became contaminated.

But fortunately, Bodhidharma took Gautam Buddha's message to China. That was a different climate. Tao was the climate in China, and Tao is very life affirmative. So in China, a new development happened: the meeting of Bodhidharma and Tao, a totally new concept.

Zen is not just Buddhism; in fact, the orthodox Buddhists don't accept Zen even as Buddhism, and they are right. Zen is a crossbreed between Gautam Buddha's insight and Lao Tzu's realization, the meeting of Buddha's approach, his meditation, and Tao's naturalness.

In Tao, sex is not a taboo; Tao has its own Tantra. The energy of sex has not to be destroyed or repressed, it is not your enemy. It can be transformed, it can become a great help in the search of your ultimateness. So in Zen, the idea of celibacy was dropped. There was no insistence on it, it was your choice, because the question is meditation. If you can meditate and live your life in a natural way, it is acceptable to Tao.

And then another transformation happened: Zen reached from China to Japan, where Shinto, the native religion, was very natural. There it became absolutely affirmative, hence it is not even talked about. There is no need, it is not a question.

You are asking, "Apparently sex was used by some Zen masters – for example, Ikkyū – as a way to transform energy. However, in no translation to date does evidence of this appear."

That does not mean that sex was a taboo. It was so natural that there was no need to discuss it. You don't discuss urination. That does not mean you have stopped urinating. You start discussing things only when you start going against nature. If you are natural, there is nothing to discuss.

Life is to live, not to discuss.

Live as deeply and intensely as possible.

Ikkyū is certainly known to have used Tantra as a way of transformation. The sexual energy is nothing but your very life energy, it is only the name. You can call it sex energy, but by your labeling it 'sex', it does not become different, it is life energy. And it is better to call it life energy, because that is a wider term, more inclusive, more comprehensive.

When you are going deeper into your center, that experience can be explained in many ways. It can be explained the way Hindus have explained it: it is realization of the ultimate, *brahmabodh*. But Brahma is not a person. The word is dangerous; it gives an idea as if we are talking about a person. Brahma is simply the whole energy of the existence.

Jainas will call it self-realization, *atmabodh*, but their self is not synonymous with the ego. It is synonymous with Brahma. You are no more – in your self-realization you are no more.

Buddha and Mahavira were contemporaries, and Buddha insisted again and again, that if you are no more, then why do you call it self-realization? That gives a very distorted description. Call it no-self realization. But Mahavira has his own reasons not to call it no-self realization – people are afraid of no-self realization; if you are going to be nothing, then it is better to remain something. And Mahavira knew that it does not matter whether you call it self-realization or not, you are going to disappear. But keep a positive word which is more attractive.

I can see Mahavira's compassion in it, but I also can see Buddha's truthfulness. He says, "If it is really no-self realization, then call it what it is. Don't deceive people."

Tantra will call it *samadhi*.

The names are different, but it is exactly life, pure life without any contamination. Once you reach to your center you can think in different categories. You can use the yoga method, then you can say this is the very center of your being: *sambodhi*. You can use the Tantra method, then you can say this is the center of your sex energy. And sex energy in Tantra is equivalent to life energy. These words have unnecessarily kept people discussing and discussing.

The reality is one. It is better to experience it.

Zen masters don't talk about it for the simple reason Zen is a very natural phenomenon. It is not anti-life, it is not escapist. But most of the Zen masters have left their household life. Tired, seeing no point in the marketplace, they moved to the mountains. It was not against the marketplace, it was simply that the mountains were more silent, more peaceful. They allowed you to be yourself without any interference.

Sex is not mentioned in the records, for the simple reason that there is no reason to record it, it is accepted. If one has lived it, and there comes a time when you have outgrown it, then there is no point to go on and on, tired and disgusted. While it is beautiful, enjoy, and when it becomes a tiring, disgusting phenomenon, then just leave it for others. But there is no reason to condemn it.

A natural person simply passes beyond stages without condemnation. He has lived life, he has known life, now he wants to know something more. He wants to know something of the eternal. He has reproduced children, now he wants to know who he is in his innermost core. He has lived the world of the outside, he has been a Zorba. Now a moment comes of turning in. The outside reality has been explored without any inhibition, then you will naturally one day turn inwards.

It is the inhibition, the repressive mentality, that goes on forcing you to think of sex, because you have never lived it. Your Christianity, your Jainism, did not allow it, or allowed it and then created guilt in you that you were doing something which should not be done. Then you are living halfheartedly. And when a thing is lived halfheartedly you never transcend, you never go beyond it.

Dance to the moment when you stop automatically.

Live everything in life so you can transcend joyfully without any guilt. That is difficult for people who have been programmed with taboos: sex should not even be mentioned; death should not be mentioned either.

Sex and death are the two points: one is the beginning, the other is the end. People are kept unaware of both. About sex, it is dirty; about death, it is dangerous and gloomy...don't talk about it. It is always somebody else who dies, don't be worried. But in reality, you are born out of sex, and you are going to die. That which is born out of sex is going to disappear in death. Sex and death are the two points of the same energy. That which appears in sex, disappears in death. And both have to be understood, because both are the most important points in your life, and both have to be accepted and lived.

But religions like Christianity and Jainism are very repressive. Their very repression makes people guilty, sinners. They cannot live their life with totality, intensity, and they cannot meditate, because meditation's first condition is to be total, to be total in everything. Then everything becomes meditation. Even making love, if you are total, then it becomes a meditation.

My own understanding about meditation is that in the beginning it must have happened to someone while making love, because that seems to be the only thing in which you can come to such a totality that time stops, mind stops, and everything becomes absolutely silent.

But that silence can be created by meditation also. The secret is known through sex, that if there is no time and no mind, you have entered into the ultimate. Through sex you enter for a single moment, and you fall back into the temporary. Through meditation you can remain in the ultimate, twenty-four hours around the clock, in an orgasmic joy. Your every moment becomes a dance.

Knowing that you are not, there is nothing to fear.

Knowing that you are the whole, there is nothing to lose.

Sex is not talked about by Zen masters, simply because it is taken for granted.

One of our sannyasins has been working with John Stevens, author of *One Robe, One Bowl*. He claims to have found ancient manuscripts never before published, in which Zen masters speak of sex as a tool for transformation. He has compiled a book of this material, which he is calling *Lust for Zen*. He anticipates that he is going to "upset Buddhists everywhere" by publishing this material.

Do it quickly, because without upsetting, it is very difficult to bring people to come to a settling. First upset, only then can they settle down in a *Zazen*.

But there is nothing upsetting to the real Zen masters; only Buddhists may be upset. The Buddhists of India will be upset, because they have borrowed the sex-repressive idea from Jainism, from Hinduism, and from Buddha's own experience.

But you cannot afford Buddha's experience, because he was first a Zorba. Even Zorba was not such a Zorba as Buddha. His father found as many beautiful girls as possible from his whole kingdom...and he became tired.

One night after much drinking and dancing, everybody had fallen asleep. He looked around – those beautiful faces... Foam was falling from their mouths, their makeup was upset, their hairdo was not in the right place...and it was disgusting. But that kind of experience is not available to everybody. It should be available to everybody, then at the age of thirty everybody is going to escape from the world. But this escape will not be out of fear.

This escape needs a new name. It is *inscape*. One has lived outside, now one wants to live inside. One is bored of repetition, but because of the guilty, life-negative religions predominating over humanity, nobody ever comes to meditation through his love life. Nobody comes to an orgasmic experience where time stops, where mind stops, where suddenly a new sky opens its doors.

Tantra has used the method in India. And in China, Tao has used its own different technique of Tantra to bring people through sexual experience to a meditative state. But it is not a necessity that you should come to a meditative state through sexual experience. You can come by the direct route, by the immediate...this very moment, through meditation.

Sex is a long way. Nothing is wrong if somebody chooses the long way; if he enjoys the journey, there is no harm. But if somebody wants a shortcut, then meditation is available as a shortcut. It is really reaching to the same experience, but by a shortcut.

And as far as my sannyasins are concerned, there is no question of renouncing anything unless something renounces you. Many things will renounce you. By and by, you will start seeing – "Why go on playing these games...?" Sooner or later you will be sitting silently, doing nothing, rejoicing in the ultimate annihilation, disappearing into the ocean, losing all your boundaries.

The second question:

Last night You said that the absolute cannot be defined by any system. However, in the relative domain of life on earth, are not seeds and seasons part of a discernable mechanism through which this limited existence functions?

The moment you say, "relative," in the relative everything can be defined, but it will remain a relative definition.

I was talking about the absolute, where all definitions disappear, where you face a chaos – no way to put it in order.

But in the relative world... That's why Albert Einstein introduced the word 'relativity' into science. The theory of relativity is a great understanding that science deals with the relative, and the relative can be defined. You can say, "This is night," and you can say, "This is day," but in the ultimate, the night disappears into the day, the day disappears into the night. In the ultimate, birth and death are one, they both arise from the same source. It is a wave arising in the ocean; you call it birth, and then the wave disappears into the ocean and you call it death.

In the relative, you can call it the birth of something and the death of something, but in the absolute, nothing is ever born, and nothing ever dies, everything simply is. This isness is so vast that it contains all contradictions.

Only one man of this century, Walt Whitman, a great poet, came to this realization through his poetry. Again and again people said to him, "You are contradictory. In one poem you said this, in another poem you said that."

Finally he said, "I am vast enough to contain contradictions." A beautiful Zen statement – "vast enough to contain contradictions." Every poet, and every musician, and every lover, and every creator, knows that in existence contradictions meet.

In existence you cannot make clear-cut divisions, everything melts into each other. It is oneness expressing in millions of ways: as a man, as a rose, as a fish...it is the same life. And this is the mystery of life – that it can become a rose, and it can become a fish, and it can become a man, and it can become a buddha.

This possibility of eternal manifestations, of infinite manifestations, makes life a joy, a song, a life worth living. If everything is explained, life will become very finite, very small, not worth living. It is the mysteriousness – you may be aware of it or not, but if you are aware, you can rejoice in it more clearly. It is the mysteriousness of life, it is its unknowability, its unpredictability, that makes it so juicy. If everything becomes predictable, mathematical, logical, life will lose all its glory and splendor.

Talking about contradictions, I would like you to know that you rejoice only in things which are beyond your comprehension. Once you understand them, you are finished with them. You cannot finish with love, because you can never understand what it is; it remains a mystery. The moment you know the formula of love – that it is just like H_2O, you are finished with it. The moment you know the exact definition of meditation, you are finished with it.

The indefinable attracts. Life remains a mystery in spite of all the philosophers, all the theologians, all the scientists doing their best to destroy the mystery. It remains mysterious, and nobody is going to destroy its mystery, because no system can contain it. It is so vast that our systems are very small in comparison. Our systems are bound to be as big as our minds are, and our minds are not very big.

Small computers can do the work that your mind does, with more clarity, with more definitiveness, with more reliability. A single computer can do the work of thousands of people, and you can keep the computer in your pocket. You can keep thousands of minds in your pocket. A single computer can contain the whole of the *Encyclopaedia Britannica*.

In my village, there was a great idiot....

His greatness was such that I have never come across any idiot of his quality. He only read dictionaries, and he became so acquainted with dictionaries, that he knew nothing else except the dictionary. He could not make a single sentence, but he could repeat the whole dictionary.

He used to write letters to the president, to the prime minister, to the governor...and he would show me his letters – ten pages, twenty pages of dictionary...just words. You could not make any sense of what he was writing, because not a single sentence was there.

And he would say, "What is the matter? I go on writing to these people – nobody answers me."

I said, "Nobody can understand your letters, they are so mysterious.

You do one thing." He brought a letter – twenty pages he had written to Pandit Jawaharlal Nehru. I said, "You write a small summary, because the prime minister may not have the time for twenty pages. So give a small summary – half a page of just the essential points."

After seven days, he said, "That is not possible. I cannot make the summary, because I don't know myself what I have written. I only write dictionaries. How to summarize it? What to leave, and what…?"

Then I said, "You send the whole letter, but be aware that nobody is going to answer you."

The governor had come to the village one time, and I told this pundit – he was a brahmin – "This is a good chance. You have been writing so many letters to the governor – I can make an appointment for you, so you can ask him directly."

He said, "I feel very nervous. In fact, I myself have forgotten what I have written to him, because I have written so many letters. But I can take the whole dictionary from which I take all those letters."

I said, "You come with me."

I knew the governor. He was an old man, Mangaldas Pakvasa, and he loved me very much. I used to stay in his house in Bombay.

I took the man to Pakvasa, and I told him, "This poor fellow goes on writing you letters, and you never answer him."

He said, "This is the fellow? I wanted to see him. Is he mad or what? He is driving me nuts! Even to have to look at his letters…I immediately throw them away. At first I used to try to read them but there are only words and words – no meaning, no sentence, no connection between those words."

I said to him, "He has brought his whole book. This is the book from which he has been writing you letters."

Mangaldas Pakvasa said to me, "Stop this fellow. He is bothering even the prime minister, the president. They have asked me, 'Who is this fellow who goes on writing?'"

The whole day his work was to write letters, beautiful letters, beautiful words. But a dictionary has no meaning. You have to make small statements which will be relative.

Relative means you can say that somebody is taller than you, but *tallness* does not exist anywhere. Somebody can be taller than you, and somebody can be more beautiful than you, somebody can be stronger than you. But always remember, it is in relation.

If you try to define something without any relativity, then what is beauty? You can say some girl is beautiful, but that is always relative. You may not have thought, but just think: if that girl becomes your wife, will she still be really beautiful? In other people's eyes perhaps, but not in your eyes. Within two days you know the whole geography of the girl, the whole territory...and now you are hooked.

In fact, everything that you say is relative, nothing is absolute.

Mahavira was so alert that he never made a single statement without using the word 'perhaps'. He would always use 'perhaps' before every sentence – "Perhaps..." – because in the absolute, nothing can be said. Somebody is perhaps beautiful – but *perhaps*, remember. When you come closer, things are going to change; it is relative to the distance.

The moon looks so beautiful from here, but the people who reached to the moon must have felt very frustrated. They looked all around – there was nothing, just bare earth. Not even grass flowers, nothing to say of roses – no water, no clouds, no river, no greenery. They did not stay there long.

And for thousands of years, poets have been singing songs of the beauty of the moon. It depends on the distance. Everything becomes beautiful if it is at a distance. As you come closer, your conception is going to change.

So relatively, everything can be explained. But in the absolute sense, everything is indefinable, everything is mysterious. You love someone, you have lived with someone for years, but do you really know the other person?

In absoluteness, you don't know. You don't know even yourself, and you have been yourself since eternity. And even now...every day you try, but you cannot say, "I know myself."

The moment you reach into the depths of your consciousness, it is so mysterious that you can enjoy it. You can rejoice it, you can dance it, but you cannot define it.

The third question:

**Last night I heard You say that our energy is based in the 'hara', and that it is expressed through the different chakras in the body.
Traditional Zen seems to emphasize Zazen as the way to come in touch with that energy, whereas You have allowed, even encouraged, Your disciples to have more freedom to explore the various avenues of expression.
Beloved Master, would You like to comment?**

I am not a traditional man at all. I am untraditional in every possible way. I am not confined to any technique.

Zen is confined, in a way, to Zazen. Zazen means just sitting and doing nothing. It is perfectly right, but my experience of the modern man is that the most difficult thing for him is just sitting and doing nothing. If you ask him to go to the moon, he can go. If you ask him to go to Everest, he can go. But just sitting? That is the most difficult thing. Finally, you will have to come to the point.

I have nothing to do with tradition. My Zen is absolutely untraditional. First, I make you jump and shout and scream, and do all kinds of gibberish. Then finally, tired, you can sit for a few moments.

I was staying in a home, and the host, my friend, was introducing me to his wife and his child. And he said, "This child is a trouble. He can't sit silently even for a single moment. He is always doing something – running..."

I said, "You can sit? Your wife can just sit and do nothing?"

The wife said, "We never thought about it, but it is true. Even my husband on holiday unnecessarily opens the car. It is doing perfectly well, but he tries to improve it. And finally it has to be sent to the garage. He cannot sit, nor can I sit. And that is the same with our child. We were not aware. You made us aware that it is not right to ask him to just sit."

I said, "First, let him go around the house seven times, and he will sit silently." And I told the boy, "Go around the house seven times."

He said, "Why?"

I said, "You just do it seven times. Just show your energy."

So he went around the house seven times, then he sat in the garden very silently.

I told his parents, "You can do the same. Go around the house whenever you feel like sitting. First, jump, scream, throw out all the garbage that is inside your head."

I am dealing with the contemporary man, who is the most restless being that has ever evolved on the earth. But people do become silent; you just have to allow them to throw out their madness, insanity, then they themselves become silent. They start waiting for the moment when I will say, "Be silent." They become tired of their gibberish. They also become aware that this gibberish is there.

I used to have camps in Mount Abu, and I used gibberish – not for two minutes, but for a complete hour. And it was such a great joy when I said to people, "Now you can be silent."

And they did such things...

One man, every day, whenever it was allowed... We used to do the gibberish in the afternoon, and as everybody was going insane, he would start phoning – that was his speciality.

"Hello...!" – and there was nobody. And he would look at me, and I would close my eyes because he felt embarrassed. There was nobody, no phone. But he was some kind of broker, so – "Hello..." And he would answer from the other end, and from both the ends for one hour... He would become tired and he would start throwing his nonexistent telephone towards me, because he was getting tired.

One hour – and then I would say, "Be silent." He would put the phone back, and he would look so joyous. And I wondered how long he would be able to do it. In the seven-day camp, after the fifth day he stopped phoning. He would take up the phone and then put it down, seeing the futility of it. But it took five days.

You have to be total, otherwise things remain inside you. You have to empty your continuous gibberish that goes on inside, "Yakkety-yak, yakkety-yak..." Don't do it partially. Don't be bothered about being seen, because nobody is looking at you; everybody is in his own insanity. This is a good time for you to say and do anything which ordinarily you will not say.

In Mount Abu one day, one of my sannyasins who used to arrange the car for me from Ahmedabad to Mount Abu – his friend, in the gibberish meditation, suddenly jumped up, threw away all his clothes, and started pulling the car towards the valley. Four persons had to prevent him, otherwise he would have thrown the car into a deep valley. When he was prevented, he jumped up on a tree, naked, and started waving the branches of the tree, and the branches started cracking! Everybody was worried – "We never expected…this man has always been sane." Somehow he had to be brought down.

When the meditation was over, he came to me saying, "Please forgive me, but perhaps these ideas must have been in me, otherwise why? I never have done such a thing before, and I cannot conceive… But in that moment I wanted to throw that car into the valley and destroy it."

I said, "You should think about it. Perhaps you have always been jealous of your friend's car."

He became silent, and he said, "Perhaps. Deep down it must have been."

"And because you were prevented from throwing the car into the valley, in your anger you forgot completely that you were naked, and you jumped on the tree. And out of anger you started shaking the whole tree. All this violence you must have carried inside you. With this much violence inside, how can you sit down silently?"

The contemporary man is the most restless man. And I am dealing with the contemporary man, not the dead of the past. I have to devise ways and methods so that you can become silent. Finally, that is the goal – Zazen. But before that you have to throw out many things. Perhaps in the past when man was much more natural, unrepressed…

In Burma there is still a small tribe in the mountains, which has never fought with anybody, which has never killed anybody. Nobody in its history has committed suicide or murder. They know nothing of Sigmund Freud, but they know a far deeper psychoanalysis than Sigmund Freud knows.

Anybody in that tribe, if he dreams, and in his dream he hits somebody, in the morning he has to confess to the elders that he has hit somebody in the dream. He has to describe the person so they can find out who the person is whom he has hit. Then he has to go to that person with fruits, sweets, to be forgiven – although it happened in the dream. But it must have been in the mind, otherwise it cannot happen even in the dream.

In that small tribe, no violence, no war, no battle…they don't have any arms. If it is possible in a small tribe, it is possible on the whole globe. If it is possible for a single man, it is possible for the whole of humanity. We have just to throw out all the garbage that comes up in our minds, in our dreams. And it affects our actions, our attitudes, our miseries, our angers, our despair. It is better to throw it before it affects your actions.

And that is the whole psychology behind meditation: emptying you, creating a nothingness in you. Out of that nothingness blossoms the ultimate joy, the ultimate bliss.

The sutra:

BELOVED OSHO,
A monk asked Daiten, a disciple of Sekitō,
"How is it when one meets the person-in-there?"
Daiten replied, "The person is not in there anymore."

When you go in, you don't meet any person, you simply meet the whole; you simply meet the impersonal existence. You *are* only on the surface; once you go deeper you disappear. The deeper you go, the less you are. And when you are not, then only have you touched the real depth.

You don't meet any person, you simply meet the impersonal existence.

Daiten was right when he said, "The person is not in there anymore if you go in." It is only when you don't go in…it is a conception, an idea. If you remain in the mind, you remain a person. The moment you go beyond the mind, the person starts melting. There comes a point *you* are no more, *everything is* – you have become one with the whole.

The monk asked, "What is *'in there'*? If there is no person, then who is there?"

Mind cannot conceive of nothingness; it can only conceive of something limited. If the person is not there, then who is there? God is there?

Buddha is reported to have said, "If you meet me in you, immediately kill, immediately cut my head! Because you have loved me, when you meditate, the image of your master may come to you. It is just an image, don't let that image prevent you from meeting the whole. Cut the head."

The monk asked, "What is *'in there'?"*

Daiten said, "Don't ask that question. That is the only question that cannot be answered. You better go in and see who is there."

Daiten is a very clear master. Without much philosophy he simply says, "Don't ask that question. Simply go in and see."

The monk then asked, "In the ocean of misery, the waves are deep.
With what can we make a boat?"
Daiten replied, "Make a boat with wood."
The monk said, "If we do, can we go across the ocean?"
Daiten replied, "The blind are still blind; the dumb are still dumb."

He is showing his frustration. This monk cannot understand. You don't have to go to the other shore of the ocean, you have to melt in the ocean. You don't need a boat for melting. The other shore will be just like this shore. You can change places, but that is not going to change your inner space.

Hence he said, "Whatever the masters say, people still remain blind and still are dumb." They don't change. They go on listening. If it is a philosophy, they can understand it, but if it is an existential experiment, they simply remain blind, deaf and dumb.

Going in is not a philosophical question. Who is there inside you? What is the point of asking when the inside is yours? Go in and see who is there. You will not find any person. You will find a pure nothingness, an existential grace, a beauty, a song without sounds, a great drunkenness, a tremendous ecstasy. You will not find any person, just experiences, but those experiences are going to transform you. Those experiences are going to change your individuality, because you will now know there is absolute silence inside, no individuality.

Then, if somebody insults you, you will not feel insulted, because *you* don't exist. He is throwing stones at nothing. Then even in your ordinary life you will function like a buddha – aware, alert, compassionate.

On another occasion a monk from Korea came to see Daiten. When the monk unrolled the sitting mat to make a bow, Daiten said, "Before you leave your country, get the single phrase!"

The monk had no answer. He could not understand what Daiten was saying to him. He is saying, *"Before you leave your country, get the single phrase!"* By "country" he does not mean Korea. By country he is meaning, before you go from your personality, the boundary that you have lived in, get one phrase. What is that phrase?

Rather than asking, the monk had no answer. He could not understand Daiten. That single phrase is *Zazen*. Before you leave your personality and your individuality and your mind, remember to sit silently without asking any question, and without creating any hallucination, and without creating any dream.

Just get one thing: sitting silently.

In Japanese it is one word: *Zazen*.

Daiten then came forward and said, "If you ask about the single phrase here, I will answer with two phrases."

He is saying that if you don't go in by yourself, and somebody else has to show you the way, the oneness of inside becomes two, a duality of the mind. Anything said is dual; only the unsaid is nondual.

You say day and it includes night; you say life and it includes death. You say man and it includes woman.

You say this – and it includes that.

You cannot say anything without implying its opposite. But inside, you can experience oneness without any duality – a pure silence not against sound, a beauty not against ugliness, a truth not against lies.

The function of the master is not to tell you what is in, but to lead you inwards, force you inwards. All that is said is in the service of that which cannot be said.

Bashō wrote:

The wild heron
sleeping –
undisturbed nobility.

Have you seen a wild heron sleeping? Bashō says, "undisturbed nobility." That's what you are when silence happens to you – an undisturbed nobility. Suddenly you become an emperor.

The insight gives you the whole universe. It takes away all that is false, and it gives you all that is truth, all that is beauty, all that is grace, all that is sheer joy.

A man like Bashō – a man of deep meditation – will start seeing it everywhere. Even in a heron sleeping, he will see an undisturbed nobility. In a wild bird on the wing, he will see immense freedom. In the sky, he will see his own nothingness.

He will start having a new sight about everything – even a wildflower will become more beautiful. Jesus says, "Look at the wild lilies in the field. They are more beautiful than even Solomon the emperor was in all his splendor."

Solomon was an ancient Jewish king of great beauty, and of great understanding. In the whole of the Holy Bible, only his song, Solomon's Song, has some truth; otherwise, everything is ordinary.

But Jesus says, "These wild lilies are more beautiful even than the splendor of the great King Solomon."

To the man of meditation, everything becomes totally new and fresh, young, alive. He radiates love and compassion and joy.

Maneesha's question:

BELOVED OSHO,

Philip Kapleau writes in his book, 'The Three Pillars of Zen':
"The drive towards enlightenment is powered on the one hand by a painfully felt inner bondage – both a frustration with life and a fear of death – and on the other hand, by the conviction that through satori one can gain liberation."

Philip Kapleau does not understand Zen as an experience. His book is beautiful. *The Three Pillars of Zen* is a good intellectual introduction, but only intellectual. Even this statement shows that the person does not understand.

Zen is not a "drive towards enlightenment." Zen *is* enlightenment; it is not a drive. But the contemporary mind thinks only in terms of drive, motives, ambitions, desires. Zen is not a motivation. It is not an effort to reach somewhere. It has no goal, it cannot have a drive.

"The drive towards enlightenment is powered on the one hand..." – it is not a drive in the first place, and in the second place, it is nothing to do with bondage, or a frustration with life, or a fear of death. It has nothing to do with fear, and has nothing to do with greed – that's what Christianity is. Unfortunately, the author of *The Three Pillars of Zen* has imposed his own conditioning on a totally different phenomenon. Zen is not Christianity.

Christianity is a drive towards the kingdom of God. It is a fear of hell, and it is a greed to be saved and to be allowed into the kingdom of God and eternity of joy. Christianity is a drive. But the author has imposed the definition of Christianity on Zen. That is absolutely wrong.

Zen is a very simple phenomenon: it is just to know yourself...here and now. It is not a motivation to go somewhere, to find something, it is simply to become acquainted with yourself. This is a basic thing.

You *are* – obviously you should know *who* you are. No drive is needed, no greed is needed, because you are not going to become something. You are moving into being. You are already it, whether you know it or not. So all that you have to do is to be a little silent, and watch inside.

Zen has nothing to do, Maneesha, with any drive, with any fear, with any greed.

It is time for Sardar Gurudayal Singh.
Put on the light!

Willie Weary, a middle-aged businessman, stumbles in to see Doctor Nutcase in his Hollywood surgery.

"Doc, I have got this problem," confides Willie Weary. "You see, my secretary, Millie, loves to make love. Every morning, when I get to work, instead of bringing me a cup of coffee, she throws me across my desk and makes passionate love to me! Then, just before lunch, she pushes me up against the filing cabinet for a quickie. And before I leave work at the end of the day, she always gives me a farewell screw."

"Hmm!" says Doctor Nutcase. "So what seems to be the problem?"

"Well, you see, Doc," explains Willie Weary, "my wife, Dottie, is a nymphomaniac. Every morning before I get up, she jumps on me and we screw until the alarm clock goes off. Then, when I go home for lunch every day, we have a quick one while I am eating my spaghetti. And then, each night we have a marathon session before we go to sleep!"

"Hmm!" says Doctor Nutcase. "I still don't see what your problem is!"

"Well, Doctor," explains Willie Weary, "I get these dizzy spells every time I jerk off!"

In downtown Los Loonies, California, three men – Leroy the black guy, Jack Jerk the white guy, and Ha-choo Wu the Chinaman – meet at Safeway Supermarket. They are all doing their weekly shopping, and they have all brought their pet dogs with them.

The first guy, Jack Jerk, begins to brag about his dog Fifi: "My dog, Fifi, is the most intelligent female dog in this state," says Jack. "She is so smart that I can tell her to go and get a packet of chocolate-chip cookies, eat half of them, and bring the rest of them to me!"

And immediately Jack snaps his fingers, and Fifi the dog jumps up and disappears behind some shelves. A minute later, Fifi comes back wagging her tail, with half a pack of chocolate-chip cookies in her mouth.

"Velly implessive!" says Ha-choo Wu. "But watchee my doggee, Chu Yoo! He velly smartest boy doggie in all world!"

Then Wu commands his dog to go and get a bottle of milk and an empty glass. Chu Yoo races off, and comes back a few moments later, pours the milk into the glass, and then stands there wagging his tail.

"Hey, that is nothing," says Big Black Leroy. Then he turns to his big black dog, named Rambo, and shouts, "Go get 'em, Rambo!"

Rambo slowly gets up from the floor where he has been sleeping, walks over, drinks the milk, eats the cookies, pisses on Chu Yoo, fucks Fifi, empties the cashbox, and goes home to rest!

Wanting to save money on their honeymoon, Bunny and Bonker Boom decide to spend the first nights of their new marriage at the home of Bunny's parents, Bob and Betty Bog.

Three days go by, and Bunny's younger brother, Little Bippo, is playing in his bedroom with his toy airplanes and listening at the wall to all the strange noises coming from Bunny and Bonker's room.

Curious, Little Bippo comes downstairs and finds his mother.

"Hey, Mom," asks Bippo, playing with his model plane, "how come Bunny and Bonker have not left their room for three days? They don't even come down for meals!"

"It is none of your business!" replies his mother.

So Bippo shrugs his shoulders and trots out of the room playing with his airplane.

A few more days pass, and even Bippo's mother begins to worry too. So she creeps upstairs and peeks through the keyhole of the young couple's room.

To her horror, she sees Bunny sitting on top of Bonker, and Bonker is trying with all his might, to push Bunny off.

"It is no good," cries Bonker. "I still can't move!"

Just then, Bippo's mom hears a noise coming from the bathroom, so she rushes down the corridor to see what is going on.

But all she finds is Little Bippo searching through all the shelves and cupboards in the bathroom.

"What are you looking for?" asks his mother.

"Just my airplane glue," replies Bippo. "I was keeping it in the Vaseline jar!"

Nivedano...

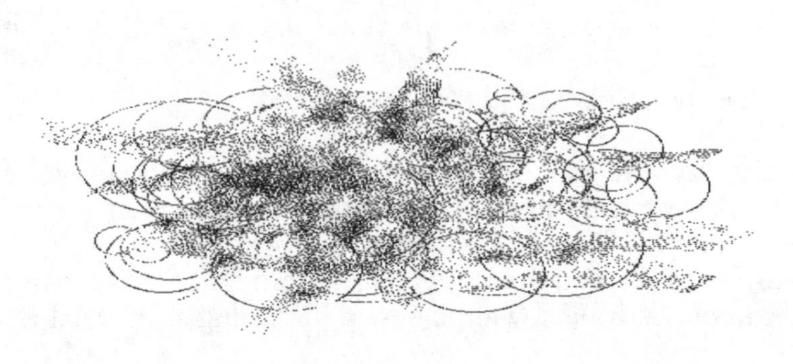

Nivedano...

Be silent. Close your eyes and feel your bodies to be completely frozen.

This is the right moment to enter in.

Gather all your energies, your total consciousness, and rush towards the inner center of your being which is just two inches below your navel, inside the body.

Faster and faster...

Deeper and deeper...with an urgency as if this is going to be your last moment. You have to make it!

As you are coming closer to the center, a great silence descends over you. And inside, you are filled with a luminosity.

At the very center there is a flame, the very source of your life, the very source of your consciousness and awareness. This is your buddha.

To make the buddha awake, only one simple method is needed: witnessing.

Witness that you are not the body.

Witness that you are not the mind.

Witness that you are only the pure witnessing and nothing else.

Go deeper into witnessing, and you will find the ultimate source of life and existence.

Nivedano...

Relax...

Let go...

Just as snow melts, let yourself melt into existence.

Gautama the Buddha Auditorium has turned into an ocean of consciousness. Ten thousand buddhas have disappeared into it.

This is the most precious experience in existence. And once you know the way to the center, you can go to the center anytime, anywhere. It is so simple, it is so close, and it is so alive.

It will transform your whole being.

It will fill you with joy, silence, love, compassion.

You will be a transformed, new human being.

Zen is only a name for this transformation.

The new man is needed around the earth, because only the new man can save this earth from destruction. The old man has created only destructive methods, war and violence. The new man will be a buddha, a man of compassion, love and peace.

Before you come back, gather all the experiences that are happening there at the center of your being, and persuade the buddha, the flame of life, to come following you and be part of your daily life. Ordinary and mundane existence can be transformed into sacred actions if the buddha is present there.

These are the three steps.

First, the buddha comes following you as a shadow.

Second, you follow the buddha as a shadow.

And third, your shadow disappears in the luminosity of the buddha, the impersonal silence, the unbounded, oceanic joy.

You disappear, but the whole existence becomes available to you. You lose nothing. You lose only shadows, and you gain everything: all or nothing. They are both synonymous at the experience of the center. They are not opposites, there is no duality in the experience of meditation.

In this silence all contradictions melt and merge into each other.

Nivedano...

Come back...but come back as buddhas, with the same grace, same silence, the same beauty, same blissfulness.

This ecstasy has to become your very heart, and this experience has to be carried into every ordinary action of your life, in your love, in your relations, in your friendships. Wherever you are, you should bring peace and joy and blissfulness, and more light.

Existence becomes more and more available to you the more you share it in your bliss, in your joy, in your laughters, in your silences.

You simply become a vehicle, a bamboo flute on the lips of existence.

The song comes from the whole.

You simply allow it.

This allowance is Zen.

Zen is a way of becoming a blessing to the whole existence.

Okay, Maneesha?

Yes, Osho.

SMALL INTERVALS OF LIGHT

BELOVED OSHO,

*A monk asked Chōro, who had been a disciple of Tanka,
"The buddhas of the past, present and future turn the great wheel
of dharma in flames of fire – is it correct or not?"
Chōro said, laughing, "I have doubts, after all."
The monk asked, "Why do you doubt?"
Chōro said, "The fragrance of wildflowers fills the pathways, but the
hidden birds don't know it is spring. Is there anyone who is not defiled
by mystic wonder?" After a long silence, Chōro concluded,
"This one spot could not be washed away even if you dumped
the waters of the ocean on it."*

FRIENDS,

First, the questions from sannyasins.

The first question:

These Zen sutras seem to come from a time when there were many enlightened ones in this world. What broke the chain of enlightenment, and left our planet with a single precious and unhidden flame of buddha nature?
How is it we have evolved into such an unenlightened planet when we were once blessed with so many masters?

The question is significant, and many of you may have wondered about it. What happened to human consciousness that it has fallen deep into darkness? Why don't we see so many buddhas?

The reason is very clear: the little man we talked about yesterday destroyed every possibility for enlightenment.

It is not just in one country. Around the world, whenever there was a man of immense consciousness, the masses were against him, the masses were violent.

One Christian was asking me – an old friend – "Do you think Jesus will come again?" I said, "I don't think, I am absolutely certain if he is intelligent, he will not come again. What you did with him last time – that's enough to prevent him from coming back. You have poisoned Socrates, Anaxagoras, you have crucified Jesus, al-Hillaj Mansoor, Sarmad..."

The masses have never been respectful to the living buddha. So many attempts were made on the life of Gautam Buddha, and finally he died from poisoning. This misbehavior of the ordinary, unconscious, but the majority of people, simply prevents.

I have been poisoned, jailed, for no reason at all...fined four hundred thousand dollars, and I don't have a single dollar with me. Twenty-one countries have closed their doors by law, saying that I cannot enter.

Sometimes it seems the politicians are the most stupid people around. They have passed laws in their parliaments that my jet airplane cannot even land and refuel on their airports, because my presence – *in* my airplane, *on* the airport – can contaminate and destroy their morality, their religion of two thousand years' standing...!

I have been expelled from Greece – threatened, and under the pressure of the archbishop of Greece, the government had to deport me. The threat was that if I was not deported, all the people who were living with me on the beautiful island of Crete – that place would be dynamited. And fifty persons at least were there with me – all would be burned alive.

The reason? I had not even gone outside the boundary of the house, but the same reason again and again: I would corrupt their morality, I would destroy their religion. Such a fear has prevented people from moving deeper into themselves.

My secretary, Anando, says to me, "You are a bad example for enlightenment. Twenty-one countries are closed for you. One country has poisoned you, jailed you, dragged you into six jails in twelve days without any evidence..."

And they have admitted it now, that there was no direct evidence of any crime, "but we simply wanted the commune to be destroyed."

One wonders why America should be worried about a small commune which was living in a desert. The nearest village was twenty miles away. We were a self-sufficient commune, and slowly transforming the desert into a beautiful oasis. But the orthodox, fundamentalist Christians became worried. The fear was that young people were moving into the commune from their flock.

And just now the Attorney General of Oregon has made the statement: "We had no reason. And we had put five million dollars into research to find some crime against him." They have come to India, they have come to Poona, they have been to Bombay. They have even gone to my birthplace, to my university, to the school, to the college...everywhere to find some hint. But they could not, because there was nothing.

I am the laziest man. I cannot commit a crime; it is too much work. If not doing anything is a crime, then I am certainly a criminal. If just being silent, rejoicing into my own aloneness is a crime, then I am certainly a criminal.

But if you behave with every conscious being in such a murderous way, certainly nobody is going to be interested in the very word 'enlightenment'. It will create fear; you will be in unnecessary danger. Of course, only these few enlightened people whom you have killed, or tried to kill, have helped humanity to become a little more conscious.

But people have seen how the masses have behaved with Jesus, how the masses have behaved with Sarmad. The masses have created a barrier for anybody interested in his own consciousness. It has nothing to do with society, it has nothing to do with the crowd. But people are afraid, very much afraid of those who know themselves. They have a certain power, a certain aura and a certain magnetism – a charisma that can take out alive, young people from the traditional imprisonment. And there are so many prisons: Christianity, and Hinduism, and Mohammedanism, and Jainism, and Buddhism...wherever there is an organized religion, it becomes militant.

Christianity clearly defines itself as a militant religion. Then it becomes a question of growing in numbers – not growing towards heights, but widening the empire. It becomes politics, it is no longer religion. All the so-called religions are just political strategies.

The enlightened man cannot be enslaved – that is the difficulty – and he cannot be imprisoned. His individuality and his rebellion make the vested interests – the priests and the politicians and the pedagogues... "It is better to finish people like Socrates – they are creating a disturbance in the mind of people."

Every genius who has known something of the inner is bound to be a little difficult to be absorbed; he is going to be an upsetting force. The masses don't want to be disturbed, even though they may be in misery; they *are* in misery, but they are accustomed to the misery. And anybody who is not miserable looks like a stranger.

The enlightened man is the greatest stranger in the world, he does not seem to belong to anybody. No organization confines him, no community, no society, no nation. His rebellion is so total that it makes the unconscious crowd antagonistic. Such a man cannot be tolerated alive; he can be worshipped when dead.

You can worship a Buddha when dead. You can worship a Jesus when dead. But not even a single enlightened person has been respected, loved, by the blind and the deaf and the unconscious masses. This has become a barrier. That's why you don't find so many enlightened people.

But if you are ready to take the risk, you are capable of becoming a buddha any moment you decide, because it is not a question of going anywhere, it is simply looking inwards.

The Hindu mythology about the history of consciousness is worth mentioning....

The first age of humanity, the very beginning, is called *satyuga*, the age of truth. Every man is naturally a buddha, just like a child – no fear, no greed, a perfect balance. To describe the balance, they say that the first age is like a table which has four legs, perfectly balanced.

The second age – one leg falls away. Still there is some balance, but that old certainty is no longer there. Because of the three legs, the second age is called *treta; treta* means three.

And the third – another leg falls away, man is becoming poorer and poorer. The third age is called *dwapar; dwapar* means two legs.

And we are in the fourth stage. It is a beautiful symbology: we have lost all balance, we are only standing on one leg. How long can you stand on one leg? And life has become inwardly poorer....

This metaphor of describing ages is not just a metaphor. It certainly has significance and meaning. It shows that man has become less and less alive, less and less connected with the totality, less and less joyful. Sadness has gathered all around, and the night seems to be unending.

And because everybody is miserable, any new child, a newcomer into the world, thinks such is life, accepts it. Everybody is miserable, everybody is in turmoil, everybody is in anxiety, so perhaps this is the way life is...unless you come across a buddha, and that has become more and more rare, more and more difficult.

When you see a buddha, the first unconscious reaction is to reject him because he offends you. His very presence is a challenge – "Why is he so happy and peaceful, and why am I in such an anguish? He should live according to everybody else, according to the crowd. Why is he living as an individual in his own right? He should be a sheep, he should not be a shepherd." They cannot tolerate it. Their own best and the highest peaks of consciousness which can make them aware of their potentialities, they destroy.

Yes, they can worship...

Before dying, Buddha said to his disciples, "Don't make my statues. If you want to remember me by something, just remember me by this tree. Plant this tree, this bodhi tree, wherever you want a memorial for me."

For three hundred years, rather than planting trees – this is the unconsciousness of man – people made temples, and made marble trees inside the temple. And finally after five hundred years, they thought, "What is the meaning of a marble tree? Why not make a Buddha?"

And at that time there was neither a photograph nor a painting of Gautam Buddha. Just by chance, Alexander the Great had come to India, and he had a beautiful Greek face. What you see as Buddha's face is really the face of Alexander the Great. Buddha is modeled on him. And it is a well-known fact – because there was nothing else to do, a beautiful face… Buddha died at the age of eighty-four; Alexander the Great was only thirty years of age. That's why all the statues of Buddha look like a thirty-year-old man, they don't show an old man of eighty-four years old, tired.

Now there are more statues of Gautam Buddha than anybody else. In Arabic, even the word 'buddha' has become synonymous with statue. It has taken a little different form; the statue is called the *budt*. But it is really the name of Buddha, because only his statues were all around the world. They have been discovered far away in Mongolia, in China, in the Caucasus, in Afghanistan. In fact, his statue became one of the most loved objects for any great sculptor. If you could make a great statue of Buddha, that showed that you were really a creative artist.

Miles of caves have been carved, turned into statues of Buddha. And the same man, while alive, we tried to kill many times. It was just an accident that we did not succeed – just as America has failed in killing me.

Two days ago a sannyasin informed me that a man has been jailed in America for one and a half years. And the charge was that he had advertised in 1984, while I was there, that he was willing to kill anybody if half a million dollars were made available to him. From this advertisement he was caught. And the sannyasin went to the jail to ask the man, "Did you receive any answer to your advertisement?"

He said, "I did, I received it from a government agency. But I am a professional killer, and I know how governments work. They will promise you half a million dollars – and they gave me the whole plan…"

We had a small lake near the entrance of the commune, Krishnamurti Lake. They had given him a plan, knowing that I always went for a drive past Krishnamurti Lake…and that is a silent place; the commune is left behind, and for twenty miles there is nobody.

"So you plant a bomb there which functions from remote control. And you hide – we will tell you where. We will take you there by helicopter so nobody can trace it. And after the car and the person in it have exploded, we will take you away in the helicopter."

But a professional killer knows perfectly well.... He simply refused. He knows that governments do this business, but they never give the money. On the contrary, you perform, and then they give you a shot, so that all evidence is removed. Instead of half a million dollars, you receive death as a reward. That is a well-known fact all around the world.

Government agencies go on killing people, and they always kill the killer. In that way money is saved, and also the evidence is removed. Knowing this, he refused. But because he had advertised, the court sent him to jail although he had not committed anything.

This new evidence shows the interest of the American government in killing me. This sannyasin is trying to find more and more sources. He wants to write a whole book about the conspiracy to murder me.

If this is the way you behave with people who are peaceful and silent and aware, and who are really indicators of your own potential, then certainly there will be less and less buddhas in the world. Or even if there are buddhas, they will remain silent. To declare is to create antagonism. There are still a few enlightened people around the world, but they don't want to be unnecessarily in trouble. I have loved trouble from my very childhood. So when it came to enlightenment, I said, "Let it be the last trouble." I am enjoying it every inch.... But it shows you how the unconscious mind has been preventing people from becoming enlightened.

I have not committed any sin, and I have been punished, dragged from jail to jail. It became known later on that the United States Attorney had asked the National Guard to arrest me. But they said, "Without any evidence, without any order from the court, we cannot do it." The U.S. Attorney General, Ed Meese, who has been accused of many crimes and has had to retire in disgrace, had even asked the commander-in-chief of the army.... And the commander-in-chief laughed. He said, "Never in history has an army been sent against a single individual. And not only that, but you don't have any evidence; otherwise why don't you ask a court first to give an arrest warrant?" They had nothing to persuade a court to arrest me.

And when I was arrested, I was arrested by twelve people with loaded guns, and I asked, "Where is the arrest warrant?" They had no arrest warrant. They had only a piece of paper on which a few names were written. I told them, "These are not the names of the people you are arresting. You can see our passports." Six sannyasins were with me – they are here – not a single name was on that paper. Still they would not listen.

And I wondered that America is thought to be a democracy, and here people are being arrested without any arrest warrant from any court, without any reason or rhyme.

And I wondered at my own attorneys, because when they started asking for bail in the court... One of my attorneys was a sannyasin. I told him, "You are starting from the wrong point. First you should ask on what grounds we have been arrested: 'You don't have any arrest warrant, and the paper you have does not have any of the names of the people you are arresting. The question of bail does not arise.'"

But the sannyasin was a young attorney, and he had called the best attorneys he knew. This is how bureaucracy works. He told me, "We will do everything. You simply be silent, because any word from you may cause trouble. Right now they don't have any evidence against you."

I still think it was wrong of my attorneys to start by asking for bail. The first question should have been, "Why have these people been arrested?" The people who arrested me should have been punished. The question about bail should not have arisen. But they started from a wrong question, and discussed bail. The six sannyasins were bailed out – everyone except me.

Even the attorney for the government said after three days of stupid talking – there was nothing in their hands, but finally he said, "I accept that I have not been able to prove any crime."

But the magistrate said – a woman magistrate... For the first time I had a thought that perhaps a woman in power may prove more dangerous than a man. That woman magistrate said, "You have not proved anything, but still I refuse to give him bail. The reason? The reason is that he is an influential man, he has thousands of followers. The maximum bail is only half a million dollars. He can jump bail; there are inexhaustible sources behind him." Not because of any crime, but because of the possibility of my jumping bail, she refused.

But the real reason was to drag me through six jails. A journey of six hours was done in twelve days. Only now do we know from poison experts that they were poisoning me in small doses; that's why it took them twelve days. If that amount of poison is given in one big dose, the person will die immediately. And they were worried that they would be condemned by the people of America, so they did not want me to die in the jail. Slowly giving me poison over a long stretch of twelve days would not kill me inside the prison, but it would have destructive effects for my whole life.

And later on they admitted, "We were not at all interested in making him a martyr, otherwise he would have been another Jesus. Then a Christianity would have followed, and we would have been condemned all around the world."

You misbehave with the enlightened people. Never, not in a single case, have you behaved with love and respect. How can you expect many more people to be enlightened? The whole atmosphere is against enlightenment.

Our effort here is to create buddhas – not one or two but millions, so that they cannot be destroyed so easily. We want to create a wildfire of awareness surrounding the whole earth. Never before has such a great experiment been done. Only individuals have become enlightened, have been tortured by the masses.

I want the world to know that this is not a place where we are going to be satisfied with one enlightened master. Thousands of sannyasins have to become buddhas.

They can prevent me from entering all those twenty-one countries, but they cannot prevent my sannyasins from reaching here. I don't have to go there to "corrupt their morality," I will send my ambassadors, my messengers. My sannyasins can do it, I don't have to do it. Even my sannyasins can destroy their so-called religions; they don't have any depth.

The second question:

Listening to You, I understand that all those beautiful Zen masters just help us open up for the bliss and ordinariness around the corner.

It's easy here, where miracles happen before breakfast and then never stop, but how to make it work the same way in everyday life and in society?

If it has really happened to you, the question will not arise. If you have imagined it, only then will the question arise.

Here, it is easy to imagine before breakfast that you are enlightened. Here, there are so many enlightened people, so it is very easy. Nobody is against enlightenment, everybody is supportive; it is easy to imagine.

The test, the fire test, will be out there in the society. If your enlightenment disappears, it has never happened. If it has happened, no society, no culture can destroy it. It is such a force, such an eternal life, nobody can even touch it, so don't be worried about society. Just let your enlightenment be a reality, not an imagination.

Once it is a reality you are no more, only enlightenment is – a flame, a fire which cannot be put out, put off. You can be killed, but your enlightenment cannot be killed. You can be crucified and poisoned, but your enlightenment remains a witness even on the cross.

And when there are thousands of enlightened people, the society will not have the courage. Where are you going to have so many crosses? If enlightenment becomes a great phenomenon around the earth, then no enlightened man or master is in danger. He can have his life unhindered, unhampered, uncrippled by the society.

The society could manage to kill Socrates, because Socrates was alone.

The society could crucify Jesus because he was alone.

I am not teaching any cult here, any creed. I want you to taste the very life source. Then nobody can take it away.

The third question:

**The other night You pierced the onion to the core;
then new protective layers sprang up.
It seems one step forward is followed by two steps backwards;
a moment's light makes the ensuing darkness deepen.
Is this part of the process?**

It is natural. You have remained with layers of personality and individuality for so long that when you drop one layer, you start feeling tense and worried – "What is going to happen?" You feel as if you are standing naked, and somebody has taken away your clothes. You immediately run and find some other clothes, some other layer of personality to cover yourself. You have always remained hidden. It is just an old habit; it will disappear.

Many times you will put the personality back, but soon you will start seeing that this personality cannot be your very existence, because sometimes you can put it off and sometimes you can put it on. It is something separate from you. And as this experience of separation deepens, you will not put any layers upon your hidden splendor.

It is not part of the process, it is part of your habitual conditioning.

It reminds me of Little Albert who reached school late as always. But today he had a perfect excuse; he said to the teacher, "It is raining, and it was very difficult. I took one step forward and I slipped two steps backwards."

The teacher said, "Okay, but then how did you manage to reach here?"

He said, "I simply started going towards home – one step forward, two step backwards... Finally, I managed to get here, but that's why I am late."

Don't find excuses; it is not part of the process. That will be an excuse, and you will feel consoled; it is just your old habit, old addiction. It takes a little time, but once you have tasted a little bit of Zen, the process has started transforming you.

It may take a little time, but certainly and surely it is going to destroy all your layers and reveal to you the reality where *you* are not, but the whole existence is. Only in the whole can you rejoice.

Separation is a false idea; you are not separate. And this separation creates all kinds of anxiety, tension, but you go on protecting yourself. But how long are you going to do it?

I always hope, even against hope, that one day you will get tired and you will drop this old garbage, and the fresh flame of joy, of bliss, of benediction will arise in you. It is already there, just the old garbage prevents you from seeing it.

The sutra:

BELOVED OSHO,
A monk asked Chōro, who had been a disciple of Tanka, "The buddhas of the past, present and future turn the great wheel of dharma in flames of fire – is it correct or not?"
Chōro said, laughing, "I have doubts, after all."
The monk asked, "Why do you doubt?"
Chōro said, "The fragrance of wildflowers fills the pathways, but the hidden birds don't know it is spring. Is there anyone who is not defiled by mystic wonder?" After a long silence, Chōro concluded, "This one spot could not be washed away even if you dumped the waters of the oceans on it."

It is a very beautiful sutra. It shows how humanity goes on missing: it turns symbols into facts, and then it lives in those fictions which have been only symbols. For example, this sutra is said repeatedly by Gautam Buddha: "The awakened one moves the wheel of dharma in flames of fire."

But Chōro is right when he says laughing, "I have doubts about it." This man is taking the metaphor as if it were factual – there is no wheel, and there is no fire.

On the contrary, *Chōro said, "The fragrance of wildflowers fills the pathways, but the hidden birds don't know it is spring."*

For a buddha it is always spring.

For a buddha even fire becomes cool.

For a buddha even the darkness of the night is a light, because he himself is light; wherever he moves his light surrounds him.

Chōro is right when he says, "I have doubts about it – this statement of moving the wheel of dharma in flames of fire." Buddha has used that symbol, but his context has to be remembered.

Just a few minutes ago, I was telling you about the difficulty of enlightenment in a world which is absolutely unconscious. This is the fire. And to move the wheel of birth and death... That is the whole work of the awakened master – to make you aware that you have never been born, and to make you aware that you will never die.

Birth and death are only episodes in an eternal existence.

This wheel of birth and death – you have to jump out of it. And certainly, because of the unconsciousness of the people, you will have to face fire. But it is only symbolic.

Inside, you will find the fragrance of wildflowers.

Inside, you will find for the first time, the eternal juices of life.

Inside, you will find that the spring has come, and a spring that is not going away; it is your very nature.

These roses will go on growing in you. This fragrance will go on becoming more and more deep, more and more mysterious.

Chōro is right. He is trying to help the monk not to get caught into a metaphor. The metaphor has its own context and its own meaning. But out of context, one can become worried: if enlightenment is moving a wheel in the flames of fire, then why unnecessarily get into such trouble? What is the point of moving the wheel of life and death? And in fire?

Life is already too much misery. If you take this symbol without understanding its context, it will look like enlightenment is inviting more misery. That's why Chōro laughed and he said, "I have doubts."

He is not saying he has doubts about Buddha, he is saying, "I have doubts about your understanding."

As far as Chōro is concerned, *"The fragrance of wildflowers fills the pathways, but the hidden birds don't know it is spring."* Only the awakened bird knows that the spring has come – the moment to dance, the moment to rejoice, the moment to experience the eternity of being. Chōro has made a very significant statement. *"Is there anyone who is not defiled by mystic wonder?"* Only the dead are not defiled by mystic wonder. The more alive you are, the more you see wonders everywhere, all around you. The whole of life is such a mystery and such a blessing. The path is full of roses and no thorns.

After a long silence, Chōro concluded, "This one spot..."

He means by "this one spot," the wonder, the experience of the mysterious.

"This one spot could not be washed away even if you dumped the waters of the oceans on it."

The man of Zen is a man who lives in mysteries. To him everything is mysterious. Nothing is to be taken for granted, everything is a miracle.

Life is a miracle, the songs of the birds are miracles, the flowers with so many colors... This whole existence, if your inner being is awake, becomes an unending series of mysteries.

Kyorai wrote:

In the thin light after sunset,
he climbs to the temple
at the summit.

In the East, two times have been thought to be mysterious, and when you are closer to the mystery of existence than any other time. In the early morning when the sun has not risen and the last star has disappeared – that light is cool because the sun is not present and the night is gone. That small interval is called in India, *sandhya*. It exactly means interval. In that space, meditation is easier.

And the same happens again at sunset. When the sun is setting and the night has not come yet, that interval again is a good moment to meditate. You will be surprised to know that because of these sandhyas, intervals, in India, prayer has been given the name *sandhya*.

My own feeling is that when the night is gone, your life is refreshed. When the sun has not risen, existence is more relaxed around you, the affairs of the day have not started yet. Sitting silently in this interval, you can enter into yourself more easily than at any other time. Hence, morning and evening have become traditionally times for prayer.

Kyorai wrote:

In the thin light after sunset,
he climbs to the temple
at the summit.

In the thin light when the sun is no more, his awareness reaches to the highest summit of the temple.

But that does not mean that you cannot meditate at any other time. It is just in India that these two moments have been thought to be very available – existence is closer to you, just a little look inwards...

But there are other mystics, for example, the Sufis, who have found the middle of the night to be the most vulnerable point to enter into the mysterious. They are also right.

In the middle of the night when everybody is asleep, when even trees are asleep and birds are asleep, and the whole world is silent, you can wake up and just sit in that silence. You will find it easier to enter into yourself.

But if you know the method of how to enter into yourself, you can enter at any moment. Even in the marketplace, doing your ordinary work, you can remain meditative. There is no need to choose particular moments. This moment is as capable of revealing the reality to you as any other moment.

Maneesha's question:

BELOVED OSHO,

In her book, 'The World of Zen,' Nancy Wilson Ross says of Zen – in particular, when working on a koan – "Again and again it is emphasized that one cannot take hold of the truth merely by abandoning the false."

Isn't truth what is left when the false is recognized for what it is? Or is there more to it?

Maneesha, Nancy Wilson Ross in her book, *The World of Zen,* has come very close to the understanding of something which is beyond the mind. But whatever she is saying is only one side of the coin. About koans she is saying, "Again and again it is emphasized that one cannot take hold of the truth merely by abandoning the false."

The problem for any intellectual is that he cannot see beyond logic. The emphasis that she is reporting is there: one cannot attain to truth just by abandoning the false. In fact, in your very abandoning it you have accepted its reality. The false has not to be abandoned; the false has just to be seen that it is false, and it disappears.

Can you abandon your shadow? Run as fast as you can, and the shadow will run faster and faster with you. You don't have to run away from the shadow, you just have to see that it is a shadow, there is no need to run away. All those who have been renouncing the world are running away from shadows, and shadows always follow you. Shadows cannot be abandoned, they can only be recognized as shadows, and what remains is the truth.

So one cannot hold the truth merely by abandoning the false. Perhaps Nancy Ross does not know any actual experience, otherwise, she would have said that the moment you abandon anything false you are giving recognition to it. Every renouncement is a recognition, is giving reality to the false.

You don't have to run away from the false.

You have just to see the false and the false falls away, and what remains is the truth.

So as far as abandoning is concerned, Nancy Ross's statement is right – you cannot abandon the false. But she does not understand why the Zen masters go on saying it. They want you to understand the false as false, not to abandon it. Just the recognition of something as false, and you are free of it. You never had it, you were just imagining it.

That's why all kinds of therapies work – even homeopathy. It has been surveyed and found that it works in almost seventy percent of cases. Only in thirty percent of cases does it fail. The reason is that seventy percent of your sickness is just false; it does not need any real medicine, it needs only sugar pills. Homeopathy works, naturopathy works, ayurveda works...any kind of thing on those cases which are false. Your so-called miracle people are working only on the false. They can remove the false, because in the very first place it was not there.

I used to have a friend, a doctor of homeopathy, and he always discussed things with me. He was a homeopathy freak. But the poor fellow one day had to enter an allopathic hospital.

I went to see him. I said, "What happened? What happened to homeopathy?"

He said, "Now I understand. You are right. If a real disease is there, homeopathy cannot work. Now I am suffering from tuberculosis, and I know those sugar pills are just sugar pills."

But there are millions of people who are helped, so there is no harm. All kinds of "pathies" should be allowed, because there are all kinds of imaginary sicknesses. Then any kind of healing will help; just the touching by a man of miracles will help.

Jesus managed miracles, but he could not do anything when he was crucified. He was supposedly the very son of God, and even God could not do anything. And he had been making dead people come to life... but I think the whole thing was a drama. Lazarus must not have died; it must have been a strategy. He must have been lying down in the cave pretending to be dead, and Jesus called to him, "Lazarus!" – and he immediately came out of the cave. But it happened only once, he could not manage...

If a man can call the dead back to life, he should not be so miserly. And Lazarus was an old friend, so it looks like a well-managed miracle.

Christians go on saying that he touched the eyes of blind people and they started seeing immediately. Either these miracles are simply invented by the disciples...because the Bible was compiled three hundred years after, so there was not a single witness.

You will be surprised to know that the Roman emperor, Constantine, called a council after the crucifixion of Jesus – three hundred years after – and in the council, by voting, it was decided that he was divine. By voting...! After three hundred years, and under the compulsion of Constantine! He was the president of the council, and he wanted to declare himself a prophet. And he did both – he declared, "Jesus is a prophet, but he is a failure; I am a prophet who is a success." And the council accepted it.

Rome became the capital of Christianity under Constantine. But they had to accept Constantine – at least for a few days while he was alive – as the real prophet. Later on, they forgot about him, but he is the man who compiled...there were many gospels. He chose a few and rejected others. There is no reason why he chose a few and rejected others, and there is every possibility that all the miracles were invented under Constantine to create the great figure of Jesus Christ.

If he was able to cure sicknesses, and to bring dead people to life, then you cannot blame the masses who were asking him continuously, shouting, when he was on the cross, "Now do some miracle!" He used to say, "God will come immediately to save me." But nobody came – nobody is there. He looked up in the sky – not even an angel, not even a single white cloud, the sky remained empty. And in deep frustration he shouted, "Father, have you forsaken me?" But he had never adopted him in the first place. It was just a bogus, hocus-pocus, holy ghost.

The false has to be known only as false. You don't have to abandon it. Your abandoning shows that you have not understood its falseness. The very understanding of the false is the emergence of the truth.

Nancy Wilson Ross is one of those intellectuals who has been trying to introduce Zen to the West. But it is not their experience. They are not themselves buddhas; they are just reporters. Hence, whatever they report – it may come very close to truth, but it cannot be the truth. Some mistake somewhere is bound to happen, because it is not their own experience.

Maneesha, there is only the false to see, and the truth reveals itself; there is nothing more. You live in unconsciousness, then the false appears as if it were true. When you wake up, the false disappears just like any dream.

Now it is time for Sardar Gurudayal Singh.

One evening, Basil and Babina Butt are making love in their bedroom when the door opens, and in walks their six-year-old son, Billy.

Basil freezes in midair in his missionary position. He turns and sees little Billy dressed up in full cowboy gear – hat, boots with spurs, six-shooter pistol, a big whip, and everything.

"What is going on, Billy?" grunts Basil Butt. "What are you doing here dressed like that?"

"Hey, Dad," shouts Billy, excitedly, "can I ride on your back like a bucking bull, while you screw Mom?"

Basil is shocked, but is beyond the point of no return, so he asks Babina. "Yes! Yes!" gasps Babina. "Quick! Climb on, Billy! And Basil, let's get going!"

So the love making increases in intensity, and little Billy is getting bounced around like a bullrider at a Wild West show.

"Yaa-Hoo!" shouts Billy, digging his spurs into his dad's ass. "Ride 'em, cowboy!"

All this drives Basil into a mad, passionate frenzy, and Bambina starts moaning and making all kinds of animal noises.

Billy is whipping his dad, urging him on, until the bucking gets so wild, that Billy throws down his whip, and hangs onto his father's hair for dear life.

At this point, Billy leans down close to his father's ear, and whispers, "Hold on tight, Dad! This is where me and the postman usually get thrown off!"

Big Black Leroy and Big Black Rufus are fighting over Mabel, the beautiful black girl who is new in town. Mabel gets tired of the two guys arguing all the time, so she decides to settle things.

"Listen, you guys!" she snaps. "You two can have a swimming race across the river, and whoever wins can be my man!"

Rufus and Leroy agree to the competition. So they walk across the bridge to the far bank, strip off all their clothes and plunge into the river.

They are swimming as fast as they can towards her, when Mabel decides that she really prefers Leroy and tries to encourage him a little. So she pulls up the edge of her skirt in Leroy's direction.

Leroy slows down.

The next time Leroy looks up, Mabel pulls her skirt up to her waist and exposes her bare contraption.

Immediately, Leroy stops dead in the middle of the river.

"Leroy, sugar!" cries Mabel. "What is the matter?"

"Dammit, Mabel!" shouts Leroy. "Pull your skirt down! My rudder is stuck in the mud!"

At the Humpty Dumpty Elementary School, one afternoon, Miss Tickletit, the teacher, gives the children their final assignment for the day.

"Now, boys and girls," she says sweetly, "I want you to open your notebooks, pick up your pencils, and write a beautiful story beginning with the words: If I had five million dollars..."

All the little kids begin writing feverishly, except for Little Albert who continues to do what he has been doing all afternoon – looking out of the window watching the little girls doing gymnastics.

Miss Tickletit sees Albert, and calls out, "Albert! Everybody else is writing, why don't you do your work?"

"Ah!" replies Albert, lighting up a cigarette. "*Work?* With five million dollars?"

Nivedano…

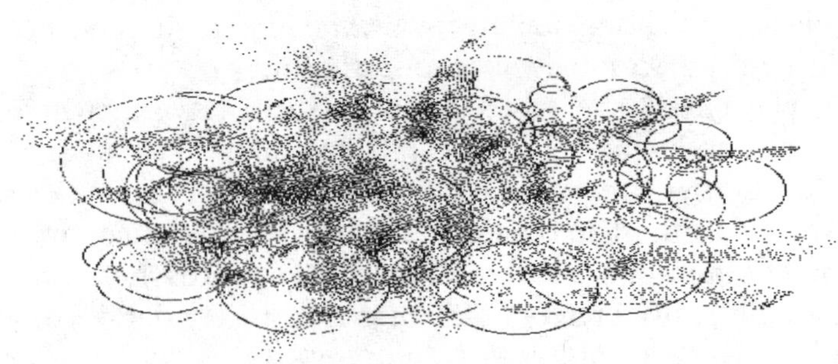

Nivedano…

Be silent…

Close your eyes…and feel your body to be completely frozen.

This is the right moment to enter inwards.

Gather all your energies, your total consciousness, and rush towards the center of your being, which is exactly two inches below the navel inside the body.

Faster and faster, with an urgency as if this is going to be your last moment.

Deeper and deeper.

As you come close to the center of your being, a great silence descends over you, and flowers of peace blossom within your being.

At the very center there is a flame, the fire of your life. It is part of the whole existence.

Symbolically, this flame is called the enlightened consciousness, the buddha; it is your intrinsic nature. You are no more, there is only a pure consciousness, unbounded.

This is a great opportunity to witness.

Witness that you are not the body.

Witness that you are not the mind.

Witness that you are only witnessing, only pure consciousness.

Relax into it....

Nivedano...

Drop all your separations. You are one with the whole.

This is the most blissful experience, the greatest ecstasy possible. You are a buddha in this moment.

If you can remain aware and relaxed around the clock, you will know the beauty and the grace of every moment, of every inch of life.

What is possible in this moment is possible in every moment. This is simply to show your potential. You have to bring all this silence and peace and this awareness to your day-to-day life.

Collect all these experiences: the silence, the bliss, the ecstasy, the divine drunkenness, and persuade the buddha to follow you. He has to come and become your very being.

He has been hiding inside you because you never went in, you never requested him. Make the request, persuade him.

These are the three steps: first, you persuade the inner light, the buddha, to come behind you; the second step, you become a shadow behind the buddha; and the third step, your shadow, recognized as shadow, disappears, and only the presence of the buddha remains.

That is your truth, and that is everybody else's truth. That is the truth of the whole existence.

Existential truth is the Manifesto of Zen.

Now, come back.

Nivedano...

Come back, but remembering, watching, silent, graceful.

Sit for a few moments just to remember where you have been, the golden path that you have gone through, the center and the silence of the center, the center and your disappearance in it.

Your witnessing has to become slowly slowly, your very life.

I don't teach any morality. To me, awareness is the only morality, the only ethics, the only religion, because out of awareness you cannot do anything wrong. It is always your unconscious mind which forces you to do wrong things.

As awareness grows, slowly slowly, your whole being becomes luminous, there is no dark spot inside you.

That day you have become a buddha.

That day is the most blessed day of your life.

Okay, Maneesha?

Yes, Osho.

THE LESS YOU ARE, THE MORE YOU ARE

BELOVED OSHO,

Shōhei – Suibi's disciple – asked Suibi, "What is the meaning of Bodhidharma's coming from the West?"
Suibi said, "I'll tell you later when nobody is around."
Sometime later, Shōhei said, "Now, there is nobody. Please master, tell me the answer."
Suibi, getting down from the Zen stool, took Shōhei to the bamboo garden. Again, Shōhei asked, "Now, there is nobody. Please master, tell me the answer."
Suibi, pointing to the bamboos, said, "This bamboo is that long, that bamboo is that short."

FRIENDS,

First the questions from the sannyasins.

The first question:

The other day You spoke about Fritjof Capra. Can You speak about the movement of transpersonal psychology, and in particular about the work and meditation of Ken Wilbur, who is said to be the founder of the spectrum psychology? Why don't such people come here? Are they imprisoned in being too established? Is Your vision and its practical consequences the problem for them?

The first thing to be understood is that I am not dealing with psychology. Psychology remains attached to the mind; it is the science of the mind. And my whole work is how to take you out of the mind, so these people will take me as if I am their enemy.

They are working out how the mind functions, whether it is personal or interpersonal, what are its conditionings and how those conditionings can be changed with new conditionings. Their whole work – whether they call it interpersonal psychology or spectrum psychology – remains confined to the mind. And my world, the world of Zen, is the world of no-mind.

We simply don't want to bother about all the rubbish that mind is carrying from centuries. If you get involved in it, you can go on digging and digging, and you will find more bullshit coming out. It is better just to take a jump out of it; it is not you. It is the whole conditioning of mankind, from generation to generation. Every mind concept has traveled to you, and it is becoming thicker and thicker every day. As time passes, you have a thicker mind, and meditation becomes more difficult.

These people are not concerned with meditation at all, hence there is no question of their being here. Secondly, they think they have found the answer. Obviously, a person who thinks he has found the answer will not go seeking the truth anywhere, but will remain confined in his own imagination.

Mind cannot be anything more than images, thoughts, sentiments, moods. Mind is not your nature, but an imposition by the society on your purity.

These people will feel at a loss here, because whatever they have been doing we are throwing out – and they have been collecting. They will get great stuff if they come – just to collect. Every evening so much rubbish is thrown. They can collect and enjoy analyzing it.

Not a single person exists in the world who is completely psychoanalyzed. Such is the depth of all past orientations. Ten years, fifteen years, people have been in psychoanalysis, and they go on talking; new dreams start coming, new thoughts start coming; they go on and they go on... When they get fed up with the psychoanalyst, they change the psychoanalyst and go on repeating the same story in another name.

But even a psychoanalyst is not aware that there is much more to your reality than your small mind.

Science remains confined to matter.

Psychology remains confined to the mind.

Meditation is an effort to penetrate beyond matter physiology, beyond mind psychology, and to find the original source of life and consciousness.

The work here is totally different, not only different, but makes all their efforts – the so-called psychologists of different schools – meaningless. It is an exercise in futility.

The second question:

In his book, 'Tao Yoga,' Mantak Chia describes the center of life energy as being just two inches inside the navel.
Is this a contradiction to Zen, which says it is two inches below the navel?
Or do they both mean the same?

It cannot be discussed and concluded; in fact, those two inches are only the average.

When you breathe deeply you touch the center, and you can find whether it is two inches behind or two inches below.

The person who has written *Tao Yoga*, Mantak Chia, does not seem to be an experienced person.

When I say two inches below the navel, I am trying to take your consciousness as deep as it can go. Those two inches are not something fundamental. *Your* center may be only one and a half inches below the navel. Just as everybody's nose differs...there is no way of concluding which nose is the fundamental nose.

Don't get into intellectual discussion. The navel you have, the consciousness you have...the path is clear, it is not far away. Just a little silence, peace and witnessing, and you will know where it is; it is bound to be different in every person.

It is possible Mantak Chia found it two inches behind the navel, but my experience is, it is two inches below the navel. And it is better to accept the idea of two inches below, because if it is two inches behind that will come in the way. It is always better to keep the goal a little farther away. If it is two inches behind, you will pass it. And everybody is going to find it a little different. Just as individualities differ, your physical organs differ.

There is no scientific way of saying where the source is. The only way is to find it. It is somewhere near your navel. Perhaps somebody may find it just behind the navel. But according to me and my experience of people, it is not behind, it is below – two inches. Only then can it manage your sexual energy, otherwise it will be too far away; there will be no connection between your sexual machinery and your life energy.

Your life energy has to reach from the sex center to the seventh center in the head, the whole golden path. So it is better, hypothetically, to make an effort of going two inches below. If you go three inches below, good – better.

Somebody may find that Mantak Chia's idea is right; it may be applicable to him. But talking in terms of the average, two inches below the navel is the right source. You will find it somewhere close by – an inch before or an inch after; don't be bothered about inches. Remember, your navel is the point, and around it somewhere is the source of your life energy, because when you were born you were connected through your navel with your mother. Your mother's life energy was moving through the navel into you; there was no other connection.

So one thing is certain, that your navel for nine months has been the connection with existence, with your mother. Everything you were getting was through the navel. But it cannot be on the surface of the navel, it can only be deep inside. Everything that is so precious, like life, has to be in a very subtle way hiding.

You can make a two-inch-wide circle around your navel. Behind, below, somewhere, you will find it – don't get fixed about inches. And you don't have any measurement inside. You cannot take your measuring tape – "How many inches deep, or back, is your life source?" It is just a hypothesis to help you to enter in. You will find it. Go as deep as possible. Don't stop if you see a little path where it is still possible to go more.

Experience is the question; don't be mathematical.

I am reminded by your question of a great mathematician, Herodotus....

He was the first man to find the principle of averages. It was a great discovery at that time, and he was so overwhelmed by it, that one day when he had gone for a picnic with his wife and seven kids – they came across a small river...

The wife was a little worried, but Herodotus said, "Wait. I will take the average depth and the average size of our kids. It will take only five minutes." He took out his measuring tape, found out the average height of the children, and ran around into that small river. At a few points he measured it and told his wife, "Don't be worried. The average depth of the water cannot drown the average height of our kids. You come on!"

But somewhere the water was deeper and somewhere it was shallow, and some child was smaller and some child was bigger... The average does not work in actual situations; it is good for mathematical calculations.

The wife was still worried, so she kept herself behind. And when she saw one child drowning, she called to Herodotus who was going ahead, "Look! I was concerned from the very beginning. I don't understand your mathematics!"

And can you believe it? Herodotus did not go to save the child, the wife had to run...! He ran back to the bank, where on the sand he had made all the calculations, to find out whether the calculation was wrong. The calculation was perfectly right, but existence does not follow your calculations.

So when I say two inches, it is only an average hypothesis. And I want it to be below the navel, because if it is behind, it will come in the way. Or if it is not behind, you will never reach to the point. So I don't want to take any risk. You may get stuck two inches behind the navel, and just two inches below will be your center. You would have missed the ultimate experience by just two inches!

There is no need to be worried about how many inches. You just gather your energy and go to the very deepest that you can. Don't leave any stone unturned.

The third question:

Is the drive towards creativity only another expression of our inability to sit quietly and do nothing?

You will have to understand two kinds of creativity. One is exactly what you are saying – it is an escape from the uneasiness of not doing anything and just sitting silently. The whole world is workaholic, and the whole world goes on driving everybody nuts: "Do this! Do that! Don't waste time!" So your whole mind is programmed for work, for efficiency. Naturally you cannot sit down silently, you have to do something. It can take the form of some kind of creation: music, poetry, sculpture, but this is not true creativity.

The true creativity comes out of sitting silently. When you are so totally quiet that there is no thought, no wave in the ocean of your being, out of this silence comes a different kind of creativity.

The first I can only call composition. The second is authentic creativity. They look alike, and sometimes the composer may even do better than the man of creativity. But the composer will never be original, he will always be copying. Only the creator can be original, can break new doors into the mystery of existence.

George Gurdjieff has gone deeply into this matter, and he has called the first, subjective creativity; it is mind oriented. And the other he has called the real objective creativity. Whatever names are given, that is not the question, but he knows the difference – that the people who created the Taj Mahal were not simply architects, they were not simply technologically knowledgeable.

The emperor who made the Taj Mahal called Sufis from all over the world – not the architects, but the Sufi mystics – to give the idea of the Taj Mahal. It was created in order to become an object of meditation. If you sit silently by the Taj Mahal in a fullmoon night, you start becoming silent. The very form of the Taj Mahal creates a certain quality in you, just as has been found about pyramids – that the very shape of the pyramid is life preserving. It detracts everything life negative.

When, in the very beginning of this century, the first pyramid was opened, they found a dead cat inside. They could not believe it. The pyramid was three thousand years old, so the cat must have died three thousand years ago. Just by accident she may have entered when they were closing it, and could not get out. But the body of the cat was absolutely fresh, as if it had just died. No stink...in three thousand years.

Then the scientists started looking at the shape of the pyramids – there must be something in the very shape of the pyramids. And now they have made pyramids for meditators, small aluminium pyramids. You sit inside and you suddenly find you are more alive, you suddenly find more silence.

We are going to create new campuses around in the pyramid shape for meditators. Even people who live inside a pyramid find it very rejuvenating. The scientists could not believe it; they themselves found that they were more alive inside the pyramid than they were outside. Something happens; just the shape of the pyramid is the thing.

Those pyramids were created by Egyptian mystics from very ancient scriptures from the continent, Atlantis, that drowned either by natural catastrophe or by man's stupidity. But in Alexandria in Egypt, they had saved everything worthwhile from the lost continents of Lemuria and Atlantis. The library of Alexandria was so big – perhaps the biggest library in the world. The Mohammedan, Khalif Omar, burned it down.

You can see the stupid logic. With the holy Koran in one hand, and a burning torch in the other, Khalif Omar entered the library and asked the chief librarian, "You have to answer a question, because the very existence of your library depends on it. Is there anything more in your library than is in the Koran?"

The librarian saw the strategy. If he said there was more, then certainly it had to be destroyed, because nothing more is needed than the Koran; it is enough. If he said...and that's what he said, being a very intelligent person, knowing perfectly well there was so much more in the library than the Koran. He said, "Whatever is contained in the Koran in a condensed form is available in the library. It is the same."

Although he tried by his answer to save the library, he did not know the fanatic mind.

Omar said, "If it is the same, then it is not needed, the Koran is enough. Why bother with so many books?" Omar burned it, and that library was so vast that it took six months for the fire to destroy it.

It had all the maps of the pyramids, and the reasoning why that particular shape is rejuvenating.

Pyramids can be called authentic creativity, but our so-called painters and our so-called musicians have no understanding of meditation. So it is just being busy without business, just doing something because the society does not accept you sitting silently.

From my very childhood, my uncles, my relatives had been telling me, "You will end up in nothing, because you simply sit and do nothing."

I said, "That's exactly what I am searching for – to be nothing."

They shrugged their shoulders; they could not understand – what kind of a man is this who does not take an insult? In their minds to be nothing is humiliation; one has to be *something!* And I said to them, "You cannot humiliate me. To be something is humiliating. When one can be nothing, so vast, so infinite, why should one be something? Something is a limitation."

So if your creativity comes out of your silence, out of your Zen, out of your meditations, then it is authentic, original. If it comes only as an occupation because you are feeling lost and there is nothing to do – a long holiday, so you start doing something.... That is not coming out of your silences, it is coming out of your crazy mind.

It happened once...

A painting of Picasso was sold for one million dollars. The woman who purchased it wanted the critics to inquire whether it was authentic, original, or a copy.

One critic said, "It is certainly original because I was present." He was a friend of Picasso; he said, "I was present when he was painting this painting, so you can take it for granted, without any doubt, that is the original."

But the woman was not satisfied. She went to Picasso himself, and she told him, "It does not matter to me, I have purchased it. I simply want to know whether it is original."

Picasso looked at the painting, and he made a strange statement. The critic was present, and the woman who had been living with Picasso was present, and Picasso said, "This is not original."

And the woman said, "You have painted it in front of my eyes, and this critic was present also. How can you say such a thing – that this is not original?"

He said, "It is true that I have painted it, but it is not original. I have already painted the same painting before. Finding nothing to do, I repeatedly painted the same painting; that is in the museum in Paris. You can go and see; this is just a copy. It does not matter who makes the copy. I have made the copy; that does not make it original. A copy is a copy whoever makes it. It has come out of my inability to sit silent; it is only a copy. But the first one is original. It came out of the silences of my being; I had no idea what I was doing. When I was painting this painting, I knew everything that I was doing. This is a mind product; the first one has arisen from beyond the mind."

Anything that arises from your silences has a beauty, a truthfulness, an authenticity. And that which arises out of the mind is only a carbon copy. Howsoever beautiful it may appear to the ignorant, it cannot be called a creative phenomenon.

If you have been to Agra to see the Taj Mahal, you will find that on the other side of the Yamuna there are the foundations of another Taj Mahal – just the foundations. The same emperor who allowed the Sufi mystics to design the Taj Mahal thought, "It is too costly to bring all these mystics from Persia and Arabia. And now that we have the model..."

It took thirty years for one thousand artists to make the Taj Mahal. He released them, and he told the architects that were available in New Delhi, "Now that the Taj Mahal is ready, you can build the same on the other side of the bank."

This Taj Mahal was going to be his wife's samadhi. It is from his wife's name that it became Taj Mahal; her name was Mumtaz Mahal. The other he was creating for himself. And the architect said, "There is no problem. We can build exactly the same thing on the other side." And they suggested, "If one is made in white marble it will be a good contrast to make the other in black marble."

They could not complete it because the emperor was imprisoned by his son, and the son was not interested at all. So it has remained only a foundation. But even if it had been completed, it would not have been a creative act, it would have been only technologically copied from the original.

And the mistake is immediately seen – they did not think of the whiteness and the communion with the full moon. Black marble does not have that beauty in the full moon. It cannot create a luminosity within you, it cannot wake you up. So even if they had completed it, it would not have been authentic and original.

If you don't have to do anything, that is the greatest moment just to be. Don't do anything. Be silent. Do only when things are necessary to be done. So much nonsense will be cut out and you will have much more energy to explore the inner.

The sutra:

BELOVED OSHO,
Shōhei – Suibi's disciple – asked Suibi, "What is the meaning of Bodhidharma's coming from the West?"

It is a traditional question. Everybody knows the answer, but it has been asked to every master, and always a different answer has been given. The question has remained the same, but because the master is different, the disciple is different and the times have changed, no master ever repeats any other master's answer.

Everybody knows that Bodhidharma came to China to convey the message of Gautam Buddha. But this answer will not be given by any Zen master. This will be too superficial, too informative, too knowledgeable, but not existential.

What is the meaning of Bodhidharma's coming?

Suibi said, "I'll tell you later when nobody is around."

Now Suibi is a very subtle master. He has already answered without answering it. He is saying, "I will tell you when nobody is around." That includes the questioner, that includes Suibi himself. "When nobody is around, I will answer it." That nobodiness is the meaning of Gautam Buddha's essential teaching.

But Suibi did not manage to satisfy Shōhei. Shōhei could not get to the point where Suibi was pointing – "I will tell you later when nobody is around." He misunderstood it, just as you would have misunderstood him.

Sometime later, Shōhei said, "Now, there is nobody. Please master, tell me the answer."
Suibi, getting down from the Zen stool, took Shōhei to the bamboo garden. Again, Shōhei asked, "Now, there is nobody. Please master, tell me the answer."

His silence is every time giving him the answer: "You don't understand. When you say nobody is there, you are there, I am there. When the questioner is not there, and the answerer is not there, you will get the meaning of why Bodhidharma came from India to China."

Shōhei goes on insisting. So finally, inside the bamboos, *Suibi, pointing to the bamboos, said, "This bamboo is that long, that bamboo is that short."*

You will not see any logical connection. There is no logical connection, but there is something more fundamentally connected. What he is saying is, "Bodhidharma came to teach suchness. This bamboo is long, so what? This bamboo is short, but there is no problem. I have never heard these bamboos discussing, 'Why are you long and why am I short?' Neither does the short one feel inferior, nor the long one feel superior. They are both enjoying existence in their totality.

"So just be, without comparing. Settle down in your own consciousness, and you will know the answer, the answer that cannot be given from outside."

Issa wrote:

Around the hearth –
the smile that bids us welcome
is also a farewell!

He is saying, the beginning is also the end, the meeting is also a departing. One has to understand this contradictoriness, this paradoxical nature of existence. The welcoming smile is also a farewell.

In a very small haiku he has expressed the very essence of noncomparative, non-relative existentialness, in which all contradictions dissolve, in which all paradoxes meet; where night is not against the day, and death is not against life; where nobody is superior and nobody is inferior; where the beggar and the emperor are the same.

This sameness, this suchness is the Manifesto of Zen: a declaration of the beauty of your individuality, and at the same time a declaration of dispersing that individuality into the universal.

The less you are, the more you are.

If you are nothing at all, then you are everything.

This is the Manifesto of Zen.

Maneesha's question:

BELOVED OSHO,

Erich Fromm has written in an essay entitled, 'Psychoanalysis and Zen Buddhism': "I have proposed that if one carries Freud's principle of the transformation of unconsciousness into consciousness to its ultimate consequences, one approaches the concept of enlightenment."
Would You comment?

Maneesha, in the first place psychoanalysis has nothing to do with Zen, and in the second place, Zen has nothing to do with Buddhism. It has something to do with Buddha, but not with Buddhism, not with the doctrine that has arisen around Buddha's words, the philosophy, the religion, the cult.

Erich Fromm, himself, being a man of psychoanalysis, looks at Zen from a particular point of view, and that is the wrong way of looking at Zen. Zen has to be entered directly, not as a Mohammedan, and not as a Hindu, and not as a psychoanalyst, and not as a communist. If you already have a framework, a pattern, then you will impose that pattern on Zen. And Zen is so innocent, just like a small child.

You can make that small child a Hindu, you can make that small child a Mohammedan, or a Christian, or a Buddhist, or whatever you want. It is a question of writing on an empty paper. The child is utterly empty, available for you to write whatever you want to write upon it. And people never look at their own conditioning....

Erich Fromm is conditioned as a psychoanalyst; hence, it seems to him to be very right that "if one carries Freud's principle of the transformation of unconsciousness into consciousness to its ultimate consequences, one approaches the concept of enlightenment."

Enlightenment is not a concept, it is an experience. And even Sigmund Freud is not enlightened. You will be surprised to know that he was not even psychoanalyzed. His disciples insisted again and again, "Why don't *you* go through psychoanalysis? Now we are ready, we can be the psychoanalysts and you be the patient" – and he always refused.

What was the fear? The same fears that are hidden in everybody – one is hiding one's wounds, one's inferiority, one's fears.

Sigmund Freud was very much afraid of death, so much so that even the mention of the word 'death' was enough to give him a fit. He would fall down from the chair, and would start foaming from the mouth. Now this man and enlightenment are as totally different as possible.

He expelled one of his most deserving disciples, Carl Gustav Jung, who was supposed to succeed him. But because Jung mentioned death three times, and caused a shaking fit for poor Sigmund Freud, Freud expelled him.

But you should not think that Carl Gustav Jung was not afraid of death. He wanted to go to Egypt. At least six times he booked his tickets and canceled them. Six times he even reached the airport and then freaked out. What was the fear? The fear was of seeing the dead bodies, the mummies of the old kings and queens. He was interested in seeing them, but was also afraid that it would give him the idea: "You are not immortal, you are also going to die. Great emperors could not save themselves." So the fear…

Psychoanalysis is a very ordinary thing, and it is very helpful to people who are going a little abnormal. Ordinarily everybody is normally crazy, but normally crazy, within boundaries. Everybody knows what his weak points are. He hides, but sometimes in some stress situation a person starts behaving beyond the normal boundaries. Psychoanalysis is helpful for bringing the fellow back to the prison – he was getting out of it.

But it is not that psychoanalysis taken to its ultimate consequences will be the same as enlightenment. Enlightenment is an effort to take you beyond the mind, and psychoanalysis is an effort to keep you within the mind. Their very processes are opposite. Erich Fromm is absolutely wrong.

It is time for Sardar Gurudayal Singh. Put on the light!

One afternoon down in Podunk, Alabama, at the Abe Lincoln Elementary School, Miss Velcro, the black teacher, is giving an English lesson.

"Now, class," says Miss Velcro, "today we are going to write some poetry. And for our theme, we are going to go back to our black roots in Africa. I want you to write a poem using that famous African town, Timbuktu."

For the next ten minutes, everybody writes. And at the end of the class, Miss Velcro says, "Okay, children, before we go home, would anyone like to read out their poem to the class?"

Two boys, Little Black George and Little Black Washington, raise their hands enthusiastically.

"Good," says Miss Velcro. "George, you read yours first."

George stands up and says proudly:

"Far away in a distant land,
Out across the burning sand,
Black men on camels march two by two,
On their way to Timbuktu!"

The classroom cheers loudly, and then Miss Velcro says, "That was very good, George. Now let us hear your poem, Washington."

Little Washington jumps up, clears his throat, and says:

"Me and my older brother Tim,
A-hunting we did go.
We came upon three pretty girls,
A-sleeping in a row.
Since they was three and we was two,
I bucked one – and Timbuktu!"

Maureen O'Murphy receives this letter from her son Patrick, at college in Dublin:

Dear Mother,

Send me fifty pounds immediately.

Your loving son, Patrick

P.S. I am so ashamed to have written you this letter asking for money, that I sent my friend Michael, to get it back, but the postman had already collected it. I can only hope that this letter gets lost in the post!

His mother replies:

Dear Son,

Don't worry, the letter was lost in the post.

Your loving mother, Maureen

P.S. I would have enclosed fifty pounds, but the postman has already collected the letter.

The Muggins family are gathered around the dinner table one evening, when young Melvin Muggins gets up to make an announcement.

"I would like to take this opportunity," begins Melvin, "to tell you all that I am going to marry Hilda Haggard, the girl across the street."

"What?" cries his father, Mr. Muggins. "Her family did not leave her any money!"

"That's right!" snaps Mrs. Muggins. "And she has not saved a penny!"

"She does not know anything about football!" shouts Little Monty Muggins.

"She is weird!" cries Little Mildred Muggins. "I have never seen anyone with such frizzy hair!"

"That's right!" shouts Uncle Mitch. "And all she ever does is sit around all day reading trashy novels!"

"And look at her clothes!" cries Aunty Mabel. "I have never seen such terrible taste!"

"That's nothing!" screeches Grandma Muggins. "You should see the makeup she paints all over her face!"

"That's all true," replies Melvin calmly, "but she has one big advantage over all of us."

"Really?" everyone cries. "What is that?"

"Well," explains Melvin, "she has no family."

Nivedano...

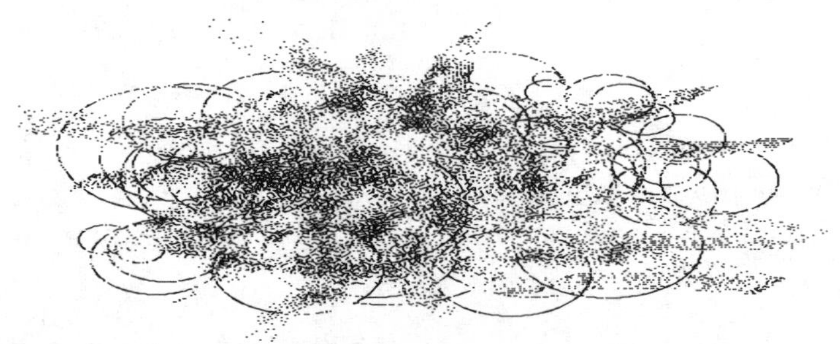

Nivedano...

Be silent...

Close your eyes...and feel your bodies to be completely frozen.

This is the right moment to enter in.

With a deep urgency, gather all your energies and consciousness, and rush towards your inner center of being which is just two inches below the navel, inside you.

Faster and faster...

Deeper and deeper...

As you are coming closer to the center, a great silence descends over you, a peace that passeth understanding.

And inside, at the center, you encounter your very self, your very buddha, for the first time. It is only a presence, a light, a flame. This flame is rooted in the eternal fire of existence.

You have been here always, and you will be here always. Only forms change, but the existential truth remains without any change. It is your ultimate being. In this ultimateness you are no more there, but the whole is. The dewdrop has disappeared in the ocean, or the ocean has disappeared in the dewdrop. This is one of the greatest moments to become a witness.

Witness that you are not the body...

Witness that you are not the mind...

Witness that you are only a pure witnessing consciousness....

The deeper this consciousness goes, the closer you are coming to your ultimate nature, the buddha.

Relax into witnessing.

Nivedano...

Just a silent witnessing, and all boundaries disappear. And suddenly, Gautama the Buddha Auditorium becomes an ocean of consciousness. Ten thousand buddhas are no longer there, only a single pure fire of awareness. This is your very nature.

Zen is not a religion, it is a manifesto of your very nature.

It is a freedom from all social structures.

It is a freedom even from yourself.

It is pure freedom.

In this freedom, all that is creative arises.

All that is beautiful blossoms...all that is significant.

A grace that you have never been aware of surrounds you.

An aura of light follows you.

Collect all these experiences before Nivedano calls you back.

You are not to become anyone, you have just to dissolve into the totality of existence. In this annihilation, you reach to the highest peak of consciousness. In that peak there is light and there is joy, and there is song and there is dance – but there is no "I" at all.

Persuade the buddha, the flame, to come behind you. It has been hiding inside your being since eternity. You have never explored the inner space, otherwise there is no need of any religion, and no need of any temple.

This very body becomes the temple.

And this very consciousness becomes the buddha.

These are the three small steps....

First, request the buddha, the internal and the eternal flame to follow you, to become part of your ordinary day-to-day life.

In the second step, you start becoming a shadow to the buddha. He takes you over; you start disappearing.

In the third step, even your shadow is no longer there, only a pure presence of the buddha.

This is not an achievement, *you are already it* – you have forgotten the language.

The Zen Manifesto is simply to remind you.

The last words of Gautam Buddha were: *sammasati* – "remember."

In a single word, everything significant is contained: *sammasati*.

Nivedano...

Come back, but come back as buddhas – peaceful, silent, relaxed.

Just for a few seconds sit down with closed eyes to remember, to make a note of where you have been, to what depth you have been able to reach; what is the taste of silence, peace, what is the taste of disappearing into the ultimate...

The last words of Gautam Buddha contain the Zen Manifesto: *sammasati*. Remember what is your inner space. Just remember.

There is nothing to achieve, and there is nothing to become. You are already that which you have been seeking in all your lives in different ways, on different paths. But you have never looked inwards.

Look in. And whenever you have time, you know the path. Just go again and again to the inner space so that your fear of disappearing is dropped, you start enjoying being nobody, and you start remembering the forgotten language.

Sammasati...

Okay, Maneesha?

Yes, Osho.

佛

SAMMASATI – THE LAST WORD

BELOVED OSHO,

Tōzan had a question about whether inanimate objects expound the dharma. Tōzan visited Isan, who recommended that he go to see Ungan.
With Ungan, Tōzan was first made aware of the truth, and he composed the following gatha *to record his experience:*
"How wonderful! How wonderful!
The inanimate expounding the Dharma –
What an ineffable truth!
If you try to hear it with your ears,
You will never understand it.
Only when you hear it through the eye,
Will you really know it."

Ungan asked him, "Are you happy now?"
Tōzan answered, "I do not say that I am not *happy, but my happiness is like that of someone who has picked up a bright pearl from a heap of garbage."*
For a while after his enlightenment, Tōzan continued to travel

around China. One day he arrived at Leh T'an and met the head monk, Ch'u. Ch'u greeted Tōzan and said:
"Wonderful, wonderful –
The inconceivable realms of Tao and Buddha!"

Tōzan responded, "I don't know about these realms.
Who is talking of them?"
Ch'u remained silent, and Tōzan shouted, "Speak!"
Ch'u then said, "No need to fight about it. That is the way to miss."
Tōzan replied, "If it has not been mentioned,
how can there be fighting and missing?"
Ch'u could make no answer to this.
Tōzan then said, "Buddha and Tao – next you will talk of sutras."
Ch'u replied, "What do the sutras say about this?"
Tōzan responded, "When all is understood, words are forgotten."
Ch'u said, "This is sickness of the mind."
Tōzan said, "Is this sickness slight or severe?"
Ch'u could make no reply to Tōzan.

FRIENDS,

Before the sutras there are a few questions from the sannyasins.

The first question:

Gerta Ital, a former famous German actress, was the first Western woman who was allowed to enter in a Zen monastery in Japan and to work with an enlightened master. She wrote two books about her path and her experience of enlightenment. When I read these books I had the impression of a very hard and lonely path. Being with You is much more joyful and playful. Would You like to say something about this difference?

The traditional Zen is hard. It takes twenty to thirty years of constant meditation, withdrawing from everywhere all your energy and devoting it only to meditation.

That tradition comes from Gautam Buddha himself. He had to find his enlightenment after twelve years of hard work.

I am changing it completely from the traditional Zen, because I don't see that the contemporary man can devote twenty or thirty years to meditation only. If Zen remains that hard, it will disappear from the world. It has already disappeared from China, it is disappearing from Japan, and it disappeared from India long ago. It remained in India for only five hundred years after Gautam Buddha. In the sixth century it reached China, remained there for only a few centuries, and moved to Japan. And now it is almost extinct from both China and Japan.

You will be surprised to know that my books are being taught in the Zen monasteries. Zen masters have written letters to me: "Perhaps now Zen will exist in India, in its original place. It is disappearing from Japan because people are more interested in technology, in science."

That is the situation in India too. Very few people are interested in the inner exploration. Here you can find a few people from every country, but these are so few compared to the five billion human beings on the earth. Ten thousand is not a great number.

Zen has to be transformed in a way that the contemporary man can be interested in it. It has to be easy, relaxed, it has not to be hard. That old traditional type is no longer possible, nor is it needed. Once it has been explored, once a single man has become enlightened, the path becomes easy. You don't have to discover electricity again and again. Once discovered you start using it – you don't have to be great scientists.

The man who discovered electricity worked on it for almost twenty years. Three hundred disciples started with him and nobody remained because it took so long; everybody became exhausted. But the original scientist continued. His explanation to his own disciples was, "The more we are failing in finding the root of electricity, the closer we are going to the very root. Every failure is bringing us closer to the discovery."

And finally, one night in the darkness, suddenly the first electric bulb started radiating. And you cannot conceive the joy of the man who had been working for thirty years. His silence…he was in awe. He could not believe his own eyes that after all this time it had happened, electricity had been controlled – "Now in our hands, how to use it?"

His wife called to him, "Come inside the bedroom, it is the middle of the night. Put the light out!"

She was not aware that it was no ordinary light, and that the scientist had called her – "Come here and be the first to see something original. You will be the first person I will introduce to the secrets of electricity."

Now, you don't have to work for thirty years to know about electricity. Nor do you have to work thirty years for the Zen experience.

The awakening of the buddha is a very easy and relaxed phenomenon. Now that so many people have awakened, the path has become clear-cut; it is no longer hard and arduous. You can playfully enter inside and joyously experience the awakening of awareness. It is not as far away as it was for Gautam Buddha.

For Gautam Buddha it was an absolute unknown. He was searching for it like a blind man, knowing nothing about where he was going. But he was a man of tremendous courage, who for twelve years went on searching, exploring every method available in his time…all the teachers who were talking about philosophy and yoga. He went from one teacher to another, and every teacher finally said to him, "I can tell you only this much. More than this I don't know myself."

Finally, he remained alone, and he dropped all yoga disciplines. He had his own five disciples, who thought that he was a great ascetic. But when they saw that he had dropped all yoga discipline, and he was no longer fasting, they dropped him. All those five disciples left him – "He has fallen from his greatness; he is no longer a saint; he has become ordinary."

But in that ordinariness, when he had dropped everything – just being tired and exhausted – that fullmoon night when the five disciples left him, he slept under the bodhi tree, completely free from this world and completely free from the very search for that world. For the first time he was utterly relaxed: no desire to find anything, no desire to become anything. And in that moment of non-desiring, he suddenly awakened and became a buddha. Buddhahood came to him in a relaxed state.

You don't have to work for twelve years, you can just start from the relaxed state. It was the last point in Gautam Buddha's journey. It can be the first point in your journey.

And the first thing Gautam Buddha did after he became awakened was to go in search of those five disciples to share what had happened to him. And when he reached those five disciples…they saw him coming – it is a very beautiful story.

They decided, "Gautama is coming, but we are not going to pay any respect to him. He has stopped being a holy man; he has started living a relaxed and comfortable life."

But as Buddha came closer, all the five disciples stood up. Although they had decided not to pay him any respect, in spite of their decision, they could see that Gautama had changed completely – "He is no more the same person we used to know. He is coming with such a silence, with such contentment. It seems he has found it." And they all touched Gautam Buddha's feet.

And Gautam Buddha's first statement to them was, "When you had decided not to pay attention to me, why are you paying such respect?"

All those five asked to be forgiven. They said, "We were thinking you were the same old Gautama. We used to know you – for five years we have been together, but you are not the same person anymore."

Enlightenment is such a transformation that you are a totally different person. The old person dies away, and a totally new awareness, a fresh bliss, a flowering, a spring which has never been there…

It took twelve years for Gautam Buddha. It need not take even twelve minutes for you. It is simply an art, to relax into yourself. In the traditional Zen they are still doing whatever Buddha did in his ignorance, and finally they drop it.

I am telling you, why not drop it right now?

You can relax this very moment!

And in that relaxation you will find the light, the awareness, the awakening.

What has happened to Gerta Ital, is not necessarily an introduction to Zen. She has been in the company of old and traditional Zen masters. I understand Zen to be a very simple, innocent, joyful method. There is nothing ascetic in it, nothing life-negative – no need to renounce the world, no need to become a monk, no need to enter a monastery. You have to enter into yourself. That can be done anywhere.

We are doing it in the simplest way possible. And only if Zen becomes as simple as I am trying to make it, can the contemporary man be interested in it. Otherwise he has so much to do – so many things to do, so many paths to explore, so many things to distract him.

Zen has to become such a small playful thing, that while you are going to sleep – just before that – within five minutes you can enter into yourself, and you can remain at the very center of your being the whole night. Your whole night can become a peaceful, silent awareness. Sleep will be in the body, but underneath it there will be a current of light from the evening till the morning.

And once you know that even in sleep a certain awareness can be present inside you, then the whole day, doing all kinds of things, you can remain alert, conscious. Buddhahood has to be a very normal, ordinary, simple and human affair.

The second question:

I cannot put it into words how much I am always touched by the beauty of Your expressions – in Your words, Your gestures and now especially in Your paintings.
What exactly happens, when You are sitting in front of an empty paper?
Is there still an urge for artistic creativity

**when one is enlightened?
Could You please tell us about Zen and art and creativity?**

Zen prevents you from nothing. It opens everything that is potential in you. If you have a potentiality of being a painter, Zen will open it – you may not have been aware of it. If there is a potentiality for poetry, Zen will open that potentiality, and for the first time you will start thinking in poetry, not in prose.

The same is true about music or dance, or scientific exploration. Any kind of original experiences, Zen allows you. It is not preventive of anything. It is affirmative, the most affirmative experience in life. It simply makes you aware of all that is hidden in you, of all that you have never looked at. It not only makes you aware, it helps you to explore that potentiality.

Zen is not a dry, desertlike experience, it is very juicy, a beautiful garden – a spring in your life where flowers suddenly start opening up. One never knows what is going to happen to him when he becomes aware. It is not a decision on your part, it is not a choice. It is a choiceless, simple experience – you start moving into a certain direction. Suddenly that direction becomes so full of life, so attractive that you can devote everything to it.

Zen is a very creative experience; it is not like other religions. All the religions are non-creative. In fact, the so-called saints don't do anything. They are not great poets, they are not great dancers, they are not great musicians. But the real and authentic saints, who are very few among the so-called saints...

Just the other day I received the information that this pope in his four years of office has made more than two thousand people saints. It is a certificate. He goes on giving certificates to all kinds of people who can donate money. Now the Catholic church owns the biggest bank in the world – the Bank of America. The Catholic church owns the greatest amount of land in the world – more than any other country.

The method in the past has been war, killing people. Thousands of people have been killed just to take possession of their properties, or they have been forced to become Catholics. A single Catholic emperor, Constantine, killed ten thousand people in a single day. He just called an assembly of all those who were not Catholics in a great auditorium in Rome, and ordered the army to shoot everybody: "We don't want anybody other than Christians in Rome." He forced the whole of Italy to become Christian…just at the point of the gun.

The whole history of Christianity is of wars and nothing else – killing and violence. And the same is true about the other religions in a lesser measure; they are destructive. They are destructive in many ways. They destroy people by creating guilt, by making them sinners, by forcing them to renounce the world and all that is pleasant, and to go into hardships unnecessarily. But those who go into hardships are respected and their hardship has nothing to contribute to the world, only sickness, only guilt. All your saints are together enforcing guilt in you.

So in this way they destroy humanity, and in other ways they kill people because they don't belong to their fold. They force people – either by the sword, or with bread. In the past they used to come with a sword, now they come with bread. The poor have been always vulnerable to being converted, either by force or by bribery. But this is not religiousness at all, this is pure politics.

Zen is an authentic religious experience. Its authenticity is in its opening of creativeness in human beings. Zen masters have never killed anyone. They have not forced anyone to their path; on the contrary, you have to go to them. And it has been very difficult to be accepted; the masters have been very choosy. Unless you show an immense desire and longing, they will not initiate you; the question of conversion does not arise.

You have to go to the well, the well does not come to you. The well does not even invite you, it is simply there, available.

The third question:

When energy goes inward it turns into thoughts, feelings, emotions, and when energy goes outward it turns into relationships with beings and nature. But when energy does not move inward or outward, it is just there pulsating, vibrating. Then it is one with the existence, one with the whole. Is this Zazen?

Exactly. When the energy is just there – not going anywhere, just pulsating at the original source, just radiating its light there, blossoming like a lotus, neither going out nor going in – it is simply here and now.

When I say go inward, I am simply saying don't go on moving in the head.

The whole society forces your energy to move in the head. All education consists of the basic technique of how to pulsate the energy only in the head – how to make you a great mathematician, how to make you a great physician. All the education in the world consists of taking the energy into the head.

Zen asks you to come out of the head and go to the basic source – from where the educational system around the world has been taking the energy, putting it into the head, and turning it into thoughts, images, and creating thinking. It has its uses. It is not that Zen is not aware of the uses of energy in the head, but if all the energy is used in the head, you will never become aware of your eternity. You may become a very great thinker and philosopher, but you will never know, as an experience, what life is. You will never know as an experience, what it is to be one with the whole.

When the energy is just at the center, pulsating... When it is not moving anywhere, neither in the head nor in the heart, but it is at the very source from where the heart takes it, the head takes it...pulsating at the very source – that is the very meaning of Zazen.

Zazen means just sitting at the very source, not moving anywhere. A tremendous force arises, a transformation of energy into light and love, into greater life, into compassion, into creativity. It can take many forms, but first you have to learn how to be at the source. Then the source will decide where your potential is. You can relax at the source, and it will take you to your very potential. It does not mean that you have to stop thinking forever, it simply means you should be aware and alert and capable of moving into the source. When you need the head you can move the energy into the head, and when you need to love, you can move the energy into the heart.

But you need not think twenty-four hours. When you are not thinking you have to relax back into your center – that keeps the Zen man constantly content, alert, joyful. A blissfulness surrounds him; it is not an act, it is simply radiation.

Zazen is the strategy of Zen. Literally it means just sitting. Sitting where? Sitting at the very source. And once in a while, if you go on sitting in the source, you can manage all mental activities without any disturbance, you can manage all heart activities without any difficulty. And still, whenever you have time, you need not unnecessarily think, you need not unnecessarily feel, you can just be.

Just being is Zazen.

And if you can just be – only for a few minutes in twenty-four hours – that is enough to keep you alert of your buddhahood.

Before the sutras, a little biographical note.

Tōzan Ryōkai, a disciple of Ungan, was born in China in 807, and died in 869.
He originally was a member of the Vinaya sect, but later became interested in Zen and set out on a journey to find a master.

The Vinaya sect is the Buddhist name of the people who are interested in the scriptures, in the words of the masters in a philosophical and scholarly way. They are mentally active, but they are not moving into the experience themselves. They gather as much knowledge as possible, they become very wise. They know all the answers that are in the sutras, but they don't have a single experience of their own.

Tōzan was first a scholar, studying all the literature – and Buddhism has the greatest literature in the world. Compared to any other religion it has more scriptures.

Just as Gautam Buddha died, his disciples became separated into thirty-two branches. Immediately there were thirty-two branches of scholarship, of different scriptures and sutras, pretending to be authentic, pretending to be the only true ones. The problem was that for forty-two years Gautam Buddha was teaching, morning and evening – a few people heard a few things, a few people heard a few other things.

In forty-two years he was constantly moving from one place to another place. Obviously there were different people who had heard different things from him, and they compiled sutras. Immediately thirty-two branches started. Gautam Buddha had not written a single word, but every branch pretended to be the authentic one – "*This* is what Buddha said..."

It is very difficult now to find out what actually was said by Gautam Buddha, and what was added by the disciples. So there is a great scholarship in the Buddhist world where people search into scriptures trying to find what is authentic and what is not.

Just recently, the same kind of scholarship has started in Europe. The professors and the very scholarly Christians have formed a special committee, the Biblical Scholars. And they are now searching for what exactly was said by Jesus, and what has been added by others – what is fiction, what is myth, what is truth.

Just a few days ago, Pope the Polack declared to all the Catholics of the world: "Don't listen to the Biblical Scholars" – because the Biblical Scholars are taking out many things which have been added to the Bible which are not true. Events, miracles, the virgin birth, the resurrection... the Biblical Scholars are taking all those things out. It is agreed that they are the most scholarly group in Europe concerning the Bible.

They meet every few months, and they discuss papers. And if you listen to them, almost ninety percent of the Bible disappears. And they are absolutely right, because for the first time they are searching at the roots from where this saying, this statement, this gospel, has come. A few are found to be in the ancient scriptures of the pagans, and those scriptures have been destroyed so that nobody can prove that Jesus ever said these things.

Even the idea of the virgin birth is more ancient than Jesus. It was a pagan god, a Roman god who was thought to be born from a virgin, and to the same god, the crucifixion happened. And to the same god is connected the idea of the resurrection. All that has been taken and compiled into the Bible. The pagans have been destroyed, their temples have been burned, their scriptures have been destroyed. Now these Biblical Scholars are trying to find ways and methods to uncover the facts from contemporary literature about when Jesus was alive.

One of the gospels was written in India – the fifth gospel of Thomas. It has not been included in the Bible, for the simple reason that it was not available to Constantine, who was compiling, and who was deciding what was to be included and what was not to be included. It was because of him that all these ideas and mythologies and fictions have been added to the life of Jesus.

The same is true about Buddhist literature: much is borrowed from

Hindu literature; much is borrowed from Jaina literature, because these were contemporaries. And a few contemporaries of Buddha have left no literature behind, but they were also teaching in the places where Buddha was teaching, so many of their teachings have been compiled and mixed with Gautam Buddha's.

A very scholarly tradition exists in Zen to find out the original teachings of Buddha. But even if you can find what is the original statement and what is not, that does not mean you can become enlightened. You may know exactly what Buddha said, but that will not make any difference to your consciousness.

Tōzan was first a scholar, and found that however you go on trying to know and find the original sources, you still remain ignorant. You become a great knower, but deep down you know nothing about yourself. And the question is not to know what Buddha said, the question is to know your own inner buddha, your own inner consciousness.

After being in the scholarly Vinaya sect, he became interested in Zen. He dropped out of the scholarly world and set out on a journey to find a master. He had been with teachers, great scholars, but none of them was a master.

And a master need not be a scholar – it is not a necessity. He may be a scholar – that is accidental. What is necessary and existential is his own knowing, his own experience.

So he went in search of a man who himself knows what is the truth, and who can tell him the way to it.

The sutra:

BELOVED OSHO,

Tōzan had a question about whether inanimate objects expound the dharma. Tōzan visited Isan, who recommended that he go to see Ungan.

His inquiry was whether inanimate objects in the world expound the dharma, the ultimate truth – whether you can find in the objective world the ultimate truth.

That's what science is trying to do – trying to find the ultimate truth in objects. You cannot find it in objects. But this is part of the Zen tradition, that also…

Isan was himself a master, but he recommended Tōzan to go to see Ungan, seeing that Tōzan was a scholar. Isan was not a scholar – he was a master, he knew his own buddhahood. But seeing that this man Tōzan was bound to ask philosophical questions, he sent him to Ungan, who was a master and a scholar.

With Ungan, Tōzan was first made aware of the truth,
and he composed the following gatha *to record his experience:*
"How wonderful! How wonderful!
The inanimate expounding the Dharma –
What an ineffable truth!"

Ungan told him to be in silence. And as you become silent, everything around you starts expounding the truth: the trees and the mountains…all the objects become suddenly aflame, afire with truth. If you are sitting silently in your own source of being, then everything in the world indicates towards the ultimate.

When he found his source he wrote this gatha:

"How wonderful! How wonderful!
The inanimate expounding the Dharma –
What an ineffable truth!
If you try to hear it with your ears, you will never understand it.
Only when you hear it through the eye,
will you really know it."

He is talking about the third eye. As you go inwards…your energy is in the head. First it has to pass the third eye. Going deeper it will pass through the heart, the fourth center – and the whole energy is at the first center. From there it can rise back to the seventh center in the head.

But if you remain hung up in the seventh center only, you will never know *as an experience* what is truth. You have to come down to the depths, to the valleys of your being. You have to reach to the very roots from where you are joined with the whole.

Ungan asked him, "Are you happy now?"

Tōzan answered, "I do not say that I am not *happy,*
but my happiness is like that of someone who has picked up
a bright pearl from a heap of garbage."
For a while after his enlightenment,
Tōzan continued to travel around China.

He is saying that unless you see it yourself, there is no other way to know it. You cannot hear it from somebody else. No buddha can preach it to you, no master can teach it to you. They all can only make gestures. They all can only indicate their finger towards the moon, but the finger is not the moon. You have to drop looking at the finger, and to start looking at the moon. When you look at the moon yourself, you know the beauty of it. You cannot know that beauty by looking at the finger pointing to the moon.

All knowledge is pointing to the moon. All sutras, all scriptures are pointing to the moon – just fingers. And people are clinging to the fingers, they have completely forgotten that the fingers are not the point. The moon is far away, the finger is only pointing towards it. Don't cling to the finger; forget the finger. Forget all knowledge, all scriptures, and look at your truth yourself.

It is not a question of your ears, it is a question of your very eye, your inner eye. Unless you look inside...you cannot know it by hearing, or by reading. Becoming knowledgeable is not becoming a buddha, but becoming an innocent child, reaching to the sources playfully without any seriousness, joyously and cheerfully, dancing... Take your energy to the very source and remain there just for a few moments, and you will be filled with a new experience which goes on growing every day.

Soon you find you are filled with light – not only filled, but the light starts radiating around your body. That's what has been called the aura, and what Wilhelm Reich was trying scientifically to prove. But he was forced into an insane asylum because people could not understand what he was talking about – "What radiation is he talking about?"

But now, Kirlian photography is able to take the photograph of your life aura around your body. The healthier you are, the bigger is the aura. In your happiness it dances around you; in your misery it shrinks. When a miserable person was used as an object by Kirlian, he could not find any aura in the photograph – the aura had shrunk inside. But when he photographed children dancing and enjoying, joyfully plucking the wild-flowers or collecting stones on the seabeach, he found such a tremendous aura around them.

The same aura has been found around the buddhas. And it is almost miraculous that although no photography was available in the times of Buddha or Krishna, the paintings, the statues all have the aura – a round aura around the head.

Once you have seen your own life source, you start seeing the same light radiating from every object in the world, every person in the world. You can see from the aura whether the person is miserable or is happy.

His master, Ungan, asked him, *"Are you happy now?"*

Tōzan was a scholar, and he knew the way a buddha speaks. And now he himself has experienced it – you can see it in his answer. He says, "I do not say that I am *not* happy, but to say I am happy will make it a very ordinary statement. To say that I am happy is not something great, and what I have found is so great that it cannot be described by the word 'happiness', it is far more. So I will not say I am *not* happy. You have to understand, it is something more than happiness. Words cannot describe it. Only this much I can say: I have found a bright pearl in the heap of garbage."

What he is calling the "heap of garbage," is his scholarship. He has accumulated so much knowledge unnecessarily, and all that knowledge was only heaping up and hiding the original being – your very roots into existence.

It is not ordinary happiness, in fact there is no word that can describe it. 'Blissfulness' comes closer, even closer comes 'benediction', still closer comes 'ecstasy'. But beyond that, no word is there; the experience is far deeper than ecstasy itself.

For a while after his enlightenment, Tōzan continued to travel around China. One day he arrived at Leh T'an and met the head monk, Ch'u. Ch'u greeted Tōzan and said:
"Wonderful, wonderful –
The inconceivable realms of Tao and Buddha!"

Ch'u greeted Tōzan, and in his greeting he said, *"Wonderful, wonderful*

– *the inconceivable realms of Tao and Buddha!* I can see in you the very meeting of Buddha and Tao."

It is the same experience. *Tōzan responded, "I don't know about these realms* you are talking about. *Who is talking of them?"*

He is indicating to Ch'u that it is beyond words – "Look inside yourself. Who is saying these words? From where are these words coming? That source is beyond the words."

Ch'u remained silent, and Tōzan shouted, "Speak!"
Ch'u then said, "No need to fight about it. That is the way to miss."
Tōzan replied, "If it has not been mentioned,
how can there be fighting and missing?"
Ch'u could make no answer to this.
Tōzan then said, "Buddha and Tao – next you will talk of sutras."

"First you mention Buddha and Tao, and then you will start talking about sutras. Once you begin to talk, there is no end to talking, and the thing you are trying to talk about is beyond words."

Ch'u replied, "What do the sutras say about this?"
Tōzan responded, "When all is understood, words are forgotten."
Ch'u said, "This is sickness of the mind."
Tōzan said, "Is this sickness slight or severe?"
Ch'u could make no reply to Tōzan.

That was the reason Isan sent him to Ungan. He was a man of great scholarship, and once he has found his own buddha, he will become a very great master. Ordinary teachers will not even be able to understand him. Ch'u was an ordinary teacher of Tao and Buddhism both. And you can see that Tōzan denied even Buddha and Tao. Those words only indicate, they don't describe. And he said to Ch'u, "If you go on, soon you will start talking about sutras."

You can see his philosophical approach. Now that he has found the truth, it is very difficult for anybody who is just a scholar even to talk with him. He will be able to defeat any scholarly person very easily.

Seeing that Tōzan is saying that even Buddha and Tao are not exactly the experience, Ch'u, as a teacher, said, "What do the sutras say about this?" He is still talking about sutras – "What do the sutras say about this unknowable, this inexpressible? You are indicating that it is beyond Buddha and beyond Tao."

Tōzan said, "*When all is understood, words are forgotten*. Once you have known it, once you have tasted it, you become silent." Of course a teacher will not agree on this point.

Ch'u, in anger, *said, "This is sickness of the mind."*

Tōzan said, "Is this sickness slight or severe?"

What kind of sickness? It is not sickness, but a teacher is confined to the mind. You say anything beyond the mind and you are simply talking nonsense. You are sick, you are mad, you are insane. A teacher is confined to the mind, a master is beyond the mind.

Ch'u could make no reply to Tōzan's inquiry whether this sickness was slight or severe.

One day the monk Akinobō, went to visit a poet friend of his.
Chatting, he mentioned that he had made a collection of poems –
one for each day of the year. He read him one:
The fourth day
of the new year;
what better day
to leave the world?
That very day was the fourth day of the first month of the year 1718.
No sooner had he finished reciting the verse
than Akinobō nodded his head and died.

Zen masters know how to live and also know how to die. They take neither life seriously nor death seriously. Seriousness is a sick way of looking at existence. A man of perfection will love to live, and will love to die. His life will be a dance, and his death will be a song. There will be no distinction between life and death.

Maneesha's question:

BELOVED OSHO,

The philosopher Karl Jaspers, writes in Volume Three of his book, 'Philosophy': "To ask real questions about reality, man must have thought, investigated, and oriented himself by

distinctions... Real is what can be measured, what our senses can perceive in space and time according to rules, what can be controlled or calculated, at least, by appropriate measures." Would You like to comment?

Maneesha, Karl Jaspers is a great philosopher, but he is not a master. What he is saying is the definition of matter. Exactly the word 'matter' comes from the Sanskrit word *matra*. *Matra* means that which can be measured. Matter means that which can be measured. And that which cannot be measured is your reality.

Karl Jaspers is confusing reality with matter. Matter is real, but reality is far more than matter; it also includes consciousness, which is not measurable. You cannot measure it by any means. How many feet of consciousness do you have, or how many miles, or how many kilos...?

Matter is that which can be measured, and consciousness is that which cannot be measured. And Jaspers is confining himself to matter as the only reality. He is absolutely wrong. About matter he is right, but about reality he is wrong, because reality is much more than matter.

Even Karl Jaspers cannot say how many kilos of consciousness he has. There is no way of measuring consciousness. And certainly, even Karl Jaspers cannot deny that he has consciousness. *Who* is denying?

I am reminded of a small story about Mulla Nasruddin....

He was talking about his generosity to friends in a restaurant. The friends said, "You are simply *talking* about generosity, but we have never seen any generous act on your part. You have not even invited us for a cup of tea."

Mulla said, "Come on! You are all invited – the whole crowd in the restaurant. Come to my home for dinner."

They could not believe it! They knew that this was a very miserly man. He had been caught just because he was boasting about his generosity.

As they were approaching his home, Nasruddin became aware about his wife, and that he had brought a trouble to himself unnecessarily. Now how was he going to convince his wife? In the first place, he had gone in the morning to fetch some vegetables, and he had not returned till evening, and now he was coming with a crowd of people.

So he told the crowd, "You understand the problem between a husband and wife. You just remain outside for a few minutes. First let me go in to convince my wife that I have invited a few friends."

So he went in, closed the door, and told his wife that by mistake he had invited a crowd – "Now you have to be a help to me."

The wife said, "What can I do? There is nothing in the house – you have been away the whole day…not even vegetables."

Mulla Nasruddin said, "That is not the point. You simply go to the door and ask the people why they are crowding there. Obviously they will say that I have invited them for dinner. You simply deny it. Simply say, 'Mulla Nasruddin has not been home since morning.' You just go and tell them, 'Go away. He is not here.'"

The wife was puzzled, but something had to be done. She opened the door, and Mulla Nasruddin was watching what was happening from the second-story window. The wife said, "He is not in the house. For whom are you waiting?"

They said, "He came with us, and he went on in front of us. We are all witnesses. He has invited us for the dinner – perhaps you don't know, but he has gone inside the house."

The wife said, "He is not inside the house."

They said, "This is strange. We came with him. He has told us to wait here. You just go in and find out. He must be inside watching, or looking for you."

The wife would not let them in. The crowd tried to go in. The crowd said, "We are all friends of your husband. Let us look inside!"

Mulla, seeing the situation, shouted from the upper story, "This is absolute nonsense! When she is saying he is not in, *he is not in!* Don't you feel ashamed challenging a poor woman? He may have come with you, but he may have gone out again from the back door."

And he himself was talking….

Just ask Karl Jaspers, "Is your consciousness measurable?" If he denies that he has consciousness, then who is denying? Either he has to deny it or he has to accept it, but in every case even his denial will be a proof of consciousness.

This is a strange thing about not only Karl Jaspers, but about all the philosophers of the world. They go on saying that only matter exists, because matter can be experienced by eyes, by ears, by hands, by all your senses. It can be measured, hence, it is the only reality. But the truth is that even those who deny the existence of the immeasurable are accepting even in their denial, consciousness. Otherwise, who is denying?

It is very amazing that a great intellectual like Karl Jaspers, a very respectable philosopher of this century, talks like a stupid man. But all philosophers talk like stupid men. His saying that only that which can be measured is real, is absolutely wrong. That which can be measured is matter, and that which cannot be measured is also real, but it is consciousness.

Our search is for the immeasurable. The measurable can be left to the scientists. The mystics are concerned with the immeasurable.

Now, it is time for Sardar Gurudayal Singh....

Captain Codfish, the old pirate, is in the Stoned Seagull Pub one night, telling stories from his life at sea.

"I had a parrot once," declares Codfish, drinking his rum. "He was the most incredible bird! He could imitate anything – Charlie Chaplin, Jack the Ripper, Marilyn Monroe, Pope the Polack...even Nancy Reagan!"

"Wow!" says Igor, the barman. "Where is he? What happened to him?"

"Ah!" cries the old pirate. "Times got hard, and I got hungry – I ate him!"

"You ate your parrot?" cries Igor in disgust. "What did he taste like?"

"He tasted just like turkey," replies Codfish. "That parrot could imitate anything!"

Paddy has a late night at the pub, and when it closes, he staggers outside in a drunken stupor. He wanders around the streets trying to remember which way to go home, and finally gives up. Paddy sits down on the street and looks all around him until a taxi pulls up beside him.

"Ah!" groans Paddy, clambering into the back and lying down on the seat. "Can you take me to number five, Fergus Street?"

The cabdriver looks around at Paddy and replies, "Hey, mister, this *is* number five, Fergus Street!"

"Ah!" groans Paddy. "Alright! But next time, don't drive so fast!"

On a foggy morning in Vienna, Austria, the two famous psychoanalysts, Doctor Sigfried Mind, and Doctor Krazy Karl Kong, meet in the little Brown Danube Cafe.

Over a table set with coffee and cream cakes, Doctor Kong suddenly jumps up, grabs Sigfried by the neck, and shakes him.

"We *must* go this time!" shouts Karl. "We have tried six times already! We *must* go to the pyramids in Egypt to see the *mummies!*"

"*Mummies?*" screeches Sigfried, collapsing into the cream cakes in a dead faint.

Doctor Kong pours coffee on Doctor Mind's head until he recovers.

"Come on, Mind," cries Doctor Kong, slapping him across the face. "We can do it! We have to explore this mystery of death!"

"*Death?*" screeches Mind, and he faints again into the plate of cream cakes.

Half an hour later, at the Vienna airport, Doctor Krazy Karl Kong is dragging Doctor Sigfried Mind by the collar onto the plane bound for Cairo.

"Come on, Mind!" cries Krazy Kong, huffing and puffing. "We have made it this far, we have got to see those mummies!"

"*Mummies?*" screeches Sigfried, falling in a faint on top of Nellie Knickers, the stewardess.

Kong and Nellie drag Mind to his seat, and strap him down. The plane takes off, and three hours later, arrives in the Land of the Pyramids. Kong carries the babbling Doctor Mind to the herd of rented camels, which are waiting to take them to the pharoahs' tombs.

Doctor Kong shouts out to their guide, Abdul Babul, "Take us to the mummies!"

"*Mummies?*" screeches Mind, fainting and falling straight off his camel, nose first, into a sand dune.

Two days later, the famous psychoanalysts and their camels arrive at the huge pyramids. Doctor Kong jumps down, lights a torch, grabs Doctor Mind by the collar, and starts dragging him into the dark, mysterious crypts.

Suddenly, in the darkness, Doctor Kong trips over something.

"What is that?" screeches Mind.

"Ah! It is alright – it is only a dead cat!" exclaims Doctor Kong.

"*Death!*" screeches Mind. And he falls over in a cold faint.

"Pull yourself together, Doctor!" shouts Kong. "We are almost there!"

And Kong grabs Sigfried by the shoe, and drags him feet first towards a huge golden coffin. "Stand up!" cries Doctor Kong, propping Mind up against the wall, and handing him the burning torch.

Then Krazy Karl Kong bends over and lifts back the heavy, creaking coffin lid. The lid falls to the ground with a loud crash, and when the dust clears, Doctor Kong is left standing with his mouth wide open, gazing at the spooky sight before his eyes.

He turns and grabs the frozen Doctor Mind by the collar and pulls his face down into the coffin.

"There!" shouts Kong, in triumph. "This is a *mummy!*"

"*Mummy?*" screeches Sigfried. But he just stares in disbelief, with his eyes popping out.

"*Mummy?*" he screeches again. "Hey, this looks more like *Daddy!*"

It is time, Nivedano...

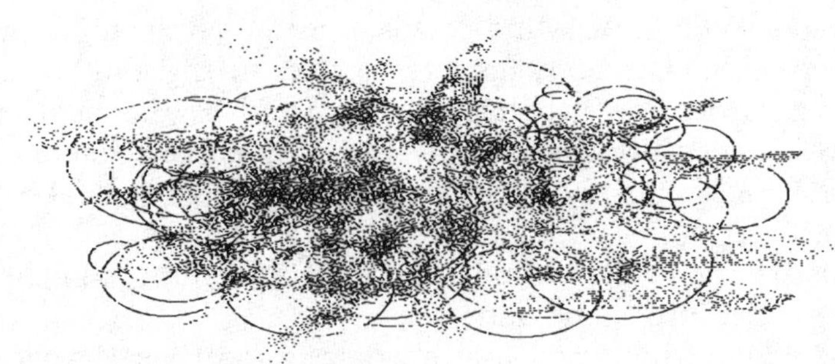

Nivedano...

Be silent... Close your eyes...and feel yourself completely frozen.
This is the right moment to enter inwards.
Gather all your energy, your total consciousness, and rush towards the inner center with deep intensity and urgency.
The center is just two inches below the navel, inside the body.
Faster...and faster... Deeper...and deeper...
As you come closer to the center of being, a great silence descends over you, and inside a peace, a blissfulness, a light that fills your whole interior. This is your original being. This is your buddha.
At this moment, witness that you are not the body, not the mind, not the heart, but just the pure witnessing self, the pure consciousness. This is your buddhahood, your hidden nature, your meeting with the universe. These are your roots.
Relax...

Nivedano...

Relax...and just be a silent witness.
You start melting like ice in the ocean. Gautama the Buddha Auditorium becomes an oceanic field of consciousness. You are no longer separate – this is your oneness with existence.
To be one with existence is to be a buddha, it is your very nature. It is not a question of searching and finding, *you are it*, right now.
Gather all the flowers, the fragrance, the flame and the fire, the immeasurable, and bring it with you as you come back.

Nivedano...

Come back peacefully, silently, as a buddha.

Just for a few seconds close your eyes and remember the path and the source you have found, and the buddha nature that you have experienced.

This moment you are the most blessed people on the earth. Remembering yourself as a buddha is the most precious experience, because it is your eternity, it is your immortality.

It is not you, it is your very existence. You are one with the stars and the trees and the sky and the ocean. You are no longer separate.

The last word of Buddha was, *sammasati*.

Remember that you are a buddha – *sammasati*.

Okay, Maneesha?

Yes, Osho.

About Osho

From his earliest childhood in India, Osho was a rebellious and independent spirit, challenging all accepted religious, social and political traditions and insisting on experiencing the truth for Himself rather than acquiring knowledge and beliefs given by others.

At the age of twenty-one, on March 21, 1953, Osho realized His enlightenment. He says about Himself, "I am no longer seeking, searching for anything. Existence has opened all its doors to me. I cannot even say that I belong to existence, because I am just a part of it.... When a flower blossoms, I blossom with it. When the sun rises, I rise with it. The ego in me, which keeps people separate, is no longer there. My body is part of nature, my being is part of the whole. I am not a separate entity."

He graduated from the University of Sagar with First Class Honors in philosophy. While a student He was All-India Debating Champion and the Gold Medal winner. After a nine-year stint as professor of philosophy at the University of Jabalpur, He left to travel around the country giving talks, challenging orthodox religious leaders in public debate, upsetting traditional beliefs, and shocking the status quo.

In the course of His work, Osho has spoken on virtually every aspect of the development of human consciousness. From Sigmund Freud to Chuang Tzu, from George Gurdjieff to Gautam Buddha, from Jesus Christ to Rabindranath Tagore...He has distilled from each the essence of all that is significant to the spiritual quest of contemporary man, based not on intellectual understanding but tested against His own existential experience.

He belongs to no tradition – "I am the beginning of a totally new religious consciousness," He says. "Please don't connect me with the past – it is not even worth remembering."

His talks to disciples and other seekers from all over the world have been published in more than six hundred and fifty volumes, and translated into over thirty languages. He says, "My message is not a doctrine, not a philosophy. My message is a certain alchemy, a science of transformation, so only those who are willing to die as they are and be born again into something so new that they cannot even imagine it right now – only those few courageous people will be ready to listen, because listening is going to be risky. Listening, you have taken the first step towards being reborn. So it is not a philosophy that you can just make an overcoat of and go bragging about. It is not a doctrine where you can find consolation for harassing questions.... No, my message is not some verbal communication. It is far more risky. It is nothing less than death and rebirth."

Osho left His body on January 19, 1990. Just a few weeks before, He was asked what would happen to His work when He was gone. He said: "My trust in existence is absolute. If there is any truth in what I am saying, it will survive.... The people who remain interested in my work will be simply carrying the torch, but not imposing anything on anyone....

"I will remain a source of inspiration to my people. And that's what most sannyasins will feel. I want them to grow on their own qualities like love, around which no church can be created; like awareness, which is nobody's monopoly; like celebration, rejoicing, and maintaining fresh, childlike eyes....

"I want people to know themselves, not to be according to someone else. And the way is in."

In accordance with His guidance, the commune which grew up around Him still thrives in Poona, India, where thousands of disciples and seekers gather throughout the year to participate in the unique meditations and other personal growth and creative programs offered there.

Books by Osho are available from all good bookshops. If you have difficulty obtaining the book you want, please write to either address listed in the back for your nearest bookshop or distributor.

For a complete catalog of Osho's books or to have your name added to our mailing list, just send us your name and address and you will receive information about forthcoming titles.

Suggested Further Reading

AND THE FLOWERS SHOWERED

TALKS ON ZEN

Commenting on 11 Zen anecdotes, Osho explores the spiritual search – speaking on emptiness and no-mind, knowledge and being; on belief and trust, repression and truth; on philosophy and religion, love and divinity; on death and disease, on happiness and living in the here-and-now.

AT THE FEET OF THE MASTER

This handsome volume of Osho's words, illustrated with black and white photos of Osho and sannyasins in the Commune, is a compilation from thirty published darshan diaries. Osho speaks directly to individuals, addressing issues concerned with their personal growth. What is a disciple? What is a master? What does it mean to take sannyas? These and innumerable other aspects of the search, as relevant today as ever, are covered.

FROM UNCONSCIOUSNESS TO CONSCIOUSNESS

4 VOLUMES

Osho's first words spoken after a period of three years of silence herald a completely new dimension to his work. It is as if he has drawn a sword and with it shredded the deceit of history, so that man, his politics and so-called religion are all totally exposed. Responding to questions solely from his disciples Osho talks on the psychology of a creed based on following; on the question of belief in God; on whether Osho is a messiah or not; the attitude of traditional holy men towards women, his understanding of the political mind-set; how he feels about Communism, why his sannyasins lead such a rich life, why their happiness is attributed to their being brainwashed or hypnotised, and many more.

GOD IS DEAD, NOW ZEN IS THE ONLY LIVING TRUTH

Osho puts the finishing touches to His portrait of Friedrich Nietzsche with answers to disciples' questions on the work, vision and madness of this controversial philosopher. A perfect companion to Osho's two-volume Zarathustra series.

THE HIDDEN HARMONY

According to Osho, if Heraclitus had been born in India rather than Greece, he would have been recognized as not simply a philosopher but as a mystic. Further, He says that if Heraclitus had been accorded his rightful status, the whole course of Western history would have been totally different. Though only fragments remain of his words, Osho finds in them a poetry that is refreshing in its simplicity and clarity. Through this series of eleven discourses, Osho acts as a via media to this mystic of twenty-five centuries ago.

I CELEBRATE MYSELF. GOD IS NO WHERE, LIFE IS NOW HERE

"I celebrate myself, and I want you also to celebrate yourself," says Osho, echoing Walt Whitman, in these commentaries on Zen anecdotes and answers to questions. He also delves deeply into the implications of the existence or non-existence of God. The idea of God is an imprisonment, says Osho, and only when one is free from this prison can one know what true celebration is.

A MUST FOR MORNING CONTEMPLATION A MUST FOR CONTEMPLATION BEFORE SLEEP

2 VOLUMES

Excerpts from talks Osho has given to His disciples and other seekers during *darshan*, the intimate evening meetings He conducted for many years. These books are divided into twelve months, of thirty-one days each, and the passages have been designed to be read chronologically rather than randomly. Osho's suggestion is, on first awakening, to read the passage designated for that morning before one's mind becomes engaged in the day's activities; and similarly, in the evening, to read the assigned passage just before going to sleep. As He explains, the words of a mystic are not theories to accept or reject, they are fingers pointing towards the transcendental.

THE SEARCH

TALKS ON THE TEN BULLS OF ZEN

The ten paintings that tell the Zen story about a farmer in search of his lost bull provide an allegorical expression of the inexpressible. Originally Taoist, they were repainted by the 12th century Chinese Zen master, Kakuan. Osho examines the deeper layers of meaning behind each painting, as well as answering questions from disciples and other seekers, in this special selection of discourses.

Osho Commune International

The Osho Commune International in Poona, India, is the world's largest meditation and growth center. It is the meeting place and spiritual home of hundreds of thousands of people from nearly every country in the world. Guided by the vision of the enlightened master Osho, the Commune might be described as a laboratory, an experiment in creating a "New Man" – who lives in harmony with himself and his environment, and who is free from all ideologies and belief systems which now divide humanity.

The Commune's Osho Multiversity offers hundreds of workshops, groups and trainings, presented by its nine different faculties:

Osho School for Centering
Osho School of Creative Arts
Osho International Academy of Healing Arts
Osho Meditation Academy
Osho School of Mysticism
Osho Institute of Tibetan Pulsing
Osho Center for Transformation
Osho School of Zen Martial Arts
Osho Academy of Zen Sports and Fitness

All these programs are designed to help people to find the knack of meditation: the passive witnessing of thoughts, emotions, and actions, without judgment or identification. Unlike many traditional Eastern disciplines, meditation at Osho Commune is an inseparable part of everyday life – working, relating or just being. The result is that people do not renounce the world but bring to it a spirit of awareness and celebration, in a deep reverence for life.

The highlight of the day at the Commune is the meeting of the White Robe Brotherhood. This two hour celebration of music, dance and silence, with a discourse from Osho, is unique – a complete meditation in itself where thousands of seekers, in Osho's words, "dissolve into a sea of consciousness."

For Further Information

This book is also available in both audio and video format. Many of Osho's books have been translated and published in a variety of languages worldwide. For information about Osho, His meditations, books, tapes and the address of an Osho meditation/information center near you, contact:

Osho International Foundation
P.O. Box 2976, London NW5 2PZ, UK

Osho Commune International
17 Koregaon Park, Poona 411 001, India